Sociology and the
New Materialism

SAGE was founded in 1965 by Sara Miller McCune to support the dissemination of usable knowledge by publishing innovative and high-quality research and teaching content. Today, we publish over 900 journals, including those of more than 400 learned societies, more than 800 new books per year, and a growing range of library products including archives, data, case studies, reports, and video. SAGE remains majority-owned by our founder, and after Sara's lifetime will become owned by a charitable trust that secures our continued independence.

Los Angeles | London | New Delhi | Singapore | Washington DC | Melbourne

Nick J. Fox
Pam Alldred

Sociology and the
New Materialism

Theory, Research, Action

Los Angeles | London | New Delhi
Singapore | Washington DC | Melbourne

Los Angeles | London | New Delhi
Singapore | Washington DC | Melbourne

SAGE Publications Ltd
1 Oliver's Yard
55 City Road
London EC1Y 1SP

SAGE Publications Inc.
2455 Teller Road
Thousand Oaks, California 91320

SAGE Publications India Pvt Ltd
B 1/I 1 Mohan Cooperative Industrial Area
Mathura Road
New Delhi 110 044

SAGE Publications Asia-Pacific Pte Ltd
3 Church Street
#10-04 Samsung Hub
Singapore 049483

Editor: Natalie Aguilera
Editorial assistant: Delayna Spencer
Production editor: Katherine Haw
Copyeditor: Kate Campbell
Marketing manager: Sally Ransom
Cover design: Shaun Mercier
Typeset by: C&M Digitals (P) Ltd, Chennai, India
Printed and bound by Ashford Colour Press Ltd.

Library of Congress Control Number: 2016936389

British Library Cataloguing in Publication data

A catalogue record for this book is available from
the British Library

ISBN 978-1-4739-4221-9
ISBN 978-1-4739-4222-6 (pbk)

Contents

About the Authors

Nick J Fox is honorary Professor of Sociology at the University of Sheffield, UK, in the School of Health and Related Research. He is the author of books and papers applying new materialist and posthuman approaches to a range of sociological topics including health, sexualities, emotions, creativity and research methodology.

Pam Alldred is Reader in Sociology and Youth Studies in the Department of Clinical Sciences, Brunel University London, UK. She has researched sexualities and sex & relationship education, gendered and sexual violence, and the views of children and young people, lesbian mothers and young mothers on inequalities and education and social policy issues. She has published on research methods, particularly feminist and discursive approaches, and is lead editor of the *Handbook of Youth Work Practice* (Sage, 2017).

Part 1

New Materialism and the Sociological Imagination

1

Introduction

This is a book designed for social scientists, and more specifically for sociologists. It is about sociology and *for* sociology: its core aim is to suggest what the new materialism can offer to a sociological imagination, and for the exploration of the social problems and topics that concern those working, studying, teaching and researching in sociology. It is the book on new materialisms that we would want to read ourselves, as we are accustomed to focusing on practical and policy issues in areas such as gender and sexuality, education, health, technology, social inequalities and so forth. Our primary concern with new materialism is as a tool to help us do social research that is both appropriate and useful; to gain fresh insights into the myriad of aspects of society and social processes that assail us on all sides; to make sense of the social world in ways that can offer solutions to social problems; and to try to frame and support activism towards environmental and social justice.

For these reasons, we do not intend to devote the next 200 pages to an exposition of the differing theories that make up the new materialisms, or engage in closely-argued point-scoring over other social science perspectives such as poststructuralism or critical realism. There are other texts that set out to do these things, and we will provide suggested reading for those readers who wish to explore them. Instead, we are going to spend our time and yours exploring the practical applications of new materialism to the practice of doing sociology – offering critical insights into the social world, developing theory that can explain human societies and cultures, and undertaking empirical research to answer specific sociological questions.

In the humanities and social sciences, 'new materialism' has become a collective term used to denote a range of perspectives that have in common what has been described as a 'turn to matter'. Possibly the best known of these in contemporary sociology is actor-network theory (Law, 1992) – an approach that recognizes non-human agency that has been applied most widely in science and technology studies. However, the variety of approaches now described as 'new materialisms' are mind-numbingly diverse, drawing on perspectives from biophilosophy to quantum physics to queer and feminist theories (Coole and Frost, 2010: 4). As the name implies, these perspectives emphasize the materiality of the world and everything – social and natural – within it. What these various approaches have in common is a concern with the material workings of power, and a focus firmly upon social production rather than upon social construction (Deleuze and Guattari, 1984: 4; Taylor and Ivinson, 2013: 666).

Materialism is nothing new within sociology, of course, and later in this introduction we will recall the rise and demise of 'old' materialist sociology during the 20th century. The new materialist sociology that is now emerging is in no way a return to this earlier emphasis, however. Instead it has taken on board insights from the 'linguistic turn' of post-structuralism and constructivism that have rejected the earlier materialism's deterministic explanations of social organization and social action, and recognized intricate links between power and resistance, language and knowledge, bodies and subjectivity (Fox, 2016; Game, 1991; Nash, 2001; Parker, 1992; Rose, 1999). Among the radical claims of new materialist theorists are the propositions that:

- the material world and its contents are not fixed, stable entities, but relational, uneven, and in constant flux (Barad, 1996; Coole and Frost, 2010: 29; Lemke, 2015);

- 'nature' and 'culture' should not to be treated as distinct realms, but as parts of a continuum of materiality. The physical and the social both have material effects in an ever-changing world (Braidotti, 2013: 3; Haraway, 1997: 209); and

- a capacity for 'agency' – the actions that produce the social world – extends beyond human actors to the non-human and inanimate (Braidotti, 2013; DeLanda, 2006; Latour, 2005).

Many of these claims run directly counter to the mainstream sociological ontology (Karakayali, 2015), and in the early chapters of this book we will look fully at the basis for these assertions by new materialist scholars. But as we begin this exploration of a new materialist sociology, it is worth noting that – both theoretically and when applied to empirical research – these statements both challenge some foundational propositions of contemporary sociology, and radically extend materialist analysis beyond traditional concerns with structural and 'macro' level social phenomena (van der Tuin and Dolphijn, 2010: 159). First, they shift sociological focus from individuals and human subjects to how relational networks or assemblages of animate and inanimate affect and are affected (DeLanda, 2006: 4; Mulcahy, 2012: 10; Youdell and Armstrong, 2011: 145). Second, they recognize that the production of the social world is due to a wide variety of forces, including desires, feelings and meanings (Braidotti, 2000: 159; DeLanda, 2006; 5). Finally, they supply a posthuman (Braidotti; 2006a: 37; 2013: 169) focus for the social sciences and social inquiry that does not privilege humans in relation to the rest of the natural and social environment.

Materialism re-booted

To begin our odyssey toward a new materialist social science, and to understand more what the turn to matter means for sociology, it is worth looking back briefly to previous sociological materialisms. Materialism was a significant feature of early sociology, most notably within the work of Karl Marx, though also for Durkheim, in whose perspective both material factors and human consciousness contributed to the production of society (Durkheim, 1984: 223), and for Weber, whose analysis of capitalism and ideology acknowledged material factors (Weber, 1930: 183).

At its most emblematic, Marx's 'historical materialist' formulation provided sociology with a means to describe and explain contemporary social processes. Its sociological analysis focused on the historical development of social institutions and practices, within a broad economic and political context of material production and consumption (Edwards, 2010: 282). This emphasis inflected materialist analysis with a concern with 'structural' or 'macro-level' forces deriving from the social relations of production; typically – in contemporary sociology – of capitalist production. All of social life, from patterns of work and material consumption to family formations and gendered divisions of labour, was explained in terms of these relations of production. Power was conceptualized as a top-down phenomenon, exerted by a dominant social class over an oppressed class of working people (Giddens, 1981: 58; Nigam, 1996: 9; van Krieken, 1991).

This materialist strand within sociology was progressively diluted during the last century. A rival 'idealist' thread (which emphasized the part human ideas, beliefs and values shape society) began with Simmel, Weber and Mead, and led through Schütz, interpretivism and phenomenology variously to interactionism, some forms of social constructionism, and humanistic sociology (Berger and Luckmann, 1971: 208; Nash, 2001: 78; Shalin, 1990). Meanwhile, the emergence of micro-sociologies focused increasingly on interaction, experiences, knowledge and eventually 'discourse' (Berger and Kellner, 1964; Mulkay, 1985; Scheff, 1994).

The feminist and post-colonial sociologies that grew in parallel with this idealist thread criticized Marxian materialism for a narrow or reductionist focus upon social class, at the expense of recognition of the power relations between genders, between races and between other social divisions, and of the interactions between these disparate and independent processes of oppression

(Barrett and McIntosh, 1982; Crenshaw, 1989; Hall, 1996; Henriques et al., 1998; MacKinnon, 1982). The demise of the Soviet bloc in the 1980s may also have undermined the authority of a sociology founded in historical or dialectical materialism (Pakulski, 1993: 287; Rojek and Turner, 2000: 635).

For all these reasons, when the post-structuralist or 'linguistic' turn in the social sciences – informed by feminist, post-colonialist and queer theory (Braidotti, 2006: 27) – sought to understand the material workings of power in social fields and to theorize resistance, it found the economic determinism of historical materialism insufficient to critique satisfactorily patriarchy, misogyny and homophobia, and rationalism, science and modernism, or to supply a critical and radical stance to underpin struggles for social justice and plurality (Bonnell and Hunt, 1999: 8; Braidotti, 2006: 24–25; Game, 1991: 12). Instead, theorists working in this perspective re-imagined class, gender, social organizations and bodies in terms of human culture and textuality (Friedland and Mohr, 2004: 2), providing new perspectives on power, resistance and social identity (Butler, 1990; Foucault, 1980; Henriques et al., 1998).

This post-structuralist trend has been criticized by some for privileging textuality and cultural interpretation within the sociological imagination, at the expense of matter and materiality (Bonnell and Hunt, 1999: 9; Rojek and Turner, 2000: 639–640). The 'new' materialisms that have subsequently emerged within the social sciences and humanities are thus in part a reaction against this textualization of the social world. However, some new materialist approaches have retained insights from post-structuralism concerning power, culture and social action, while resisting longings for sociology's earlier reductionist materialism. However, the new materialism radically extends the scope of materialist analysis beyond both traditional concerns with structural and 'macro' level social phenomena (van der Tuin and Dolphijn, 2010: 159) *and* post-structuralism's concern with construction (Coole and Frost, 2010: 7; Taylor and Ivinson, 2013: 666). It addresses issues such as identity, interpersonal relations or sexuality, often regarded as the remit of micro-sociology because of their concern with how thoughts, desires, feelings and abstract concepts contribute to the social world (Braidotti, 2000: 159; DeLanda, 2006: 5).

Why a new materialist sociology?

In our view, there are a number of key reasons why the new materialisms offer opportunities for sociology, and we want to set these out now, though we will revisit this question throughout the book.

First is the emphasis that new materialists place upon ontology (concern with the kinds of things that exist) rather than epistemology (which addresses how these things can be known by an observer). Historically, sociology stepped away from ontological concerns, to focus upon how knowledge of the social world may be gained (De Castro, 2004: 283–4). The debates over whether it is possible to know a social world beyond human constructs (or even if there is such a world independent of human thought) has divided the sociological community, but has also contributed to barriers between quantitative and qualitative research approaches that appear to deal with different aspects of the social. New materialist scholars regard their own efforts to re-focus on ontology as a means to cut across an irresolvable argument between two self-contained belief systems (realism and idealism), but also as necessary to address assumptions about what matter is and what it does (Barad, 1996: 163, see also Karakayali, 2015).

Second, while there is some divergence across the new materialist terrain, the distinctive ontology advocated by new materialist scholars has been described as 'flat' or 'monist' (as opposed to 'dualist'), rejecting differences between 'natural' and 'cultural' realms, human and non-human, 'base' and 'superstructure', micro and macro, and perhaps most significantly for sociology, mind and matter (van der Tuin and Dolphijn, 2010). By challenging any distinction between the materiality of the physical world and the social constructs of human thoughts and desires, it opens up the possibility to explore how each affects the other, and how things other than humans (for instance, a tool, a technology or a building) can be social 'agents', making things happen. So sociology from a new materialist perspective would become 'post-anthropocentric' (Braidotti, 2011: 327), shifting humans from the central focus of sociological attention, and facilitating this 'post-human' sociology to engage productively with the world beyond the human: with other living things, and with the wider environment of matter and things.

New materialism's flat ontology also marks the rejection of any sense of social structures (for instance, 'patriarchy', 'neo-liberalism' or 'masculinity') as 'explanations' of how societies and cultures work (Latour, 2005: 130). There are no structures, no systems and no mechanisms at work in new materialist ontology; instead there are 'events'; an endless cascade of events comprising the material effects of both nature and culture that together produce the world and human history. Exploring the relational character of these events and their physical, biological and expressive composition becomes the means for sociology to explain the continuities, fluxes and 'becomings' that produce the world around us. We explore these issues in detail in Chapter 4.

Third, many of the leading new materialist scholars – notably feminists, postcolonial scholars and queer theorists – have developed or adopted their perspectives on the world because they are socially and politically engaged, and have sought a framework that is materially embedded and embodied (Braidotti, 2011: 128) – a perspective that is capable of use both to research the social world and to seek to change it for the better. While post-structuralism and social constructionism provided a means to break through top-down, determinist theories of power and social structure, the focus upon textuality, discourses and systems of thought in these approaches tended to create distance between theory and practice, and gave the sense that radical, interventionist critiques of inequities and oppressions were merely further constructions of the social world. The turn to matter offers a re-immersion in the materiality of life and struggle, and a recognition that in a monist world – because there is no 'other level' that makes things do what they do – everything is necessarily relational and contextual rather than essential and absolute.

These three reasons, in our view, supply the logic for why sociologists might choose to apply new materialism to both empirical research problems and to social theory. We find in the new materialisms – and in the scholarly work of new materialist social theorists, philosophers, feminists and posthumanists – a perspective on the social and the natural world, on social processes and on social identities that addresses key sociological questions. It offers a means to move beyond artificial divides in sociology between agency and social structure, culture and nature, mind and matter, human and non-human, power and resistance, continuity and change, reason and emotion that have constrained both social understanding and the sociological imagination.

Exploring the consequences of a monistic, materialist ontology will be the central theme throughout the book, from our questioning of an opposition between humans and their environment in Chapter 3; our rehabilitation of emotions as productive of social life (Chapter 7); and our re-making in Chapter 9 of issues of epistemology in social research. Our intention is to provide a critical overview of the application of the new materialisms within social science research and scholarship (see Fox and Alldred, 2014 for a review of pathfinder new materialist social science), in order to assess what these social theory developments mean when translated from social philosophy into sociological usage and into empirical social inquiry.

New materialism offers a means to move beyond the anthropocentrism that takes the human as the measure of all things, and allows us to take a fresh look at the ways in which the non-human has important and pervasive effects – on a daily basis – upon the social world and on all our lives. It supplies new insights into topics from gender and sexuality to climate change, and provides a materialist perspective on the processes of doing research and engaging in social activism. It also suggests a means to shift sociology from being a form of what Deleuze and Guattari (1988: 372) called 'Royal' science – one that treats its objects as stable entities that are reproducible so long as their contexts are controlled, and become instead a 'minor' (or we might suggest 'transgressive') science, that sees its purpose as seeking out singularities and variability, flows and singular events in the social world, and recognizing the possibility for change and transformation.

Challenges for a new materialist sociology

Given this logic for a sociological new materialism, the consequent challenge is to establish a workable sociology that may be used productively to theorize human societies and cultures, to inform research into issues of sociological concern, and also to provide a foundation for social action to change and enhance the social world. While a new materialist sociology will need to engage with the main topics that sociologists explore – social stratifications, social divisions and inequalities, work, religion, families and relationships, media, sexuality and so forth, it also must be able to supply a useable account of some more fundamental sociological issues. Among these are:

Continuity. How is it that societies and cultures sustain a substantial degree of stability of social formations (for instance, nation-states, democracy, capitalism, local and regional accents and identities, gender roles) over time, seemingly independent of the turn-over of the human individuals of whom they comprise? What are the material processes needed to explain this (for instance, enduring mechanisms and/or structures)?

Change. Despite these continuities in social formations, societies and cultures do change, sometimes quite radically. What material processes enable social change, and how may these be reconciled with the processes that sustain social continuities?

Social divisions and inequality. The social world around us seems inexorably split apart by social divisions (for instance, between genders, or races, or social classes), and marked by inequalities that follow these dividing lines. How are these divisions and inequalities sustained?

Power and resistance. Following on from the last point, how do certain individuals (such as a monarch or dictator), particular elements in a society (a social class or a gender) or social groupings (such as a trade union or a management team) wield power over others? And conversely, how do others resist this exercise of power?

Subjectivity. What is the relationship between a society and the thoughts, feelings and actions of the individual humans within it, and how does each affect the other? In some ways (and in some sociologies) many of the previous sociological issues revolve around this interaction; but how to understand it from a sociological perspective?

'The social'. This final concept is the very subject-matter of sociology. Different sociologies have understood this social stuff in a variety of ways, but for all, 'the social' is something that sociologists have argued cannot be reduced either to

the cognitions and emotions of individual humans, or to the realm of biology, chemistry and physics. But what exactly is the social, of what does it comprise, and how does it work?

The history of sociology may be seen as efforts to address these foundational questions, with the success or failure of a particular perspective judged in part upon the extent to which it satisfactorily addressed some or all of them. Particular sociological theorists have placed different emphases on some rather than other of these questions, and indeed on what these concepts mean. Thus for example, power may be understood entirely differently by a Marxist sociologist (as a top-down coercion) and a post-structuralist (as a bottom-up discipline of the body or self). Each new reading has brought new opportunities to think about aspects of these fundamentals; arguably the success and relevance of a new materialist sociology rests upon the extent to which it opens up novel questions for sociologists to ask, and consequently new avenues for theory and research.

The aim that we have set ourselves in this book is to take new materialist concepts and develop a sociological imagination that addresses issues in a way that is intellectually coherent and useable, that asks novel questions, and offers sociologically interesting answers. Our first task will be to translate what are often abstract new materialist theoretical perspectives and concepts (often developed outside the social sciences), into ideas and tools that will address the particular needs of sociologists, and that will be our starting point in the next chapter. What might the new materialisms mean for our subject? How do new materialist perspectives recast some core sociological assumptions or concepts? We will consider the ways in which new materialism transforms the object of sociological study (human societies and cultures), and thus our sociological imaginations, and the consequences for sociological research practices and for social transformation.

Structure of the book

We have divided the book into three sections. Part 1 of the book establishes the framework for the development of new materialist sociology, and sets out to demonstrate the radical impact of new materialism on some core sociological concepts, and its capacity to cut across dualisms including culture/nature, structure/agency, human/non-human, and mind/matter. Chapter 2 introduces the scholarly perspectives of new materialist authors, and shows how these transform some of the foundational concepts in sociology, most specifically agency and structure; nature and culture; subjectivity and objectivity. Chapter 3 considers the interaction between humans and their natural and social contexts. It challenges the dualism of nature/culture through a post-anthropocentric and posthuman concept of 'environment' that sees humans as fully integral to the physical and social world. Chapter 4 develops a new materialist perspective on some core issues in sociology. It begins by re-thinking the topics of social organization, social institutions and social 'structure' in terms of new materialism's 'flat' ontology. It then develops a materialist approach to social stratifications such as 'class', 'gender', and 'race'. We show how these stratifications are based not upon social divergence, but upon aggregations of disparate bodies into social categories. This provides a new point of departure for re-thinking social mobility.

If these early chapters seem tough theoretically, readers may wish to flip ahead to Part 2, in which we apply the approach to more specific sociological issues, returning later to the theory chapters. In this second part of the book, we address an aspect of sociological study that has became a major focus during the 'cultural turn': the relationship between the social world and human subjectivities and identities. New materialist ontology has a rather different take on these latter conceptions, and we explore this through a series of materialist analyses of social production of social formations and subjectivities. Chapter 5 explores creativity, and we use this analysis as a way to interrogate the production of human culture, from science and technology to the arts and to social forms and institutions. In Chapter 6, we develop a materialist sociology of sexuality that regards it not as an attribute of a body or individual, but as the product of an affective flow between bodies, things, ideas and social institutions that produces sexual (and other) capacities in bodies. We reflect on what this means in relation to 'sexualization' and the development of sexual identities. Chapter 7 explores emotions. We argue that emotions are a part, but only a part, of a more generalized affective flow that links human bodies to their physical and social environment, and as such contribute to the production of many aspects of the social world and human history, including social change and social stability, and to subjectivity. Finally, in Chapter 8 we offer a materialist view of 'health' as the capacity of a body or a collectivity of bodies to affect (to act, feel or desire) or be affected by biological, physical and social elements. We make connections back to creativity and emotions, to develop a new approach to health and care that elides biological and social views of embodiment and identity.

The final part of the book turns to the practicalities of doing social research and the challenge of developing a public and engaged sociology. Chapter 9 develops the concept of a 'research–assemblage' that comprises researcher, respondents, data, methods and contexts, and we develop this way of thinking about research to assess, critique and potentially engineer research methods and methodologies that shift the relationship between researcher, researched and audience. In Chapter 10, we explore a new materialist approach to social engagement, politics and activism, based on a non-reductive perspective on power, subjectivity and resistance, drawing sociology towards social action and struggles against injustice and inequalities.

Writing what we believe is the first textbook on new materialist sociology, we are keen to make it as accessible as possible. Some readers will read from cover to cover, but others will use it more like a tool-box, picking and choosing the parts that can be used to address specific problems. We would suggest that if you are in the latter camp you read the next three chapters, as these provide the main foundational perspectives of a new materialist sociology, and Chapters 9 and 10, which explore how new materialism provides a new ontology to underpin social research and an approach to social change. The middle section of the book provides insights into how new materialist sociology addresses more specific aspects of the social world, and can be dipped into, using the index to find specific tools for specific questions.

There is always a risk that a textbook may 'dumb down' or over-simplify the subject matter presented. With new materialist thought in all its diversity and vibrancy, that is a danger that we recognize all too clearly. For readers seeking stronger fare, we attempt to accommodate you through signposts, citations and suggestions for further reading, to enable you to forage among the burgeoning materialist literature in journal papers and edited collections that we reference along the way.

As we draw this introduction to a close, a note on our use of the term 'new materialism' in what follows. We have already recalled the 'old materialism' of sociology, and set out the clear divergences between that and the perspectives we are writing about here. Consequently, we feel it is unnecessarily clumsy to repeatedly use the term 'new materialist' in the coming pages. For that reason, towards the end of Chapter 2 – once we have the reviewed some key new materialist theories, we shall thereafter refer to our position simply as 'materialism'. This will both offer conciseness *and* assert our view that the perspectives we are developing are the rightful heirs to that name. Where there is any possible confusion with historical materialism, we will be careful to make this distinction clear.

Further reading

Barad, K. (2003) Posthumanist performativity: toward an understanding of how matter comes to matter. *Signs, 28*(3): 801–831.

Coole, D.H. and Frost, S. (2010) Introducing the new materialisms. In: Coole, D.H. and Frost, S. (eds.) *New Materialisms: Ontology, Agency, and Politics.* Durham, NC: Duke University Press, pp. 1–43.

2

Foundations
New Materialism and the Sociological Imagination

In the introduction we identified some of the key claims of the new material-isms, and how and why these offer possibilities for a sociological imagination. These new materialist propositions and perspectives have emerged from a wide variety of philosophical, feminist and social theoretical positions, and in this chapter we will unpack the roots of these claims. We will survey the work of some key new materialist thinkers from Bruno Latour and 'actor-network the-ory' to Rosi Braidotti and 'the posthuman'. We will use these to establish more formally the core features of new materialism, and use these to set out the foun-dations, the concepts and the tools for new materialist sociology, and consider what they may bring to the sociological imagination.

As was noted in the introduction, new materialist ontology[1] cuts across 'the mind-matter and culture-nature divides of transcendental humanist thought' (van der Tuin and Dolphijn, 2010: 155), thereby putting into ques-tion other social theory dualisms including structure/agency, surface/depth; reason/emotion, human/non-human, and animate/inanimate (Braidotti, 2013: 4–5; Coole and Frost, 2010: 26–27; van der Tuin and Dolphijn, 2010: 157). Take, for instance, the sociological models that explain social organi-zation in terms of some kind of surface/depth dualism. This dualism underpinned Marx's historical materialist model of society of, on one hand, a 'base' – comprising the economic rules that govern material production and consumption within a specific social system (such as capitalism or communism), and on the other a 'superstructure' made up of all the cultural norms, roles and rituals, laws and politics of a society that grow up within the constraints of the economic base.

Few contemporary sociologists now adhere to this crude base/superstructure model, which implies that the entirety of human endeavour – public and private – is determined by the economics of a society. However, this surface/depth dualism has been a feature of other social science theories, from evolutionary models that regard human culture as surface phenomena overlaying a biological drive to sexually propagate the human species (Tooby and Cosmides, 1989) to critical realism (Danermark et al., 2002), in which the daily lives of people and their interactions obscure a 'deep' system of rules or social mechanisms, which it is the ultimate aim of sociological analysis to uncover (Karakayali, 2015: 733). New materialist scholars such as Connolly (2010: 179) and DeLanda (2006) have rejected these surface/depth models, and by contrast have argued that everything that goes on in the social and natural world should be judged on its own terms, without recourse to notions of a deeper mechanism or structure (or a 'higher' governing power such as God or Gaia).

Cutting across this surface/depth dualism reflects the broader 'monistic' or singular theme running through the new materialism (Braidotti, 2013: 95; Gatens, 2000). New materialism, it is argued, rejects, or is 'transversal' to, many of the dualisms that have been devised to manage knowledge (and hence exercise authority) in the past, including those within social science knowledge and theory (see, for example, Alldred and Fox (2015a) on the history of the hetero/homosexual dualism in psychology). Perhaps most significantly, this monism removes a distinction between a 'physical' world of things and bodies and a realm of thoughts, social structures and cultural products (matter vs. mind); between a 'reality' independent of human thought and the social constructs that humans produce to apprehend that reality, or even between animate and inanimate. At the same time, this monism opens up the possibility of multiplicity and diversity that exceeds and overwhelms the dualities it replaces.

So the new materialisms have not developed in any linear way from earlier sociologies, and we must start our project of developing a 'new' materialist sociology without the benefit of a simple recourse to either an earlier sociological materialism or to post-structuralism, or merely because 'new' is 'better'. The influences and propositions of the new materialisms derive from bizarrely (almost embarrassingly) disparate perspectives, including – in alphabetical order – actor-network theory, artificial intelligence, biophilosophy, evolutionary theory, feminism, Foucauldian genealogy, neuroscience, non-representational theory, posthumanism, queer theory, quantum physics and Spinozist monism (Anderson and Harrison, 2010; Ansell Pearson, 1999; Barad, 1996; Best, 1995; Braidotti, 2006b, 2013; Clough, 2008; Connolly, 2011; Coole and Frost, 2010; Deleuze, 1988; Grosz, 1994; Haraway, 1991; Latour, 2005; Massumi, 1996; Spinks, 2001; Thacker, 2005). This litany of influences together inspires a project that extends from concerns with issues of identity and human need to the forces of international economics and ecology (Coole and Frost, 2010: 28).

To help us find our way through this web of theory and concepts to see more clearly what a (new) materialist sociology will look like, we begin by examining critically some of the propositions in the work of influential new materialist scholars. From these disparate yet interwoven threads, we will draw out what we suggest are the key features of the turn to materiality, in terms of how new materialism addresses the social theory dualisms of nature/culture, agency/structure, mind/matter and human/non-human. This will in turn lead us to assert some core propositions for a sociologically-coherent and critical new materialist sociology, which we will apply in subsequent chapters in terms of its implications for sociological research, ontology and epistemology, and applications to policy and practice.

New materialism: four voices

Both because of their significance to new materialist theory, and to supply a breadth of perspectives, we have chosen to summarize briefly some key ideas from first Bruno Latour's actor-network inflected assemblage theory, then the Spinozist ontology of affects and assemblages in the individual and collaborative work of philosopher Deleuze and psychoanalyst and activist Guattari, next the feminist physicist turned social theorist Karen Barad, and finally the feminist, posthumanist philosophy of Rosi Braidotti. We will identify the main elements of their analyses, and use these to draw out core issues relevant to the development of a sociological application of the new materialisms. Though we have done our best to draw out the key points, some readers may find what follows in this section difficult and abstract. If the going gets too tough, readers may prefer to skip forward to subsequent chapters, and return to these theorists later.

Bruno Latour: (re-)assembling the social

Actor-network theory (ANT) will be familiar to some sociological readers, particularly those working in the arena of science and technology studies, where its recognition of non-human agency has been used successfully to explore interactions between humans, technologies and the contemporary social world (Law, 2009). ANT gains its most powerfully new materialist and generalized presentation in Latour's (2005) *Re-assembling the Social*, which sets out to develop a full-blown materialist theory of the social, and an agenda for a new 'sociology of association' (ibid: 9). Latour builds on core principles of ANT, most notably by ascribing agency to transient relational networks (Law, 1999: 4) or assemblages (Latour, 2005: 7) comprising both human and non-human 'actants' (2005: 54). These networks are consequently heterogeneous, and extend beyond what is traditionally considered 'social', to include 'texts, devices, architectures' (Law, 1992: 379). From this perspective, social life is heterogeneous engineering, 'in which bits and pieces from the social, the technical, the conceptual and the textual are fitted together' (ibid: 381).

While ANT's main sociological focus has traditionally been on studies of science and technology (Callon, 1986; Latour, 1999), Latour's broader concern has been to criticize sociology's view of 'the social' as a distinct domain of reality that provides the context within which events of all kinds occur, and that can be revealed through the specialized methods of social scientists (Latour, 2005: 4). His contrary view is that 'the social' is not distinct from other materialities; consequently the appropriate task for a sociologist is not to describe and explain 'social forces', but to explore how a range of heterogeneous elements from the physical, biological, economic, semiotic and other 'realms' may be assembled to produce this or that social aggregation (ibid: 5–6). Such aggregations (which might be a nation, a corporation, a social institution, a social category or an aspect of human culture) are thus the outcome, not the cause of interactions. Sociology should not restrict itself to studying social ties, but instead become a 'sociology of associations' that can 'travel wherever new heterogeneous associations are made' (ibid: 8), in order to understand how the social is continually assembled from non-social associations.

This sociology of associations does not restrict itself to studying the traditional conception of social actors – human beings – but considers also the interplay between humans and non-human entities. One particular casualty of this re-formulation of the sociological project is what Latour (2005: 9) terms 'critical sociology', which we take to mean approaches including both critical realism and Marxism, that seek to 'explain' the social in terms of 'deep' or underlying structures or mechanisms. For Latour, these perspectives epitomized the kind of sociology he rejects, as offering as 'explanations' precisely those social formations (for example, capitalist social relations, patriarchy or the neoliberal market) which – in his view – are the very things that need themselves to be explained (ibid: 130–131). Unfairly, but perhaps unsurprisingly, as a consequence Latour and other ANT theorists have been criticized for failing to address the political exercise of power (Alcadipani and Hassard, 2010: 420) or structural determinants of action (McLean and Hassard, 2004: 507–510).

In our view, the principal contribution of Latour's ANT to the new materialist project is in its extension of the sociological imagination beyond its limited concern with 'social forces' (and thus also the limited range of acceptable sociological questions or controversies that may be posed), to address a wide range of materialities. It fundamentally challenges sociology to shift its ontology to study heterogeneous associations, many of which draw in elements that lie outside the traditional limits of sociological inquiry.

Deleuze and Guattari: the microphysics of social production

Together and separately, the philosopher Gilles Deleuze and psychoanalyst and social activist Félix Guattari have arguably emerged as the most influential new materialist scholars within the arts, humanities and among social sciences such as education and geography, though currently less so within sociology. Their sheer volume of work and the range of novel concepts in their materialist ontology has contributed to their significance for a number of feminist and queer theory scholars (Braidotti, 2000; Gatens, 2000; Grosz, 1994), as the foundation of DeLanda's (2006) assemblage theory of interaction, organization and society, and in the so-called 'affective turn' in the social sciences (Clough, 2008; Leys, 2011; Thrift, 2004) that has re-focused scholarly attention upon matter and its dynamic and productive capacities. Deleuze and Guattari's work also has spawned a large secondary literature, including a series of edited collections on sociologically-relevant topics including race (Saldanha and Adams, 2013), sexuality (Beckman, 2011), the body (Guillaume and Hughes, 2011) and research methodology (Coleman and Ringrose, 2013).

In many ways, Deleuze and Guattari's materialism is cognate with that of Latour and other ANT theorists, particularly in their ontological emphasis upon relationality and in their model of power as potential capacity to affect (Massumi, 1988: xvii). However, they offer a more fully worked through ontology: one that supplies a detailed microphysics of social production that is amenable to tasks in both social and cultural analysis and radical politics. Drawing on their exegesis of Spinoza's 'monist' philosophy – that rejects any notion of the transcendent, or of base/superstructure or surface/depth dualism (Deleuze, 1988) – DeleuzoGuattarian materialism regards human bodies and all other material, social and abstract entities as relational, having no ontological status or integrity other than that produced through their relationship to other similarly contingent and ephemeral bodies, things and ideas (Deleuze, 1988: 123; Deleuze and Guattari, 1988: 261).

These contingent and ephemeral materialities gain substance and shape as they are drawn into *agencement* (a French term roughly equivalent to 'arrangement', but now more commonly translated as *assemblage*). Assemblages develop in unpredictable ways around actions and events (Deleuze and Guattari, 1988: 88), 'in a kind of chaotic network of habitual and non-habitual connections, always in flux, always reassembling in different ways' (Potts, 2004: 19). For example, a sexuality-assemblage (Fox and Alldred, 2013) accrues around an event such as an erotic kiss, which comprises not just two pairs of lips but also physiological processes, personal and cultural contexts, aspects of the setting, memories and experiences, sexual codes and norms of conduct, and potentially many other relations particular to that event (see Chapter 6).

What holds assemblages together, Deleuze and Guattari suggested, are the capacities of assembled relations to affect or be affected. This capacity, which – following Spinoza – Deleuze (1988: 101) called simply an *affect,* is a 'becoming' (Deleuze and Guattari, 1988: 256), or in other words, a force that achieves some change of state or capabilities in a relation (Clough, 2004: 15; Massumi, 1988: xvi). Such change may be physical, biological, psychological, social, political or emotional. The flow of affect within assemblages is consequently the means by which lives, societies and history unfold, by 'adding capacities through interaction, in a world which is constantly becoming' (Thrift, 2004: 61).

Affect replaces the more familiar sociological conception of 'agency' in DeleuzoGuattarian ontology. Critically – because all relations (human and non-human, animate and inanimate) have affects – this means that non-humans as well as humans can be agentic (as in Latour's ANT). This elides any distinction between physical/biological materiality and the expressive realms of concepts, thoughts and feelings. To the extent that a relation in an assemblage can affect or be affected, it may be understood as material, thus opening to materialist analysis a range of materialities that spans the physical (geological formations or genetics) to the expressive affects of human thoughts, beliefs, desires and feelings.

The DeleuzoGuattarian project was concerned principally with what assemblages do, what they produce, and in particular with their micropolitical consequences for bodies and for social formations. Like ANT, their ontology rejected any notion of transcendent or multiple levels: without determining structures, systems or mechanisms, social production is entirely due to the forces or affects within assemblages. Deleuze and Guattari (1988: 88–89) described assemblage micropolitics in terms of a dynamic 'territorialization' (a process of 'specification') and 'de-territorialization' ('de-specification' or 'generalization') of the capacities of bodies and the other relations within assemblages, continually in flux. So for instance, a stone may be territorialized into a 'tool' by the hand that uses it to hammer or grind; it is de-territorialized back into a stone once it is cast aside. Similarly, during childhood a mix of physical and cultural forces may territorialize humans into male or female genders, an attribution that for many (but not all) remains in place life-long.

Deleuze and Guattari saw themselves very much on the side of de-territorialization and resistance. In relation to mental health, they advocated a de-territorializing 'schizoanalysis' (Deleuze and Guattari 1984: 273); more generally – as a strategy for living – they promoted 'nomadology' (Deleuze and Guattari 1988: 23). A commitment to deterritorialization and the nomad is intrinsically political, always on the side of freedom, experimentation and becoming, always opposed to power, territory and the fixing of identity (ibid: 24). This focus has led to adoption of DeleuzoGuattarian philosophy by some feminist and queer scholars such as Elizabeth Grosz, Patricia Clough and Rosi Braidotti (of whom more below).

Karen Barad: materialist onto-epistemology

Barad's background as a theoretical physicist, along with her feminism, has provided her with a very different starting point for her new materialism: quantum mechanics. More particularly, she focused on the work of the physicist Niels Bohr and his 'Copenhagen Interpretation' of how – at a quantum level – the act of observation inevitably affects the phenomena it seeks to study.[2] Barad (1996, 2007) extended Bohr's conclusions beyond the quantum level to include the world of the everyday, arguing for a view of the world that is always physically and socioculturally contextual, and which therefore must take account of the part observers or researchers play in its production.

Barad has based her thesis upon the insights of Bohr concerning the influence of the measuring process at the sub-atomic or quantum level (Barad, 2007: 198), where materials do not conform to the Newtonian/Cartesian expectation of observer-independence. Unlike an apple falling from a tree, at a quantum-mechanical level, the very act of observation seems to determine the outcome of sub-atomic interactions; consequently it is impossible to separate out the effects of the observation from the object, indeed, it becomes meaningless to talk of a pre-existing or independent object (Barad, 1996: 169–170). Bohr referred instead to 'phenomena', meaning specific instances of interactions between particles, but also of interaction with observers/measurement devices/theories. Phenomena are thereby entirely contextual, rather than absolutes, and there is no way to reveal the pure 'essence' of reality (ibid: 170). For Bohr, Barad has argued, an observation 'cannot be meaningfully attributed to either an abstract object or an abstract measuring instrument', but instead to the always already contextual phenomenon (1996: 172).

Bohr's Copenhagen Interpretation thus provided Barad with a generalized basis for a more contextual and 'local' research perspective on how objects behave, in both the natural and social worlds; a view to which Bohr himself assented, according to Barad (1996: 167). If there is a reality, Barad has argued, it is one constructed by 'things in phenomena' (1996: 176), in other words, in the inter-actions (or as Barad (1996: 179) has it, 'intra-actions') that constitute a phenomenon, event or action. These intra-actions within a phenomenon, Barad contends, constitute an 'agential reality' that necessarily include both object and observer, as well as both sides of nature/culture and word/world dualisms (ibid: 177). In this way, matter and meaning are inextricably fused (Barad, 2007: 3).

This quantum mechanical understanding of the intra-action of phenomena provides a new perspective, Barad has argued, on both natural and social science inquiry. Using what she called a 'diffractive' understanding (Barad, 2007: 71) of Bohr's work (by reading it alongside social theorists including Donna Haraway, Judith Butler and Michel Foucault), she has suggested that all knowledge should be seen as situated. Scientific inquiry is not neutral: every research design, method or theory is an 'agential cut' that reflects a particular power-laden effort to create 'knowledge' (2007: 185). However, this recognition of social and local forces is not a recipe for pessimism about the outcomes of research. That scientific knowledge is constructed, she suggests, does not mean that science doesn't work, while 'the fact that science "works" does not mean that we have discovered human-independent facts about nature' (2007: 40). Rather, it is precisely because science *is* socially constructed that provides reliable knowledge about reproducible phenomena (Barad, 1996: 186).

For the broader sociological new materialist project that we aim to develop – and in particular for the task of undertaking empirical research on the social, Barad's Bohrian 'onto-epistemology' (2007: 185) offers two important contributions. First, by drawing the researcher into the research, to become part of what we will call a 'research-assemblage' (Fox and Alldred, 2014) when we consider social inquiry in Chapter 9, it provides the means to transcend conventional epistemological arguments in the social sciences that have favoured either 'realism' (a commitment to disclosing a reality independent of the human mind) or constructionism (which sees human constructs as an inevitable limit to what can be known of the world), thus marking a decisive shift of focus from epistemology to ontology.

Second, Barad's onto-epistemology makes the point (also made by Deleuze and Guattari but from a different starting place) that ontologically, culture and nature cannot be differentially privileged and that 'constructedness does not deny materiality' (Barad, 1996: 181). It offers a foundation for scientific practice that is 'material-cultural', based not upon a distinction between independent observer and independent object of inquiry, but in 'the movements between meanings and matter, word and world, interrogating and re-defining boundaries … in "the between" where knowledge and being meet' (ibid: 185). Barad's work thereby supplies an agenda for a critical new materialist social science that can both reveal the specific 'agential cuts' that disguise the simultaneous materiality and discursivity of scientific inquiry (1996: 188), and show how applying a certain theoretical framework or a particular study methodology to a research problem produces specific phenomena (1996: 179–183). We shall return to this aspect of Barad's analysis when we consider research methodology later in the book.

Rosi Braidotti and the posthuman

Of the new materialists reviewed here, Rosi Braidotti offers the most thoroughly developed and penetrating critique of 'anthropocentrism': the pervasive post-Enlightenment humanistic outlook that has regarded the human (and more typically, the male human) as the centre of concern, and the 'measure of all things'. Anthropocentrism is, of course, foundational to the social and human sciences that have emerged over the past 200 years, which dissect the human body and soul in ever-increasing detail and offer solutions to how humans should conduct themselves.

Braidotti's work has drawn upon a range of embodied feminisms and materialisms, from de Beauvoir and Haraway to Foucault and Deleuze (Braidotti, 2011: 128), but has adopted 'nomadology' – a concept and philosophical position devised by Deleuze and Guattari to be emblematic of de-territorialization (Deleuze and Guattari, 1988: 382) – as the basis for a philosophical trajectory developing a notion of 'nomadic thought'. This latter she has described as 'a non-unitary vision of the subject ... that is densely material [and that] invites us to rethink the structures and boundaries of the self' (Braidotti, 2011: 3), but that is quite distinct from an anthropocentric and individualist view of the self. Instead of exploring the body as the product of discourses of law, medicine, science and so forth, as in the 'linguistic turn' of post-structuralism, Braidotti's interest has been in the materiality of the lived and living body (2011: 130), and in developing an embodied and embedded, feminist and materialist, nomadic and 'posthuman' theory of the body and subjectivity (2013: 51).

In this posthumanist project, the racial, sexual and natural 'others' of modernity and humanism become 'positive and pro-active alternatives' that express both the crisis of the majority and the becomings of minorities (2013: 37–8). Braidotti's writing is consequently replete with discussions of 'becoming-animal', 'becoming-woman' and 'becoming-minoritarian'. Thus, the 'nomadic becoming-woman' moves beyond an essentialist understanding of female specificity, tracing a 'zig-zag path' that encompasses issues from global social justice to creativity (2011: 41). Philosophical nomadism contests 'the arrogance of anthropocentrism', allying instead with the productive and transformational forces of zoë or 'life in its inhuman aspects' (2011: 139). This monistic philosophy of becoming challenges essentialist dualisms such as man/woman, human/animal, minority/majority, and:

> rests on the idea that matter, including the specific slice of matter that is human embodiment, is intelligent and self-organizing. This means that matter is not dialectically opposed to culture, nor to technological mediation, but continuous with them. (2013: 35)

This analysis is congruent with the other materialisms already reviewed, which have sought to reinstate vital, self-organizing capacities to what is traditionally conceived as inert matter, and to break through the social theory dualisms of nature/culture (2013: 2) and mind/body (2011: 99). The resulting 'radical neo-materialist' and 'posthumanist feminist' perspective cuts across natural and social science boundaries, drawing neurology and phenomenology, artificial intelligence and cultural theory into juxtaposition (2011: 132). Braidotti has used her conception of the posthuman as the philosophical foundation for what she has called the 'post-humanities', the successor to the anthropocentric humanities. The subject of the post-humanities is not 'Man' (2013: 169) but rather the processes of change and becoming of the natural and social world, and an ecology of the human and the non-human in which neither is distinguished from, or privileged over the other. (We will re-visit this posthuman perspective when we explore new materialist understanding of 'the environment' in Chapter 3.)

In practice, this means shifting focus away from essentialist and organic notions of 'life' towards a concern with practices and flows of becoming, and of complex assemblages that cut across natural and cultural domains, thereby eliding also the traditional division between the 'sciences' (exclusively ascribed concern with nature and technology) and the 'humanities' (concerned with all things human, social and cultural) (2013: 172). This supplies a model for a new posthuman synergy between the physical sciences, social sciences and humanities. Braidotti has argued for a new science that is 'ethically transformative, and not bound to the economic imperatives of advanced capitalism', a 'minor science' that recognizes its material subject as complex, assembled from disparate materialities, and relational (2013: 171). While she may have had the natural sciences in mind, this argument for a posthuman science seems equally relevant to the social sciences and sociology.

Propositions for a new materialist sociology

Though these four summaries of new materialist scholars do not exhaust the breadth of the new materialisms (we might, for instance, have also considered Bennett's (2010) explorations of vibrant matter and 'thing-power', DeLanda's (2006) realist re-thinking of Deleuzian assemblage theory, Haraway's (1991, 1997) posthumanist science studies or Massumi's (1996) exploration of affect), they do reveal a tapestry of concepts that make new materialism distinct from both historical materialism and the ontology of autonomous entities that underpins mainstream sociology (DeLanda, 2013: xiii). Latour's project re-assembles nature and cultures, and challenges a division between 'micro' and 'macro' sociologies, turning the 'social forces' such as patriarchy or neoliberalism that have been often used to explain social phenomena into the things that themselves need to be explicated. Deleuze and Guattari supply ontological concepts that can help to flesh out this change of focus, with their emphasis on assemblages rather than entities, and on affects in place of agency, while also offering a sociologically and sociologically-viable micropolitics of assemblages as 'becomings', always in flux. Barad challenges social science to shift its focus of debate over social inquiry from epistemology to ontology, firmly situating the sociological observer as part of the events being researched, and 'meaning' as part of materiality. Finally, Braidotti offers an intellectual, ethical and political agenda for the new materialisms in which embodiment, subjectivity and ecology are parts of a posthuman project that transcends the humanities, social and natural sciences.

With the benefit of these theoretical insights, what then might the imagination of a new materialist sociology (or sociologically-inflected new materialism) encompass? To structure our answer to that question, we might begin with the ontological claims that we set out in the opening pages of this book concerning what matter does, the relationship between nature and culture, and social production. We will re-work and develop these in the light of the new materialist theorists we have reviewed, and the tendency of all four to cut across dualisms such as nature/culture or mind/matter, favouring instead monistic explanations that at the same time open social processes, and hence sociology, to flux and multiplicity (van der Tuin and Dolphijn, 2010). These propositions will seek to refine understanding of what a 'materiality' signifies, with the aim of establishing a framework for materialist sociology, and to consider how this challenges some of the foundational sociological conceptions of both the social world and how social inquiry is to be undertaken. At this point, we will simply sketch out the broad features of a new materialist sociology; we will add more detail to our model throughout the book, as we explore different areas of sociology.

1. A focus upon matter

The starting point for a new materialist sociology is its ontological orientation, which asserts a strict focus upon 'matter' (though as will be seen in a moment, matter comes in disparate forms). This orientation marks a clear shift away from the concerns of post-structuralist and other idealist sociological theories. These latter perspectives emphasize the constructed character of the social world; consequently constructs, language, systems of thought and discourses have been the focus of concern, both theoretically and as objects of social inquiry, displacing the sociological observer from the materiality of the social and natural world (Coole and Frost, 2010: 3).

New materialist sociology's concern is with social production rather than social construction, and consequently extends to examine matter's capacities: how it interacts, affects and is affected by other materialities, and how material forces produce both the world and human history from moment to moment. New materialism emphasizes matter's capacity for self-organization (or 'autopoiesis'), or even its 'vitality' (Bennett, 2010). We see this not as imputing 'life' to matter, but recognizing that new materialism's monism means that matter is ontologically free (Braidotti, 2013: 56): it is not 'opposed' to anything else (for example, 'mind' or 'spirit'), nor is there anything inside or outside matter that makes it do what it does.

2. Explore what matter does, not what it is

If new materialisms shift away from constructionist concerns with how human constructs and meanings produce the social world, the perspectives we have surveyed do not simply adopt a realist notion of a multitude of individual material entities each located within its own bit of space and time (Coole and Frost, 2010: 7). For all the new materialist scholars surveyed earlier, materialities – bodies, objects, organs, species and so forth – should be regarded not as ontologically-prior essences, each occupying distinct and delimited spaces, but as *relational*, gaining ontological status and integrity only through their relationship to other similarly contingent and ephemeral bodies, things and ideas (Deleuze 1988: 123; Haraway, 1991: 201).

This relational ontology has led new materialist scholars to assert that matter is to be studied not in terms of what it is, but in terms of what it does: what associations it makes, what capacities it has to affect its relations or to be affected by them, what consequences derive from these interactions. This relationality, and the concepts to describe it, are perhaps most fully developed in Deleuze's (1988) ontology. This adopts Spinoza's notion of an *affect* (Deleuze, 1988: 101), meaning simply the capacity to affect or be affected, in place of a conventional conception of 'agency'. An affect represents a change of state or capacities of an entity (Massumi, 1988: xvi) – a change that might be physical, psychological, emotional or social; as such it is a 'becoming' (Deleuze and Guattari, 1988: 256). Affects are what links matter to other matter relationally, within *assemblages* (Blackman, 2012; Deleuze and Guattari 1988: 88) that work rather like machines, inasmuch as they do something, they produce something, according to what Clough (2004: 15) calls an 'affect economy' of forces. Of course as matter within assemblages is affected it may acquire new capacities to itself affect; this goes on repeatedly within assemblages, in a 'rhizomic', branching, reversing, coalescing and rupturing flow (Deleuze and Guattari, 1988: 7). Materiality is consequently plural and complex, uneven and contingent, relational and emergent (Coole and Frost, 2010: 29). We will apply this ontology of assemblages and affect economies throughout the rest of this book, as we look at different topics in sociology.

3. Human agency is not privileged

This understanding of matter's inherent capacity to affect has an important consequence. Rather than being merely inert stuff that may or may not be moulded by human agency, consciousness and imagination (Barad, 1996: 181; Coole and Frost, 2010: 2), the conventional hierarchy of matter (from the 'raw materials' of rocks and gases, through to simple life forms and onwards and upwards until we reach human agents) is flattened. Matter is not to be evaluated by its essence, but by its capacities to affect (Bennett, 2010: 3).

This undermines the emphasis on humans as exclusively productive of the social world, with profound implications for the concerns of social researchers (typically with human lives, experiences and identities), the kinds of data that are to be collected, and the sorts of research questions that should be posed. However, it also reflects a broader shift. Since their inception, the social sciences have been marked by their *anthropocentrism*, which privileged the human being and her social, psychological, economic, political and spatial interactions with her environment as their focus (Berger and Luckman, 1971; Giddens, 1982: 11; Mills, 2000 [1959]: 3). A materialist turn in sociology redresses this anthropocentric focus, recognizing humans as one materiality among many (Braidotti, 2006b: 41). This has the consequence of cutting across animate/inanimate and human/animal dualisms that underpin the natural and social science understandings and systems of privilege. In this way, all matter is emancipated from anthropocentric hierarchies.

Recognition of the multiplicity of matter's capacity for affectivity cuts across one of sociology's favourite dualisms: agency/structure (DeLanda, 2006: 10). Of even greater significance, however, is the challenge this poses to the conventional distinction drawn between natural and social worlds. If matter, or more specifically how materialities affect or are affected, becomes the focus for social scientific exploration, then the distinction between 'natural world' materialities – 'things' such as physical objects, bodies or nervous impulses – and 'social' materialities from cultural practices to rules of social conduct, becomes irrelevant. It no longer makes sense to compare and contrast natural and social worlds; instead we should acknowledge a singular, yet multiple and rhizomic materiality. We explore this fully in the next chapter when we consider environment, and again in Chapter 8, when we look at health and sociology. However, this new monism of materialism has some other surprising consequences, as revealed in the next proposition.

4. Thoughts, memories, desires and emotions have material effects

If a focus upon what materiality does enables new materialist ontology to transcend the dualism of the natural and the social, then it also provides the means to transcend the conventional dualism between mind and matter (Barad, 2007: 152; Coole and Frost, 2010: 26–7). Because thoughts, ideas, memories, feelings, desires, and collective abstractions and 'constructions' can all materially affect and be affected by other relations in an assemblage, they can be treated in exactly the same way as other (seemingly more 'material') relations (Deleuze and Guattari, 1988: 89; see also Barad, 1996: 181). Barad (1996: 188) describes the 'intra-actions' between matter and knowledge that produce phenomena, while Deleuze and Guattari (1988: 88), DeLanda (2006) and Latour (2005) consider how the physical and cultural assemble together to produce bodies, social formations and events.

This proposition marks a radical divergence from the exclusive focus in earlier materialist sociologies upon macro-structures, social institutions and economic relations noted earlier. It draws into the materialist domain aspects often regarded as the 'subjective epiphenomena' of events: knowledge, meanings, interpretations and social constructs, beliefs and values, as well as memories, reflections and aspirations. To the extent that all of these have the capacity to affect or be affected, they must be considered as productive relations within material phenomena or events (Barad, 2007: 152; Haraway, 1997: 129). With this focus upon the materiality of actions, interactions, subjectivities and thoughts, new materialism cuts across a conventional mind/matter dualism (van der Tuin and Dolphijn, 2010: 166), not by an anthropocentric privileging of human *constructions* of 'reality', but by recognizing the dynamic, generative and rhizomic *production* and actualization of the world, in which both matter and meaning play a part.

The significance of this latter ontological move for the new materialist sociology that we develop in this book must not be under-estimated. By drawing the supposedly separate realms of the 'objective' and the 'subjective' into one plane, with no 'other' or 'outside' or 'deeper level', this new materialist perspective on how the world and human history are continually actualized and realized, cuts across the rival epistemologies of realism (that asserts a deep reality independent of human construction) and constructionism (that denies that such a reality might ever be known). Epistemological issues of how humans can 'know' the world appear as anthropocentric hubris, now sidelined by ontological concerns with what the world is (or rather, with what it *does*). As Barad (1996) has shown, human observers are ineluctably caught up in the actions they attempt to describe and explain, and rather than bemoaning a failure of objectivity, from a new materialist perspective, this reveals how thoughts, desires and interpretations are part of the on-going production of materiality.

5. Material forces act locally

Together, the previous propositions supply a relational ontology, in which multiple relations assemble or associate as a consequence of their capacities to affect or be affected. The fifth proposition addresses the forces between these relations.

The workings of power within modern societies have been a key concern throughout sociology's history (Giddens, 1981: 49). In Marx's historical materialism, power was relational but top-down: a process by which material social relations are exerted: by one class over another, or by the state upon a certain class (Jessop, 2012: 4; Nigam, 1996: 8–9; van Krieken, 1991). Post-structuralism has offered an alternative perspective, arguing that power in the contemporary world is not coercive and 'top-down', but instead disciplinary or governmental, concerned with controlling the minute details of human conduct in daily life (Foucault, 1990). It is a phenomenon revealed and deployed at the level of actions and events; as Foucault (1982: 789) put it, power 'acts upon actions'.

The new materialisms similarly break with top-down conceptions of power, and focus on the forces (or affects) operating at the level of actions and events. The monism of new materialist ontology – of relational materialities assembled by their capacities to affect and be affected – requires that power is seen not as something outside or beyond the flow of affects in assemblages, but *as* this flow itself (Braidotti, 2013: 188–9). Power is a transient, fluctuating phenomenon – a momentary exercise by one relation over another; only if replicated in multiple events over time and space, does it acquire a more regular patterning, which in traditional sociology has then been seen as a thing in its own right (for instance, as 'patriarchy' or 'neoliberalism'). However, this regularity is illusory: power has continuity only as long as it is replicated in the next event, and the one after that. Resistance to power, in the same way, is processual and transitory rather than something that stands outside of material affectivity. We explore power in greater detail in Chapter 4 when we unpick a new materialist perspective on social structure and organization, while in Chapter 10 we look at 'resistance', in relation to social change and sociological activism.

6. The materiality of sociology

Of course, these propositions about how materialities work also apply to sociology and to sociological research, and the final proposition asserts a need to understand sociology as a material and affective process. A new materialist sociology must be reflexive about how it contributes to the production of the world, social and natural, and what assemblages it is drawn into. This is pertinent when it comes to considering sociological research. Conventionally, social inquiry (like other scientific inquiry) has been anthropocentric, regarding the researcher as the prime mover in the research enterprise, whose reason, logic, theory and scientific method gradually imposes order upon 'data' to supply an understanding, however imperfect, of the world (and its social construction).

Applying the new materialist ontology of assemblages and affects developed in the preceding propositions to sociology itself, requires that we treat the researcher and the researched event, plus the many other relations involved in social inquiry such as the tools, technologies and theories of scientific research, as relations within a *research-assemblage* productive of a variety of material capabilities in its human and non-human constituents. This research-assemblage is shaped by affects and produces relations of power and resistance in just the same way as any other materiality, undermining any recourse to notions of the 'objectivity' of research (cf. Barad, 1996: 185). We take this up in detail in Chapter 9, while Chapter 10 will examine the associated issue of how sociology engages with social policy, social change, power and resistance. These latter chapters will consequently review the issue of precisely what a materialist sociology should do.

Applying the new materialist imagination sociologically

With the benefit of a review of new materialist scholarship, and the subsequent development of six propositions for a new materialist sociology, we can now set out more explicitly a sociologically-useable formulation of an ontology to which we shall refer from here on simply as 'materialist' (losing the prefix 'new'). By setting out these propositions at this point in the book we offer an agenda for what follows, as we turn to consider the practicalities of doing materialist sociology and undertaking materialist research. We will expand on the points we have made as we progress through the book, developing the understanding of the approach and making connections with materialist scholarship and with studies that have used such approaches. This will provide the means for students and scholars to apply a materialist sensibility to sociological topics, and to foster a materialist sociological imagination based upon a materialist understanding of the social.

To illustrate how we intend to use materialist ontology to elucidate issues in sociology, we will apply the principles we have just set out to a topic that is central to contemporary social life, and a concern for sociologists of all methodological and theoretical hues – the challenges deriving from the ageing profile of Western industrialized countries. Our aim here is not to do a full-blown analysis of ageing: such an enterprise would be premature here, given we have not yet set out some other core aspects of materialist ontology (such as the elision of nature/culture to be considered in Chapter 3, or the materialist re-thinking of social stratification that we shall explore in Chapter 4). What we will do is to take some 'data' (descriptive statistics and an extract from an interview), and use these to establish a materialist approach, using some of the concepts we encountered earlier, specifically *relation*, *assemblage*, *affect* and *micropolitics*.

Ageing is a feature of contemporary industrialized countries, a consequence of declining birth rates and rising longevity due to improvements in health (United Nations, 2013). Official statistics suggest this trend will continue into the future, posing challenges for financial support and care of older adults by younger generations (via direct cash transfers within families, or through taxation and pensions) (Office for National Statistics, 2012; United Nations, 2013).

Whereas such 'macro-level', aggregated data might be the starting point for a conventional sociology of ageing (while other sociologists might choose to focus upon the experiences of ageing through observation and interviews), our fifth materialist proposition above emphasized how power and resistance operate at a local level, 'acting on actions' in the myriad events that make up the social world and produce the flow of history. So our materialist starting point is necessarily concerned with what happens in the *events* that constitute 'ageing', rather than with some abstracted generalization. To focus at the level of an 'ageing event', consider this extract from an interview with Mr L, an older adult who Nick interviewed (Fox, 2005) as part of an ethnographic research study on older people and care in Australia and Thailand. Mr L lived with his wife at 'Springwood', a residential facility for older people (of a type known in Australia as 'hostel accommodation'), comprising self-contained units plus some communal spaces and employing a range of medical and non-medical support personnel. Here he is talking about his daily life at Springwood.

> The change in the government made a lot of difference here. Not the level of care but the availability of staff coming to you. We can press that button and it might be 10 minutes or even longer before a girl [care assistant] comes. In that time you could be lying on the floor. You could have had a heart attack. At night time, you can walk around here looking for the sister and you can't find her. Nobody at the nurses' station, so if there is somebody in a bad way, it's a hell of a problem trying to find somebody sometimes. ... Each person has got a care list but in a lot of cases the girls don't even read it. They don't know what they're supposed to do. They say they haven't got time to read it and we have had the Aged Rights Advocacy [representative] here and it's in their statement that the girls should read everybody's nursing care plan so that they know what they've got to do. But if you upset the girls, they can make it awkward for you. ... I guess this goes on everywhere, in every home. There's others a lot worse than this. We visited quite a lot of places before we came in here and some of them were like a jail, you know. ... This one at least is nice and airy and open and bright – everything is on the same level. It's got a lot going for it but it's the shortage of staff that is the problem. They can't do enough about that here ... it's down to the government. I don't think they care enough about older people.

To address the *first* and *second* of our propositions, our analytical focus needs to be firmly upon materiality, and its relationality – what it does rather than what it is. So a materialist analysis begins by trawling these two sources of data, to make sense of how a wide range of materialities have been assembled (to use Latour's and Deleuze and Guattari's terminology). In these data, we can discover both 'local' relations (in the interview), and some of the contexts (suggested by the official statistics). The resulting 'ageing-assemblage' is a cloud of 'intra-acting' (Barad, 1996: 179) material relations, which might be represented thus (in no particular order):

> Mr L – Mrs L – 'Springwood' residence – concrete and glass – health – medical facilities – care assistants – care plan – management – other residents – memories – fear/anxiety – Aged Rights Advocacy – government – money – national care policy – ageing population – time

No doubt there are many other relevant relations that cannot be picked up from the few data presented here, and in practice we would use multiple interviews or observational data to generate a more complete understanding of the 'ageing assemblage' (see, for instance, Alldred and Fox, 2015b). However, this will suffice to illustrate the approach.

Our *third* proposition is about how assembled relations affect or are affected by each other, shifting attention away from the anthropocentric privilege supplied to human agency in conventional sociology, and ascribing this 'affective' capacity to all kinds of matter. The *fourth* proposition meanwhile has recognized that thoughts, memories, emotions and desires – through their ability to affect – are also material. To learn what an assemblage does, and the consequences for those relations assembled within it, the next step is to use the interview and observational data to reveal how the assembled relations affect, and are affected. So in this assemblage we might identify how staff affect residents physically and psychologically (and *vice versa*); the effects of the built environment on residents' moods and behaviour; how money is used to provide care to older adults; the way governmental policy affects care and in turn how the quality of care produces anxiety or fear in residents; how memories affect residents' daily preferences and decisions; the demands on staff time from multiple duties; how care plans affect what care is provided; dialogues between ageing advocates and management, and so forth.

Patricia Clough (2004: 15) has suggested we think of the mix of affects in an 'event' (an interaction, action or other assemblage) as an 'affect economy' that shifts bodies and other relations 'from one mode to another, in terms of attention, arousal, interest, receptivity, stimulation, attentiveness, action, reaction, and inaction'. This affect economy makes an assemblage do what it does and produce the capacities of all the assembled relations, from human bodies to government policy. It both holds an assemblage together and may drive it apart, and comprises affects that range from the natural (such as the physical properties of concrete or glass), the biological (for example, physiological processes of ageing), through the psychological (emotions and memories), to the sociocultural (for instance, social interactions between staff and residents). The affect economy mediates the micropolitics of the assemblage, or to put it in sociological terms, the processes of power and resistance that shape social organization and subjectivities.

This analysis draws into assemblage both natural/physical and cultural/psychological relations, and also the 'micro' of embodiment and human experiences and the 'macro' of government policy and demography (Youdell and McGimpsey, 2015: 119). Recall again our *fifth* proposition about the local nature of power and resistance, and the absence of a 'structural' level in this materialist ontology. This means that if a materialist ontology is to work sociologically, it is these affects or forces – and these alone – that must produce everything, from a human's social identity or a body's capacities, through to the continuities and social regularities that we discern in social life (in this example, 'macro-level' things like a national care policy or an ageing population). They must also generate the kinds of social 'entities' that sociology has conventionally called structures, mechanisms, systems or discourses, of which 'ageism' is an example.

How is this possible? In Chapter 4, we will address this when we consider a materialist sociology of organization, and how a materialist sociology moves beyond 'structural' models of the social. For now, we might simply note that a 'local' event (such as described by Mr L here) assembles the 'micro' of experience and subjectivity with the 'macro' of laws, policies, economies and so forth – as mediated by local affects. So, for instance, in this illustration, macro-level factors such as declining birth rates, increased longevity and government economic austerity are mediated locally by the reduced service that staff can provide as a consequence of tight budgets and demands on time. Meanwhile, an affect economy such as the one described by Mr L at 'Springwood', if temporally and spatially reproduced at other locations, may eventually manifest to outside observers as a broader social formation or 'structure'. For instance, pressures on staff time and a consequent lack of attention afforded to residents, reproduced over time, and in many other parallel facilities, little by little produce an apparent pattern of inter-generational inequality which is then labelled by sociologists and by activists alike as 'ageism'.

This example has demonstrated the kind of analysis that can be undertaken by applying the materialist propositions that we have developed in this chapter. It establishes a dynamic understanding of an event that draws micro and macro, natural and cultural, human and non-human into assemblage. However, it clarifies an important point about materialist analysis: sociologically, the focus of interest and concern rests entirely upon the micropolitics of what goes on within assemblages. Much of what will follow in this book will be devoted to micropolitical exploration of material affect economies in different fields of sociological concern. We will conclude this chapter by exploring two micropolitical processes that we will encounter throughout our materialist sociology.

The micropolitics of social production

To understand what goes on inside assemblages, we shall apply two concepts to aid us, derived from DeleuzoGuattarian materialism. The first, 'territorialization' (Deleuze and Guattari, 1988: 88–89), we noted earlier addresses how affect economies in assemblages produce specific capacities in bodies and other relations. We see this as an 'ecological' *specification* process not unrelated to the French agricultural notion of 'terroir', which acknowledges how features in the immediate physical environment establish a vine's or a beehive's capacities to produce certain qualities in wine or honey. Similarly, affects deriving from relations in assemblages specify or 'localize' the capacities of a body or other relation.

Territorialization/specification is not absolute, because other affects may de-territorialize/generalize and then re-territorialize/re-specify a body, re-shaping the possibilities and limits of what a body can do, continuously and unendingly. The most obvious case in the illustration above was the territorialization or specification of Mr L and his wife by natural and sociocultural affects in terms of age. Meanwhile care assistants were territorialized by their employment, by time and by the requirements to follow care plans.

The second analytic concept we use to explore assemblage micropolitics is a distinction between 'aggregative' and 'singular' affects (Fox and Alldred, 2014).[3] Aggregating affects act similarly on multiple bodies, organizing or categorizing them to create converging identities or capacities. In our example, Mr and Mrs L were aggregated by the Springwood assemblage into a category of dependent residents, establishing their status, capacities and others' expectations; meanwhile the care assistants were aggregated as 'the girls' with other statuses and capacities. Aggregation is very widespread in human cultures, producing the social stratifications of gender, race and class that we shall look at in Chapter 4, as well as other social categories such as 'delinquent', 'criminal', 'heterosexual' and so on. Prejudices and biases may aggregate people according to specific physical or behavioural characteristics, while the discourses on human conduct documented by Foucault (1976, 1979, 1981, 1990) aggregate bodies through discipline or governmentality.

By contrast, other affects produce a singular outcome or capacity in just one body or other relation, with no significance beyond itself, and without aggregating consequences. Singular affects in Mr L's account included his effort to summon a care assistant to provide help, or the effect the home's architecture had on his mood. Events will usually comprise many singular affects, from a smell that triggers an emotion to a memory that produces an action or a decision. Such singular affects may act on occasions as micropolitical drivers of de-territorialization, enabling bodies to resist aggregating or constraining forces, and opening up new capacities to act, feel or desire – a dis-aggregation described by Deleuze and Guattari (1988: 277) as a 'line of flight'. As such, they will be of interest to us as we explore resistance from a materialist standpoint.

These two dynamic processes of specification/generalization and aggregation/dis-aggregation will be our ways into exploring the micropolitics of assemblages. In our illustration, they can provide us with an assessment of the dependency culture of Springwood, as mediated by micropolitical processes including cultural understandings of ageing, the institutionalization of aged care in both architecture and social interactions, as exacerbated by economic austerity and staff shortages. At the same time, there remain possibilities for singular affects and lines of flight (Fox, 2005) – resistance is always possible. A full-blown analysis of Springwood and its residents and staff would seek to reveal the granularity of materiality and how it produces both the daily lives of older adults and the broader material circumstances of ageing in a developed country. It would establish a basis for a critical perspective on the materiality of human ageing, recognizing how the natural and the cultural together contribute to this aspect of the social world. It would also provide a means to think differently about ageing, to take an ecological, post-anthropocentric and posthuman view of time and its effects on matter in all its human and non-human forms (Braidotti, 2013: 111ff.).

It is appropriate therefore that we turn in the next chapter to consideration of 'the environment', in which we explore more broadly the significance of the micropolitical processes of specification and aggregation.

Summary

In this chapter, we have introduced the new materialisms, and by exploring the main features of just some of the leading scholars, have established the principles of a materialist sociology, which we shall apply in the rest of this book. These principles address how a materialist sociology understands materiality, the relationality of materialities, the ways that capacities are produced in materialities and the micropolitics of power and resistance in materialist sociology.

(Continued)

(Continued)

In the final section of this chapter, we set out a model for how we shall develop a materialist sociology in subsequent chapters. We introduced the key concepts of relations, assemblages, affects and micropolitics, and showed how these can be used to address an event sociologically. We will use this approach repeatedly as we look at different sociological topics, both in terms of materialist and posthuman theory and in terms of practical social research and policy. Our next chapter starts on that exploration, as we turn to the intra-actions between 'nature' and 'culture'.

Notes

1. Ontology concerns propositions about the fundamental nature of things and the kinds of things that exist, while epistemology addresses how these things can be known by an observer.

2. The Copenhagen Interpretation was Niels Bohr's proposition that quantum particles exist in multiple states, and are only brought into a specific state when interacting with an outside agency such as an observer. Because for a single particle this state may vary from observation to observation, this makes the universe uncertain and unpredictable.

3. Our terms aggregative and singular replace Deleuze and Guattari's (1984: 286–8) terminology of 'molar' and 'molecular' affects, respectively.

Further reading

Barad, K. (1996) Meeting the universe halfway: realism and social constructivism without contradiction. In: Nelson, L.H. and Nelson, J. (eds.) *Feminism, Science and the Philosophy of Science*. Dordrecht: Kluwer, pp. 161–194.

Braidotti, R. (2013). *The Posthuman*. Cambridge: Polity.

Latour, B. (2005) *Re-assembling the Social*. Oxford: Oxford University Press.

Law, J. (2009) Actor network theory and material semiotics. In: Turner, B. (ed.) *The New Blackwell Companion to Social Theory*. Oxford: Blackwell, pp. 141–158.

Youdell, D. and McGimpsey, I. (2015) Assembling, disassembling and reassembling 'youth services' in Austerity Britain. *Critical Studies in Education*, 56(1): 116–130.

3

Environment

Humans, Posthumans and Ecological Sociology

Introduction

In the previous chapter, we considered the ways in which materialist scholars and researchers have conceptualized the world in terms of its materiality, and made some suggestions about how this perspective affects the ways in which a materialist sociological imagination might develop. We developed a set of propositions to guide the practice of a materialist sociology, and also identified an emphasis on exploring assemblage micropolitics. To develop this imagination further, we will focus in this chapter on a foundational issue in sociology: the relationship between humans and their environment.

Our intention here is to bring to bear a materialist perspective on the specific ways in which sociology has considered environment, and in the process, explore some foundational dualisms for sociology: culture/nature, human/non-human and agency/structure. These dualisms, we would argue, contribute to an 'anthropocentric' focus for sociological discussions of environment, in which the human and the cultural are privileged over environment, nature and other species (Stevens, 2012). Our objective will be to explore the consequences for sociology of adopting an alternative materialist sociology of environment that cuts across such dualisms and applies the 'flat', monistic ontology of materialism outlined in Chapter 2.

Historically, culture/nature dualism has been a neat way to set limits on the concerns of the social and natural sciences, respectively (Barad, 1996: 181; Braidotti, 2013: 3; Fox and Alldred, 2015). At first sight, it seems fair to ascribe phenomena such as patterns of atmospheric pressure or the operation of living cells and organs to the 'natural' world and others such as industrialization or sexuality to an alternative realm: the 'social' world. But what happens when we start to explore embodiment, anthropogenic climate change, or the effects of the built environment on human well-being? It swiftly becomes clear that the natural and cultural are intertwined and that a culture/nature dualism imposes a false division to understanding these complex processes. More and more, social and natural scientists in fields as disparate as epigenetics, macroeconomics and environmental science are recognizing that we need to cut across these artificial distinctions, and work across disciplinary boundaries to formulate new questions and solutions (Landecker and Panofsky, 2013; Meloni, 2014; Niewöhner, 2011: 281).

So we begin this chapter with a look back at how sociology has conventionally addressed the physical environment. We shall argue the need to move beyond sociology's anthropocentric privileging of the human over the non-human (Haraway, 1991: 11), to develop a perspective on the environment that, rather than differentiating the realms of human and non-human, draws culture and nature into one affective assemblage. Drawing on the work of Haraway, Braidotti and Guattari, we will promote a 'posthuman' and ecological sociological perspective that sees humans as fully integral to the 'environment', re-thought as the world of physical and social relations that is both productive of – and produced by – the on-going flow of events that comprise the history of the Earth and the universe.

Sociology, humans and the environment

The word 'environment' is applied in a variety of ways, both in everyday usage and in different scientific disciplines. Earth sciences such as geology and climatology use 'environment' to set the parameters and boundaries of their subject areas; biological scientists regard it as the ecological setting that has affected (and continues to affect) the differential evolution of the panoply of species and the behaviours of life-forms; physical and social geographers and architects consider environment as the back-cloth for their studies and practices concerning places and spaces; health scientists see it a repository of hazards afflicting humans and other animals. Finally, social sciences such as sociology, economics and political science treat 'the environment' as the broad social context for human action, and differentiate between the physical and biological environment on one hand and on the other, the social and cultural environment (Dunlap and Catton, 1979: 245). They also increasingly use the term to refer to the global physical milieu of the Earth, often implicitly or explicitly considering this as a fragile and limited resource that is under threat from human culture.

Social scientists have engaged variously with issues concerning environment and ecology. First, they applied a broad notion of environment as a context for social action, in which 'the environment' is basically everything that is not part of a human body, a product of human agency, or a human construction (Dunlap and Catton, 1979; Walker, 2005: 80), and analysed the interactions between society and the environment – usually focusing upon how to manipulate the natural environment for the benefit of human kind, for example, to manage water or food supplies (Pretty and Ward, 2001: 209), or to enhance human health (Hoehner et al., 2003, Swinburn et al., 1999). In its original formulation, this amounted to what Catton and Dunlap (1978) called a 'human exemptionalist (or exceptionalist) paradigm', which, as Stevens (2012: 580) has put it, asserted:

> a fundamental separation between humans and the rest of the animal world, culture being a uniquely human quality that is more variable and able to change more rapidly than purely biological traits; that humans have freedom of choice, subject only to social and cultural factors; that sociologists should focus on a social and cultural environment that is discrete from biophysical considerations; and that human ingenuity and problem-solving shows a cumulative progression that can continue to expand *ad infinitum*.

Second, social scientists sought understanding of the part that the physical environment has played in shaping human existence: for instance, the particularities of climate and geology that determine cultural stability or environmental events such as frequent flooding; longer-term climatic changes that affect human endeavour (Urry, 2009); or the psychological and social effects of the built environment (Halpern, 2013) or countryside (Watkins and Jacoby, 2007). They contributed to debates about the effects of the environment on humans, pointing to the social, psychological and cultural mediation of links between health and ill-health and the material environment (Dunlap and Catton, 1979: 254; Nettleton, 2006: 89; Schulz and Northridge, 2004), and offered critical insights into public understanding and construction of environmental hazards (Dunlap, 1998).

Finally, since the 1990s sociologists addressed concerns that 'the environment' as a system is progressively being damaged by human social and economic activity. Furthermore, it must now be protected from the ravages of an 'anthropocene' era (Braidotti, 2013: 79; Steffen et al., 2007) in which the physical attributes of our planet are increasingly affected (possibly irrevocably) by human activity (Dunlap and Catton, 1994: 24). Social theorists offered a critical perspective on environmentalism and the construction of a 'risk society' (Fox, 1991; Matten, 2004; Mol and Spaargaren, 1993; Shrivastava, 1995); explored the problems and challenges scientists face when recommending cultural or behavioural changes to address threats from the environment (Wandersman and Hallman, 1993); and suggested methods to assess quantitatively people's concern with environmental threats and 'ecological consciousness' (Dunlap et al., 2000). This scholarship reflects broadly what Dunlap and Catton (1979) have designated as a 'new ecological paradigm', in which humans – though still distinct from the rest of nature – are part of the global ecosystem, and are governed by the same 'ecological laws' as other species, which they may not flout with impunity (Stevens, 2012: 580).

As we will see later, these environmental sociological angles have all depended upon sustaining a distinction or an opposition between humans and environment, and a view of the environment as 'conceptually subordinate to society' (Walker, 2005: 80). Humans and their social products are to be defined as distinct from the great mass of 'everything else', be that the rocks and seas studied by geology and geography, the animals and plants of the 'natural world', or the built environment. Despite environmental sociology's shift from the exceptionalist to the ecological paradigm, it has remained fundamentally *anthropocentric* (Stevens, 2012: 8).

This anthropocentrism may indeed be ingrained within sociology. As Haraway (1992: 65): 157–8) has noted, 'nature' has long been culture's 'Other', used as a justification for colonialism, racism, sexism and class domination, and this dualism bled over into the foundational premises of the social sciences (Shalin, 1990: 8), reinforced by the 19th century differentiation between human social life and the forces of nature then being revealed in theories of genetics and natural selection. This opposition of nature and culture has subsequently manifested at points throughout sociology's history, from Durkheim's insistence on the social as a causal agency independent of biological processes, Weber's antinaturalism (Benton, 1991: 12), and Marx's view that humans are unique in their ability to produce the *means* of subsistence – for instance, by farming or industrialization (Seidman, 1992: 57). It is reflected in the differences claimed by social scientists between 'natural' and 'social' times (Newton, 2003); and in the view that the legitimate focus of sociology should be human social constructs, including 'environment' and 'climate change' (Fox, 1991; Murphy, 1995).

Evidencing anthropocentrism: health and the environment

To illustrate this sociological oppositional stance between environment and human culture, which with few exceptions defines how sociology has engaged with the natural world, consider the ways that the social sciences have conceptualized the relationship between 'environment' and 'human health'. We can identify five discrete models for this interaction:

First, human health has been seen as threatened by environmental factors such as floods, drought or climate change. This is a view widely held in public health and associated social science literature, in which the environment is a potentially dangerous place, full of hazards for unwitting humans (for example, see Douglas, 1992: 29). The usual consequence of this perspective is an effort to find scientific, technological or social means to overcome these environmental threats.

Second, improvements to the environment have been regarded as means to enhance human health. This is the obverse of the first perspective, and requires intervention by humanity against a risky environment, for example by developing more effective and efficient means of growing food crops, improving the built environment to provide sanitation, or by building defences against natural hazards such as floods (Halpern, 2013: 10–11; Mitchell and Popham, 2008).

Third, social scientists have identified more recently how improvements in health threaten the environment by degrading or exhausting its natural resources, for instance through exponential population growth, economic development or over-fishing or unsustainable farming practices (McMichael, 2013). Critical social science responses to this have been to argue for the need to build environmental resilience into social development, and to recognize the finite resources of planet Earth (Poland and Dooris, 2010; Westhoek et al., 2014).

The fourth perspective is a specific sub-case of the third, addressing the negative impacts of human healthcare on the environment: for example, run-off pollution from pharmaceutical manufacture, oestrogens from contraceptives and even waste water containing anti-bacterial mouthwash causing negative effects upon river life. The response here is to develop initiatives that seek to reduce this negative environmental impact by managing healthcare systems (Lange et al., 2002; Sarmah et al., 2006).

Finally, some 'Gaia'-inspired holistic conceptions have regarded humans as part of a self-regulating environmental system. Over an extended span of time, this will compensate for the excesses of human social and economic activity, possibly quite dramatically, and in ways that will have very negative consequences for human health, including radical population reduction or even extinction (Kirchner, 2002; Lovelock, 2007).

All these five perspectives are grounded in an implicit human/environment opposition. In all but the last, humans and their well-being implicitly or explicitly inhabit the privileged pole of the opposition. The fifth is a dystopian vision of how the environment will eventually bite back against human depredations, restoring nature's privilege over human culture, with the human era just a fleeting moment in the Earth's history. Though the polarity of privilege may be reversed, the implicit dualism of human/environment remains (Braidotti, 2013: 85).

Some sociologists have offered resolutions to the anthropocentrism and nature/culture dualism inherent in such social science engagements with environment. Ted Benton (1991) suggested that antagonism by sociology towards the natural sciences is a defensive response against movements such as sociobiology or evolutionary psychology that seek to reduce social processes to biology. What sociology needed, he argued, was a more sophisticated reaction that could enable social and natural sciences to co-exist and even integrate. A bias toward modernity and the West has rendered sociology inadequate to address global environmental challenges, Gavin Walker (2005) concluded, because of its failure to recognize the dual character of humans as both cultural and biological. In his view the solution lay in a synthesis between environmental sociology and cultural anthropology, applying the latter's sophisticated Weberian conception of 'culture' to incorporate broader biological and environmental factors into an understanding of human life (2005: 99–100). In similar vein, Paul Stevens (2012) called for an 'ecosociology' that recognized environmental contexts as part of the human experience of embodiment, and extending ideas of 'the social' beyond the human, as a means to address issues of environmental sustainability, to 'help humanity come to terms with its unique, but not pre-eminent role in the global system' (2012: 579).

All of these assessments – in one way or another – have recognized constraints inherent in mainstream sociology's orientation that limit engagement with the 'natural world'. None, however, has adopted a radical ontological solution that cuts across the very dualism that sets the social and the natural in opposition. This is the starting point for the materialist approach that we will develop here, adopting the alternative flat, monistic ontology that we set out in the previous chapter. To explore this, we will stick initially with the specific issue of the relationship between human health and the environment, before broadening this to offer an alternative to environmental anthropocentrism.

When exploring potential cause/effect interactions between 'health' and 'environment', materialist ontology starts from the view that there are not pre-existent, fixed entities such as bodies, infectious agents, animals, plants, diseases, fossil fuels, atmospheric conditions, climates, coastlines, economic and political systems, consumers, motor vehicles, governments and all the other things that are implicated in a putative health/environment interaction. Rather, all these myriad materialities are relational, gaining form and continuity through their engagements with the other material relations with which they assemble, and through their 'becomings'. To this list of materialities we must add the expressive relations deriving from human minds, cultures and societies, such as beliefs, desires and values, ideas and feelings, political movements and institutions, ideologies and discourses, and so forth, all of which can materially affect other constituents of an assemblage.

These disparate relations accrete around specific events. Consider, for example, an initiative by public health staff in a city council to improve child health by reducing the number of vehicles using the roads during peak times, thus cutting pollution and road traffic accidents, and encouraging people to walk more or use bicycles. This policy is quite complex, and the relations involved may be represented (in no particular order) by the following assemblage:

> cars – public transport – bicycles – roads – fossil fuels – renewable fuels – pollution – schools – work places – shops – services – housing – workers – transport infrastructure – local employers – environmental campaigners – council leaders – urban planners – obesity – climate change – etc.

No doubt many other relations are also involved, but this is sufficient for the example. In the materialist ontology, this assemblage is the product of the affect economy between its component parts, and the capacities these affects establish in both human and non-human relations. It is these capacities that may enable the development of a viable public transport system. Of course, the assemblage is dynamic and always 'becoming-other', with relations and affects shifting continually, so there is no final guarantee of the outright success of such a scheme. If there are powerful forces in the assemblage (for example, cultural beliefs or entrenched local opposition) that disrupt the forces favouring success, then the development will falter and fail. By contrast, assuring that powerful affects (a flow of funding, political patronage, local support) are encouraged will improve the chances of success.

It is important to note that in this formulation, humans are not privileged actors over other relations: cars, roads and environmental beliefs are all affective in this assemblage, while the outcomes depend as much on the capacities of the non-human or inanimate components (for example, the pollution products of carbon fuels or the existence of cycle lanes) as upon those of school children or local campaigners. Because all these different relations are part of a shifting and unstable assemblage, and all are 'affective': affecting and being affected as they interact, it is ontologically unsustainable to retain an opposition – implicit or explicit – between human bodies and culture on one hand, and all the other physical and biological stuff that constitutes 'the environment' on the other. Indeed, human bodies, thought, ideas, memories, aspirations and so forth are drawn into a single assemblage alongside all that other 'stuff' that conventionally has been called 'material'.

This application of a materialist ontology of assemblages and affects, and the rejection (as we noted in Chapter 2) of any notion of another 'level' of systems, structures or mechanisms determining what assemblages do and produce, establishes the materialist approach as quite distinct from each of the five conventional approaches to thinking about human health and environment set out earlier. In each of those, humans were ontologically positioned as different from, indeed opposed to their environment. In the flattened monistic ontology of materialism, human and non-human are drawn into assemblage by their capacities to affect or be affected. Understood in this way, *'human' bodies and other 'human' relations in the assemblage are inseparable from – and have the same status as – 'environment'.*

Environmental sociology: beyond anthropocentrism, towards the posthuman

It is this monism that provides the means for a materialist sociology to break down the distinction between humans and the 'environment', or between human and non-human, and the nature/culture dualism that has given sustenance to the mainstream environmental sociological imagination. However, the point of this exercise is not simply to provide a neat philosophical trick that enables us to claim that humans are part of the environment. Rather than being the end-point of the analysis, an assessment of human/environment assemblages must be the start of a new way of thinking sociologically about nature and culture, with practical implications for how we understand and how we research the social and natural worlds, and also for how – ethically – sociology engages with the non-human. Removing the privilege from humans, human cultures and human endeavours by cutting across the nature/culture divide in this way has implications, both for a human culture that has often benefitted from this privilege, and for sociology, which has defined itself in part via this opposition. As a justification for this materialist ontology of environment, and to begin to consider what opportunities it affords to sociology, we draw on the perspectives of two materialist scholars, whose analyses bear on this matter.

The feminist biologist turned social theorist Donna Haraway has provided one of the most trenchant and comprehensive commentaries upon the negative consequences of nature/culture dualism for social justice and social change, beginning from the recognition of increasing and inevitable convergence of the organic and the inorganic in our contemporary technological society (Haraway, 1991, 1997). Haraway explored the proliferation of technologies and associated scientific perspectives that increasingly impinge upon human bodies. As a hook for her argument, she focused in on the notion of the 'cyborg': an admixture of flesh and technology that is not simply a *Terminator*-style creature of science fiction but to be found all around us in the contemporary world – the product of scientific and medical innovations that link bodies to inorganic matter, ranging from hip replacements and false teeth to gene therapies and test-tube babies.

However, she argued that, historically, along with the cyborg, those entities labelled as 'apes' and 'women' have also – in their different ways – unsettled the 'evolutionary, technological and biological narratives' (1991: 2) that have been founded upon an easy distinction between the natural and the human. These narratives (and the dualism they foster), Haraway concludes are not neutral: they are grounded in colonialism and racism, patriarchy and sexism, and the capitalist appropriation of nature for the exclusive benefit of culture (1991: 150). Cyborgs, simians and women all transgress the leaky boundary between these domains (1991: 154), and consequently provide the means to reveal the continuities between humans and the rest of the material universe, and the means to overturn many other dualisms including those that oppress specific individuals, groups, classes, genders and species (1991: 157, 177). Such transgressions, Haraway (1997: 270) argued, have the potential for 'tearing down a Berlin Wall between the world of objects and the world of subjects', revealing that nature and culture are inextricably tied up in all bodies.

The feminist philosopher Rosi Braidotti acknowledged Donna Haraway as 'my travel companion across multiple nomadic paths of reflection' (Braidotti, 2006a: 197); she writes of her aspirations to move beyond humanism and to champion a posthuman sensibility built on Haraway's commentaries. For Braidotti, the justification for overturning a nature/culture dualism lies in the recognition, cognate with Haraway's, that the interests of humans are not divorced from the interests of other living things and of the physical Earth.

Braidotti traces a trajectory for posthumanism that is beyond both humanism and 'anti-humanism'. Humanism provided the post-Enlightenment challenge to religious authority by elevating secular human reason over all else, including God (Carroll, 1993: 117), and thereby supplying the basis for progressive social and political change that extended from the literary Romantic movement to the French revolution to Marxism, first-wave feminism, anti-slavery campaigns and sexual liberation. Anti-humanism rejected this anthropocentric focus, and – most recently in the shape of post-structuralist theory – presented an alternative to what became an ossified and conservative humanism by the 20th century, and proclaimed the death of 'Man' as an intrinsically progressive force (Braidotti, 2013: 23). The human who had been the measure against which everything else was to be assessed physically and morally, turned out to be white, male, able-bodied and exploitative of all other life-forms (other than those fortunate few animal species such as cats, dogs and chimps that are individualized and anthropomorphized) (Braidotti, 2006a: 200; 2011: 82, 88–89).

However, while fully sympathetic to this latter critique of humanism, Braidotti has argued that anti-humanism risks throwing out the progressive achievements of humanism concerning solidarity, social justice and equality (2013: 29); additionally, it would be an ironic act of humanist hubris for humans to assert that the end of humanism was under their control (2013: 30)!

For these reasons, Braidotti has advocated an alternative 'posthuman' project grounded in the same monistic materialism that we set out earlier, in which matter and culture are not dialectically opposed. Posthumanism cuts across the humanist/anti-humanist opposition by emphasizing the vital capacities of all matter – animate and inanimate – for self-organization and 'becoming' (Braidotti, 2011: 16), in the sense that matter is continually affected and affecting. Sexual, racial and natural diversity considered by humanists as markers of categories of otherness (see Chapter 4), now are recognized as aspects of the multiplicity and rhizomic capacities of matter (2011: 139), and:

> act as the forces leading to the elaboration of alternative modes of transversal subjectivity, which extend not only beyond gender and race, but also beyond the human. (Braidotti, 2013: 98)

This understanding of the posthuman supplies Braidotti with the basis for an eco-philosophy that establishes a continuum between human and non-human matter (2013: 104), and between human subjectivity and planetary ecology (2006b: 41). This in turn has provided her with a posthuman ethics for an engagement with the environment, based on a new sense of inter-connectedness between human and non-human; 'an affirmative bond that locates the subject in the flow of relations with multiple others' (2013: 50).

These readings help us to set the parameters for a materialist sociology of the environment, within which – as we noted at the end of the previous section – humans and their bodies are now fully integrated ontologically. This means that human skin no longer has the weird property it had in dualist sociology – of separating everything human that is inside it (flesh, thoughts, cultural beliefs, feelings, desires) from everything else 'environmental' that is outside. Materialism's rejection of a distinction between nature and culture is not some arbitrary hang-up over dualisms. Rather, it is a necessary re-thinking that recognizes first – as Haraway has noted – that the nature/culture division was founded upon a supremacist politics of sexualization, racialization and naturalization of the West's Others; and second, as Braidotti has concluded, that the materialist act of refusing and overturning this politics of sexism, colonialism and anthropocentrism is a serious act that requires a new eco-philosophy and ethics that affirms the commonalities and connectedness of all matter.

Materialism, sociology and 'sustainability'

What does this mean for the practice of sociology, and in particular for the ways that sociology may research the issues surrounding the environment and humans' embeddedness within it? To begin this synthesis, how might a materialist sociology re-make the 'health and the environment' example we explored earlier, concerning an initiative to improve child health by reducing urban car journeys? Though the terms of that initiative have been framed firmly within an anthropocentric framework that privileges human health, we analysed it from within a materialist and non-anthropocentric perspective, to explore the health/environment assemblage to reveal an affect economy of multiple human and non-human relations and forces.

However, the analysis that we have developed subsequently in this chapter suggests that we need a more radical re-making of this 'problem' of child health and road traffic, and more broadly how we might address issues involving humans and their 'environment'. In an ontology that does not distinguish between human and non-human, culture and nature, and does not privilege humans over other matter, it no longer makes sense to explore this problem in terms of 'improving child health' by altering the environment, as if 'child health' were an entity separable from the rest of the stuff, or that 'the environment' was an entirely independent realm to be controlled and if possible manipulated to human benefit. Of course, this does not mean that we must abandon any effort to change the world, including changing aspects of it associated with human lives in ways that might, *inter alia*, improve health. But it does mean that we need to change how we think about things like 'child health', in line with the materialist ontology we developed in the previous chapter. You will recall that earlier we identified an assemblage of relations surrounding this event:

> cars – public transport – bicycles – roads – fossil fuels – renewable fuels – pollution – schools – workplaces – shops – services – housing – workers – transport infrastructure – local employers – environmental campaigners – council leaders – urban planners – obesity – climate change – etc.

The model for materialist sociology that we developed at the end of Chapter 2 suggests that, as with any event (which might be an observed activity, interaction or occurrence), we might explore this event though some general questions:

- What relations are assembled?

- What are the affects (and the affect economy) between these relations that assemble them and thereby produce the event?

- What are the capacities produced in the different relations by this affect economy – what can the human and non-human relations do?

- What are the micropolitics of the event assemblage – what does the event reveal about which relations in an assemblage are powerful?

(Incidentally, the latter question is of particular interest, as it opens the door to not only describing an event, but also making sense of why it is the way it is, and conceivably, manipulating the affect economy to change what an event does. We will have a lot more to say about this in Chapter 9, when we consider materialist sociological research.)

Analysis of this assemblage in terms of these questions will reveal a multiplicity of affective flows; for instance, an 'employment' flow that connects employers, workers, workplaces, houses and economics; an 'education' flow between children, schools, houses and so on; a 'transport' flow of roads, modes of travel, fuel, pollution, housing, schools, workplaces and so forth; and a 'climate' flow of fossil fuels, industry and transport, the atmosphere, the sun etc. The capacities of these affective flows produce the events associated with the assemblage, including economic production, education, traffic congestion, poor air quality, climate change and deleterious health outcomes. The micropolitics of the assemblage reflect the disparate ways power flows through it, including the development of a city environment that bring workplaces and current and future generations of workers into proximity; the economics and physical logistics of managing daily transport; the economics and politics of cheap energy; and the democratic and technocratic processes of planning a city to achieve a range of sometimes contradictory objectives such as financial prosperity and human health/well-being.

This monist analysis suggests that the issue of improving 'child health' is caught up in a highly complex assemblage, with multiple affective flows and contradictory micropolitics. Traditionally, public health interventions and social science analysis of such complex assemblages have sought to isolate a specific cause/effect flow of affect in the assemblage and intervene accordingly (for instance, banning all 'school run' journeys by parents transporting children to and from school, and providing an alternative public transport system). The materialist analysis that we are developing here suggests another approach, which would aim for a more holistic engagement with the assemblage. Significantly, this would not make a foundational distinction between humans and 'the rest', instead adopting a posthuman sensibility that neither privileges nor denies human aspirations, values and desires. The stages in this process would be:

- Seek a comprehensive understanding of the affects and the micropolitics that surround the interactions between children and transport.

- Critically evaluate how the assemblage sustains particular patterns of social, economic and political power.

- Address the contradictions that emerge between the different affective flows between relations (for example, between the needs of industry and the health of citizens).

To these, we suggest a fourth stage:

- Explore multiple ways to engineer *sustainability* into the assemblage.

This latter point requires further justification, as it introduces sustainability as an objective for this materialist analysis. Sustainability is a contested concept (Braidotti et al., 1994; Lockie, 2016; Ratner, 2004), which draws into assemblage a range of natural science, ecological, economic, political, social justice and other perspectives on the interactions and conflicts between nature and culture. Given both our flat ontology of events and affects, and the arguments in this chapter about the need to move beyond nature/culture dualism, we are disinclined to treat sustainability either as a point of conflict between human desires and natural environmental limitations, or in terms of how negative or positive feedback loops may enable continuity of systems. What a materialist perspective on assemblages suggests is that, indeed, most assemblages are not sustainable and have within them contradictory affects that will lead them to fall apart or transmogrify into something else in a day or an hour or a minute (Deleuze and Guattari, 1984: 5). After all, the universe, we are told, is not sustainable, some time in the future it will either expand to infinity and slowly chill to near absolute zero, or collapse into a singularity; one day the Earth will fall into the sun and be utterly transformed materially. Nor would we aspire toward an earth-assemblage or any other kind of assemblage that was immune to becomings or lines of flight.

An alternative view of sustainability more in line with a materialist ontology of affects and becomings needs to focus upon potentials and capacities (Braidotti, 2011: 312–3; Parr, 2009: 161), and be marked by an ethics that favours differentiation, rhizomes and becoming-other, but moves beyond the usual narrow focus on human potential, to instead encompass the capacity of all matter within an inclusive 'environment' (that includes humans) to become other (Guattari, 2000: 20). The posthuman ethics that underpins becoming counters forces and affective flows that constrain the environment's potentialities – be that by exhausting natural resources, filling the atmosphere with greenhouse gases, or limiting human possibilities through poverty, inequity or threats to health – fostering in their place affects that enhance human and environmental potentiality.

From such a perspective, the challenge of pollution and child health is re-constituted, not specifically to reduce air pollution from road traffic (and other sources), but in terms of dis-assembling and then re-assembling the affective flows and consequent micropolitics that we identified earlier, to engineer interactions in the assemblage that establish and foster a range of potentialities for the myriad relations in the assemblage – human and non-human. This would establish not only a 'sustainable' road traffic policy, but also contribute to reducing carbon emissions, enhancing working conditions and making the city a generally more conducive place socially, psychologically and physically. The improvements in child health that derive from this re-engineering are one amongst a number of positive outcomes.

This re-formulation provides the basis for a materialist perspective on environment that is not only theoretically grounded in the monist perspective on the world that we have adopted in this book, alongside the arguments from scholars such as Haraway and Braidotti, but also provides a means to translate into a research agenda for the sociological study of environment. This agenda, we would suggest, is energized first by the monistic ontology that draws humans fully into the environment to which they have for long been ontologically differentiated in contemporary sociology, and second, by the assemblage/affect approach that focuses not upon single entities, but upon the affectivities and micropolitics of assemblages. Practically speaking, this means designing and undertaking research that is capable of exploring the constellations of relations that assemble around events, and of unpicking the affects, the capacities and the micropolitics that produce these assemblages.

The challenge for sociology of the perspective on environment that we have set out here is to recognize that human endeavours are far less independent of the non-human world than is sometimes supposed. There is an inclination when undertaking sociological research to focus on the cultural at the expense of the natural (for instance, by adopting an interview-based design and develop an interview guide that addresses human interactions, values, beliefs, feelings and desires, without taking account of the broader 'environment' around the participants). If, as we have argued here, this nature/culture dualism should be dissolved, then it behoves sociological researchers to ensure that their designs can take account of the ecological breadth of affects that are involved in what might at first glance seem entirely 'cultural' (or 'micro-sociological') activities and events.

As an aside, while we have focused in this chapter on environment, there are other areas of sociological inquiry in which non-social relations are of great significance – most notably, those associated with bodies and embodiment. The 'sociology of the body' (Shilling, 2012; Turner, 1984) emerged in the 1980s and 1990s as a topic of interest, while biology and other aspects of the 'natural world' are implicated in sociological areas including gender, race, sex, health and sport. Sociology has not traditionally dealt particularly well with issues of embodiment, often 'bracketing' the biological body in ways similar to those we considered earlier in relation to the environment, in order to focus on the social side of embodiment. It has been feminism, queer studies and post-structuralism that have taken the lead in developing theoretical models of the body (Game, 1991; Grosz, 1994; Haraway, 1991), and the new materialisms have been keen to offer new perspectives on the body that cut across a nature/culture dualism (Cutler and MacKenzie, 2011; Fox, 2012). In Part 2 of this book, we intentionally focus upon areas such as sexuality, emotions, creativity and health that traditionally have been treated in precisely this 'culturally-exclusive' way, to explore them ecologically, across a materialist nature/culture continuum.

Returning for now to the main topic of environment, we will conclude this chapter by considering in detail a further example of how a materialist analysis may enhance sociological analysis of environmental issues.

Lives in a post-industrial landscape

Over the past half century, many developed countries have experienced de-industrialization, as heavy industries such as mining, engineering and car manufacture have struggled financially in a globalized market-place. Whole swathes of both the UK and USA suffered as these industries diminished, as home-grown products were replaced with cheaper overseas goods and new knowledge-based economies gradually replaced heavy industry. There have been huge social and economic consequences, many of which are of core concern to sociology. Towns and cities in areas such as northern England, south Wales and some of the northern states in the US have suffered high rates of unemployment, with consequences for social deprivation, crime and health (Strangleman et al, 2013; Walley, 2013). Male unemployment and a new family dependency on women's income have led to a 'crisis of masculinity', shifting gender roles away from male dominance (Mills, 2003: 53). Trade unions have been weakened, with effects on workers' rights, and growth in part-time, casualized and semi-skilled employment (Nayak, 2006) – a marginalized 'precariat' (Standing, 2014), blamed for its 'dangerous' lack of social allegiances.

As we wrote this chapter, a news story broke about the Nottinghamshire village of Trowell, in the heart of the English Midlands, which brought into focus some of the complexities associated with de-industrialization. This part of the world was once dominated by deep coal mines, and communities grew up around the pits during the 19th and 20th centuries; often the mines were the only employers in these villages. But by the 1980s alternative fuels such as gas and nuclear, plus political antagonism toward the then powerful mining trade unions, led to coal pit closures across the UK, devastating the social and economic life of villages like Trowell. Miners lost their jobs, and in these rural locations young and old had to leave the village to find work. Industrial landscapes of pit-heads and slag heaps gave way to green fields, wildlife and open country as the deep mines closed one by one.

Against this trend, a private coal mining company finally obtained approval in 2015 (after a protracted battle with local people and local government planners) to begin open-cast mining in Trowell. Their application was to excavate a vast

(Continued)

(Continued)

swathe of the countryside close to the village, to extract around 1.3m tonnes of coal over five years; with re-landscaping, locals feared their landscape would be devastated for twice that long. Feelings in the community toward the proposal were divided. Over 1,200 locals signed a petition objecting, fearing negative consequences including the mine's visual impact, noise, air pollution, and road traffic increases as the coal was carted away (as well as concerns over carbon release from further fossil fuel use). But some former miners in the village took a more positive view of the plan. They saw it as a way to bring traditional employment (particularly male employment) back to the community, and to reinstate what they saw as a proud history of coal mining that had been destroyed when the deep mines were closed. The matter was finally settled when a government minister over-ruled local councillors and gave the go-ahead to the open-cast mine development in June 2015 (*Nottingham Post*, 11 June 2015).

What might a materialist analysis make of this event? This example provides an opportunity to explore the analysis of environment that we have developed in this chapter, because of the wide range of natural and social relations in the assemblage. These include:

- Physical stuff like the coal under the ground, the land and the landscape it is in, the machinery needed to dig it out and transport it, the power stations that will burn it and the electricity and pollution it will produce.

- The humans who will work at the mine and those in the community who will both benefit and suffer from the development.

- Biological things that make up the ecology of the proposed mining location, such as vegetation and trees, birds and wild animals, micro-organisms and organic molecules that make the soil fertile.

- Economics, and the flows of money and resources that will flow through the mining enterprise and into the pockets of shareholders, workers and the local community.

- The social processes associated with both industry and its management and governance.

- The politics of planning, industrial development and protest.

- Regulations governing coal extraction, safety, employment and so on.

- The past experiences and memories of locals.

- Hopes, fears and other emotions.

It is the breadth of these different relations and the scope for them to affect and be affected by each other that makes this materialist analysis of the event so interesting and potentially rich sociologically. The affect-economy in this assemblage includes obvious affects such as the physical, biological and chemical processes that produced coal deposits in the first place and that enable it to generate electricity when burnt for fuel. Affective interactions between coal, money, mining, machinery, and miners turn a subterranean mineral millions of years old into a product to be sold commercially and burnt for fuel and at the same time provide work and wages to local people. Planners and local councillors, planning laws and procedures, a petition, and a government minister interacted in a complex affect-economy that produced decisions, appeals and finally approval for this open-cast mining enterprise.

However, this event-assemblage includes other significant affectivities. The community campaign for and against the open-cast mining application suggests that memories of both the earlier mining history, and of the following de-industrialization when the pits closed were powerfully affective. De-industrialization had devastating consequences on Trowell and other mining communities (Strangleman, 2001: 256). These were economic, as families lost their main source of income – with knock-on effects on the community's disposable income and infrastructure; social, affecting boys' job expectations and aspirations (Nayak, 2006), and impacting gender relations once men were no longer the main family earners; and cultural, destroying a way of life built upon co-operation, solidarity and working-class values (Strangleman, 2001: 255). For some former miners, their memories of earlier days inspired positive responses to the proposal, with the expectation that the open-cast mine would provide a return to good wages and traditional male employment patterns.

Meanwhile, for others in the community (and for local councillors who opposed the application) perhaps their memories of the earlier mining era were more negative – of air pollution, grime, destruction of the environment and danger. Along with the contrasting green fields and wildlife of the post-mining landscape, these recollections contributed emotions and a new community spirit that fuelled a campaign and petition against the new mining enterprise, and the original decision by local planners against the development. Memories and emotions contribute in this way to the assemblage and the capacities it produces (we will have more to say about the social productivity of emotions in Chapter 7), though it is important to note that in this example all these affects were effectively side-lined by the final, top-down decision by a government minister who favoured business and enterprise, and allowed the mining development to proceed.

There are many other affects that could be identified in this event, and a materialist analysis can reveal the myriad ways that the social, economic and the political are intricately caught up with biology and the geology and geography of the landscape. It is hard to tease apart these realms when the affect economies of events like de-industrialization and re-industrialization cut across nature and culture; indeed such an effort to compartmentalize social and natural sciences seems pointless and foolish. Issues of environmental sustainability are no longer simply about physics, chemistry and biology, nor just about economics and politics. They are all these things, but also caught up with emotions, memories, gender relations, masculinities and many other affects. Perhaps more remarkably, it turns out that understanding things like changes in contemporary gender relations – considered to be the exclusive domain of social scientists – turn out to be tied up with flows of minerals, money and energy.

This example suggests how a materialist 'sociology of associations' (Latour, 2005: 8) transforms the sociological imagination in relation to environment, drawing human and non-human relations into a single realm, rather than setting them in opposition. Yet, if the task of a materialist sociology of environment is not only to analyse but also to improve the world, this is in many ways disheartening, as its outcome (a mining operation that will disrupt both the natural and cultural environment of a village, against the wishes of many inhabitants) in no way embraces the perspective on sustainability that we developed earlier. Environmental sustainability, in that view, entails encouraging assemblages in which affects and interactions foster human and non-human, natural and cultural, capacities and potentialities.

If anything, we see here quite the opposite – an environment, a landscape, and all the animate and inanimate things in it, that have been repeatedly exploited for economic and political purposes: first by the development of industrial mining, then through a forced de-industrialization, and now in the pillage of the remaining coal for short-term profit (with a consequent contribution to anthropogenic climate change). A contrary, sustainable resolution would seek ways to enhance the capacities and 'becomings' of all elements of the assemblage – from the interactions between earth, air and water, nitrogen and water cycles of the physical environment, to the productive life-courses of the multiplicity of plants and wild animals, to the opportunities for humans to work, play and interact productively – and to do all this in ways that do not oppose humans to other materialities.

Summary

This chapter has taken as its focus what might have seemed to some a very particular area – environmental sociology. Our intention, however, has been to address one of the foundational components of a materialist sociological imagination: the interactions between the natural and the social, and the

> need to cut across this conventional sociological dualism. We have sought to reveal an alternative, monist ontology of environment in which humans are not separate from, but part of an ecology of the natural and the social. This provides not only the basis for a materialist environmental sociology and approach to sustainability, but also the basis for a post-anthropocentric and post-human project that we will continually revisit in the remainder of the book.

Further reading

Braidotti, R. (2013) *The Posthuman*. Cambridge: Polity. Ch 2.

Haraway, D. (1992) Otherworldly conversations; terran topics; local terms. *Science as Culture*, 3(1): 64–98.

Stevens, P. (2012) Towards an ecosociology. *Sociology*, 46(4): 579–595.

4

Society
Beyond Systems, Structures and Stratification

Introduction

While the previous chapter focused upon the 'natural' environment within which our lives are lived, now it is time to examine in more detail the social and cultural 'environment' that is the context for social action and social identities. This social world, with all its divisions, inequalities and cultural formations has been considered in many different ways by sociologists. Durkheim (1976 [1915]) conceived of a 'collective consciousness' that provides the shared beliefs, ideas and moral attitudes which unified society; Parsons (1951) spoke of a social system; while Bourdieu (1990: 88) discerned distinct cultural 'fields' with their own laws, axioms and power relations.

Our focus here will be upon these social 'contexts' of social action, and how sociologists have considered aspects such as social backgrounds or a society's normative discourses on behaviour as 'structuring' or determining the limits of, and the possibilities for, action. This contextualization is the basis for the distinction made in conventional sociology between human agency (as a productive force) and the social formations, institutions and structures that have been seen as determining or even oppressing this agentic production. We will draw on Latour's (2005: 9) proposition of a 'sociology of associations', and use this to develop a materialist perspective on social organization. In particular, we want to pick up the issues noted towards the end of Chapter 2 concerning materialism's monist ontology, and how this forces us to re-think sociological understandings of culture, social systems and casual mechanisms. This perspective rejects entirely any sense of structures, systems or underlying mechanisms, finding a basis for both power and resistance in the micropolitics of the affects that assemble 'events'.

With the benefit of this re-working of structural explanations, the second part of this chapter explores a topic that has sometimes seemed emblematic of sociology: the exploration of social stratification and social divisions. The sociological categorizing of people into classes, genders, races and so forth has been foundational to our discipline, and was significant for sociology's historical materialist roots and a focus on the classed nature of capitalist society (Marx, 1959: 70). However, it has been less clear whether sociological notions such as class and gender are just that: concepts used to analyse the complexities of the social world, or intended as an *accurate description* of the social divisions and differences that manifest in the world. We will argue that – from a materialist, relational perspective – classes, races and genders are *aggregations* of dissimilar persons, rather than categories and collectivities of individuals that possess some foundational similarities to one another. We will also apply a relational analysis to Bourdieu's notion of capital – social, cultural, physical and so on, which has been appropriated in recent theories of social class. We will draw all these threads together at the end of the chapter in an example, looking at social mobility from a materialist perspective.

Materialism and the 'sociology of associations'

The 'duality of agency and structure' is one of those issues in sociology that perennially re-surfaces whenever scholars have sought to set out the ontological and epistemological bases of our subject (DeLanda, 2006: 9–10). It has led to divisions in terms of theory, between 'macro-sociology' which explores the broad shape and power structures of a society and a 'micro-sociology' that addresses the experiential and agentic aspects of social life. This dualism sometimes also influenced choices of research methods, with quantitative approaches generally favoured to examine social organizations and 'structural' matters such as social divisions or social mobility, with qualitative methods reserved to study individual action and resistance to power. Meanwhile, the relative emphasis ascribed to agency or structure in different sociological theories has waxed and waned, depending upon whether the sociological wind has been blowing in favour of recognizing the relative autonomy of social actors (Wrong, 1961) or the determining or constraining forces of the social order (Shilling, 1997).

However, this agency/structure distinction reflects a broader dualism intrinsic to much sociology, that has differentiated between an 'everyday level' comprising the minute-to-minute interactions between social actors, and another 'structural level' in which social forces somehow regulate or govern these interactions. Manifestations of this conception of 'another level' – regarded as where the engine of society 'really' resides, and therefore as the holy grail for sociological attention – include notions of an economic 'base' in Marxian sociology (Marx, 1971), upon which cultural life is overlaid; ideas of social systems that govern social interactions in sociologies ranging from Talcott Parsons' (1951) structural-functionalism to Niklas Luhmann's (1982) systems theory; and in critical realist notions of a 'deep' stratum of social mechanisms that constitute the powers that shape social phenomena (Danermark et al., 2002: 59). In all of these models, social interactions and human agency are not fully autonomous, but are shaped by social structures, systems or mechanisms.

As we saw in Chapter 2, materialist scholarship is generally marked by a rejection of such dualistic notions of the world, in favour of a 'flat' ontology in which matter is self-organizing (as opposed to having its capacities determined by something external like a system or mechanism). The model of materialist sociology that we developed at the end of the last chapter reflects this monism, setting out a social ontology of relational, affective materialities that assemble and disassemble, according to the forces or affects that they exert over each other, and whose capacities to do, feel or desire emerge within these assemblages. This flux of assemblages and affects is the means whereby the social world is produced and reproduced, and from which the flow of history derives. With this simple ontology as the basis for a materialist sociology, then as Latour (2005: 7–8) has pointed out, it follows that there is no longer any place for overarching 'social structures' or 'systems' or underlying 'mechanisms' that determine how relations assemble. The task is no longer to reveal the social forces at work behind the scenes in law, science, religion, organizations or elsewhere; in this monist social world 'there exists nothing behind those activities, even though they might be linked in a way that does produce a society – or doesn't produce one' (2005: 8). This, however, does not mean we should abandon analysis of power and inequality, just that we must shift our analysis from a 'structural' level to focus on the micropolitics of events, activities and interactions.

Adopting what Latour calls a 'sociology of associations' (2005: 9) requires a different view of human bodies, things, ideas and all the other stuff that make up the kinds of ecological assemblages that we explored earlier in this chapter. Such a materialist sociology, according to the social philosopher Manuel DeLanda (2006: 9–10) marks a break from 'organic' models of society that have shaped sociology widely, from Parsonian functionalism to Giddens' structuration theory. These latter sociologies are based on a 'superficial analogy between society and the human body' (2006: 8), and depend upon 'relations of interiority' (2006: 9), meaning that component elements (the 'organs') have inherent attributes or properties that are manifested only when constituted with other specific elements within a whole (the 'organism'). So, for example, 'teachers' and 'students' manifest their particular properties when interacting together as elements within a school or college (the whole), while retaining these inherent attributes even if removed from that setting.

By contrast, monists such as Deleuze and Guattari replace the 'organism' with the 'assemblage' – a different model of collectivity based upon 'relations of exteriority' (DeLanda, 2006: 10–11). Relations of exteriority mean that any component (such as a human body) may be detached from one assemblage and plugged into another, within which it will have differing interactions and consequently exercise different capacities. So a component may become a 'learning-body' when it is part of an assemblage in which it interacts with 'teaching-bodies' – these capacities in turn establish the assemblage's capabilities as a 'school' or 'college'. But detached from this assemblage and plugged in elsewhere, the former 'learning-body' may manifest entirely different capacities (for instance as a 'worker' or a 'lover') as it interacts with other bodies in a 'workplace-assemblage' or a 'sexual relationship-assemblage', respectively.

This has a number of consequences for how we understand both the parts (relations) and the wholes (assemblages). First, we cannot predict what a body (or thing or abstract concept) can do until we observe its interactions in a particular assemblage. Second, neither is it possible to predict what an assemblage can do by simply documenting its components, we need to explore relations' capacities when assembled together. This 'empiricism', incidentally, establishes the need for a materialist sociology firmly based upon observation of actual events. Third, power and resistance cannot be treated as properties of an individual or group; rather, they are contingent capacities that emerge in particular relational contexts – this analysis will be particularly important when we explore social action and social change in Chapter 10. Finally, it means that unlike 'organisms', assemblages are highly unstable and continually in flux as relations join and leave.

DeLanda's explanation of how and why an assemblage does what it does provides a foundation for a monistic sociology, in which there is no 'other level' structuring what goes on between assembled relations, but at the same time cannot be reduced to the essential properties, attributes or actions of individuals. Assemblages do not exert some kind of force over relations: these forces are a consequence simply of how relations affect, and are affected by, other assembled relations. This model of a sociology of associations – denied any recourse to 'social forces', 'structures' or 'systems' as explanations of activity and events – is a radical departure from dualistic sociologies. It poses challenges that must be worked through adequately, in order that a materialist sociology can provide both an ontologically-convincing model of society that accounts for both continuity and change, and to offer models for social inquiry that do not merely offer 'explanations' in terms of social structures or extraneous social forces. For instance, we need to find a way to explain 'social inequalities' without invoking concepts such as 'class' or 'neo-liberalism', or gendered violence without positing 'patriarchy' or 'hegemonic masculinity' as its causes, as if these 'explanatory' concepts are foundational and do not themselves need explaining.

Sociology claims a distinct perspective on the world through its focus upon the 'more-than-individual' processes that produce the social world and human history, and sociologists have developed a vocabulary of terms to aid this perspective. To clarify the way a materialist sociology of association understands social production, we now wish to explore its perspective on some key sociological concepts: 'organizations', 'social institutions'; and 'social structures'. To illustrate our analysis, we have used examples from economic sociology that make connections between these, with 'a commercial business' as our organization, 'work' as the social institution, and 'neoliberalism' as an example of a social structure.

Social organization

In sociology, organizations can range in size from a small club through to an entire national governmental apparatus. The term organization may be used both as a noun and as a verb (Cooper and Burrell, 1988: 92), to refer both to an entity ('an organization') and to the process of organizing. Both senses of organization require some re-thinking from a materialist perspective.

In terms of the former (organization as entity), the preceding discussion of assemblages and 'relations of exteriority' is immediately applicable and this may be illustrated by using a commercial business as an everyday example of 'an organization'. Such an organization may be considered as an assemblage (Cooper and Burrell, 1988: 105; DeLanda, 2006: 86ff.) comprising human relations (workers, bosses, owners and shareholders, customers, suppliers, distributors and so on) and a range of non-human relations (buildings, raw materials, products, transport, capital reserves, cash and so forth). This business organization gains continuity (and the appearance of being a thing-in-itself) from the affects between these multitudinous relations, which we may conjecture include interpersonal employee relations, hierarchies and authority (DeLanda, 2006: 68ff.), flows of money and debt, legal frameworks governing business and employment practices, and relations with other businesses who are the business's suppliers, distributors and customers. These flows together produce the capacities of human and non-human elements (staff, customers, products etc.) and thereby the capacities of the business to produce and trade. These latter capacities may include becoming a relation within other assemblages such as 'the economy' or 'import/export markets' (DeLanda, 2006: 86).

This dynamic understanding of organizations shifts the concept towards the second sense of 'organization-as-process', a topic that has been of interest to sociology since Weber studied bureaucracy and its 'iron cage' (Weber, 1930: 181) and Parsons (1951) set out rules for social systems. More recently, organization and efforts to organize have been criticized from postmodern and post-structuralist perspectives as endeavours established within a wider modernist and humanist project. In this view, organization seeks to order and rationalize a chaotic world, so as to achieve specific objectives (Cooper and Burrell, 1988; Fox, 1993: 49; Mumby and Stohl, 1991: 327). In the example of the business organization, these objectives are typically oriented at producing some kind of output that is commercially viable, that is, profitable; other organizations will have different objectives.

A materialist perspective on the fluxes and fluidity of a monist social world of assemblages and affects provides a novel angle on these commentaries. Organizations appear far less static and structural, and far more contingent and fluid when understood as assemblages drawn into being by flows of affect between relations whose capacities are entirely contextual to a particular assemblage. They can be pulled apart to reveal the affect economies that make them work (and that make them fail), using as a toolkit the micropolitical concepts of specification (territorialization), aggregation and lines of flight that we introduced in Chapter 2 (Patton, 2006: 28). This opens the possibility to understand the part that organization-assemblages play in both sustaining continuities in the social world, and also the fragility of these assemblages and the possibilities of becoming-other. We will have more to say about organizations in the discussion of social mobility towards the end of this chapter.

Social institutions

Sociologists have used the idea of a social institution to refer to something distinct from a social organization, typically referring to an apparently stable, pervasive and enduring building-block of society. Examples of social institutions include the family, religion, marriage, education, or work, though as Martin (2004: 1249) notes, sociologists have also made a case for more 'physical' things such as schools, universities and mental hospitals, plus a further 'amazing array of phenomena' (from taxation to sport) to be included in the category. In her review of the literature, Martin found that most sociological conceptions described social institutions as 'controlling, obligating, or inhibiting' (though occasionally facilitating and empowering), while many equated them with ideas, norms, values, or beliefs, or recognized the part that practices, rules, procedures, customs, and routines played in their constitution (2004: 1251).

According to Martin (2004: 1253–4), social institutions serve the sociological purpose of explaining continuities and stability in social life, and the means whereby social order is legitimated and sustained. So, for example, 'work' as a social institution (Albiston, 2010: 25) will refer to something other than a specific instance of working or of 'my work' (which could be analysed simply as an assemblage comprising a worker, the materials used, the products of labour, wages, the location and physical environment of work, work-mates and so on). It implies instead a more generalized or abstracted notion of expending labour, with or without recompense, an established, conventional and widespread aspect of daily life in a society or culture. This helps to stabilize 'the familiar, material horizon of ordinary lives' (Coole and Frost, 2010: 34), establishing a set of 'complementary social practices and meanings that form taken-for-granted background rules that shape social life' (Albiston, 2010: 27).

However, we have already acknowledged (in relation to organizations) that a materialist sociology is fairly dubious about social order and continuity, recognizing flux and becoming as endemic to matter. Looking at the so-called 'social institutions' identified by sociologists, it is questionable just how institutional they really are in a contemporary Western culture. Marriage – supposedly a cornerstone of society – has been decried widely as a pernicious social formation based on patriarchy, monogamy and until recently heterosexism (B. Fox, 2015), while work has been criticized since sociology's inception as an alienation or source of *anomie* (Marks, 1974: 331). For these reasons, a materialist sociology may wish to treat a notion of a social institution with some caution.

To the extent that a materialist sociology might seek to understand the part that events such as work, marriage and those other practices conventionally designated as social institutions may play in the production of continuity and stability, this may be understood in the affectivity of myriad repetitions and habituations of individual work events across time and space. These are continually made present within event-assemblages through aggregative memories and experiences, and continually reinforced by every further act of working.

Structures, systems and mechanisms

We turn finally to a category of entities that has been employed variously throughout the gamut of social theory as a means to invoke determining causes or 'social forces' as 'explanations' of social events, whereas – as Latour (2005: 7–8) argued – they are really the things that need explaining by sociology. Notions of social structure, social systems and social mechanisms have waxed and waned in sociological popularity, and we are not minded to attempt a genealogy here, or to further differentiate these various models (for a review, see Martin, 2014: 5–9). We feel justified in drawing them together on the basis that they have in common a dualist model of society in which 'human agency' is pitted against a distinct realm of social formation (sometimes described as a 'base' or a 'deep level', and sometimes – as in Giddens' (1981: 27) structuration theory – simply as a 'medium') that in some way shapes, constrains or on occasions facilitates action. Structures, systems or mechanisms are the location of power, while resistance is a feature of oppressed human agency.

Our concern here is less to do with whether it is a structure or a system or a mechanism that is used as the justification for this kind of explanation of social phenomena, and more with how these may be used implicitly or explicitly to justify the action of various social forces (often conceived as working at a 'macro' or inhuman level) on human actions. These 'explanations' are regularly invoked in relation to perceived patterns or replications of particular social formations, often in relation to social divisions, inequality or social disadvantage, and considered as productive of constraints or limits on human action or of outright oppression. Examples that spring to mind of such 'explanations' include capitalism, racism, patriarchy, modernism, post-modernism, heteronormativity, neoliberalism, hegemonic masculinity, rationality, science, and religion.

Beyond 'social structure': the case of 'neoliberalism'

To explore how a materialist sociology would make sense of such explanatory social forces, we will consider one of the explanations frequently used within contemporary sociology: 'neoliberalism' (Jessop, 2002). This we take to mean a set of practices and a philosophical and policy orientation towards individualized self-interest and the market as the foundation for most if not all human interaction. A swift trawl of recent literature reveals that sociology is replete with studies that conclude that features of contemporary life are under neo-liberal influence. So, for instance, neoliberalism is implicated in contemporary education policy (Lipman, 2011), food security (Lawrence et al., 2013), health (Coburn, 2014), the global spread of English (Piller and Cho, 2013), the management of universities (Lorenz, 2012), home ownership (Rolnik, 2013) and sport (Silk and Andrews, 2012)!

To initiate a materialist re-conceptualization of neoliberalism, it is helpful to differentiate between on one hand those practices that take place within a market environment, and on the other those policies, political decisions and efforts by major commercial interests such as multinational corporations that encourage the development and expansion of a market solution and who seek to break down barriers to free market transactions between producers of goods and services

(Continued)

(Continued)

and consumers. The kinds of practice that are considered to be influenced by neoliberalism could be summarized at its simplest as an assemblage comprising:

commodity – individual A – individual B – money

An affect economy that is termed neoliberal or marketized would mediate the interactions between these relations according to market principles, such that the commodity may be traded by A in return for a mutually-agreed sum of money from B. This capitalist market relation, Deleuze and Guattari (1988) have argued, is highly de-territorialized, in the sense that it is not constrained by contextual factors (for instance, the relative statuses of A and B, which would have precluded such open transactions in feudal or other social forms). In practice, this pure capitalist transaction is trammelled by relations that inhibit its completion such as sales taxes, regulations on safety of goods or consumer protection, international trade controls, geographical barriers and so forth. Whole areas of social life have traditionally remained off-limits from markets, including education, healthcare and religion, though this is no longer the case.

Recognizing these constraints on 'free markets' leads us to address the second aspect of contemporary neoliberalism: the efforts made by governments and corporations to promote further neoliberalization, through policies, laws and de-regulation. Neoliberalism, it has been argued, has an aggressive policy agenda promulgated by a coalition of free-market politicians, entrepreneurs and right-wing social philosophers who aim to break down all barriers to this pure market-driven model of social interaction, to bring it as close as possible to the idealized assemblage outlined above. Pro-business government policies have dismantled trade barriers within and between countries, and enhanced markets through increased productivity, while controlling wages.

The aims of this movement are purportedly both to facilitate trade and therefore the flow of profit and economic growth, and to promote an individualized model of social interactions, as outlined in the infamous proclamation by 1980s UK Prime Minister Margaret Thatcher that 'there is no such thing as society'![1] Neoliberalization has successfully opened up public services such as healthcare to market forces, and translated many UK state schools into relatively autonomous 'academies' that control their own budgets and are free to appoint unqualified classroom staff on salaries below nationally-negotiated rates.

Returning to materialist sociology's re-conceptualization, the earlier discussion of social institutions is relevant here. Rather than claiming neoliberalism as some kind of overarching social force, it may be seen as a slow drip of a repeated, routinized and habituated pattern of interactions (Barad, 2001: 94–96), memories, experiences, and outcomes that aggregate subsequent aspects of life within an assemblage that mediates a market-oriented affect economy. We may add into this assemblage some of the other factors we have just noted: free trade initiatives, low prices, and rules that facilitate market interactions. These relations all contribute to an affect economy that encourages marketized transactions.

We hope that this example shows how something that has been treated as an 'explanation' in some sociological studies can be re-thought as a relational assemblage, in which the relations are progressively aggregated and territorialized by a specific economy of affects or 'intra-actions' (Barad, 2001: 95). 'Macro' relations such as government policy may be incorporated indirectly into the assemblage in terms of the affectivity of those policy initiatives as they influence human and non-human relations. The same type of analysis may be used to re-think other 'explanations' such as patriarchy or rationality, in the process making them the things that need to be explained, as we have tried to do here with neoliberalism.

Social stratification: differentiation or aggregation?

We now turn to another concept in sociology where materialist theory forces a re-think: social stratification. This will in turn lead to the final focus of this chapter, the related topic of social divisions, which addresses 'the classification of populations, differential treatment on the basis of labelling or attributions of capacities and needs, and modes of exclusion that operate on this basis' (Anthias, 1998: 506): all social processes with material consequences.

Sociology, particularly in its quantitative moods, has often addressed the stratifications (and consequent divisions) it has observed among members of societies, most notably in terms of gender, race and social class, though also by ageing, education, occupation and sexual orientation. Among these, some like gender and race were at one time considered to have some kind of underpinning in human biology, though in both these cases – as we will see in a moment – this connection has been revealed to be spurious. Social class has been considered the most purely 'social' – both an outcome and a determinant of other social processes.

However, the importance of social stratification for the study of social divisions poses an immediate ontological question for sociology, which we need to address before we can develop a materialist approach to social divisions. Are 'gender', 'race', 'class' and other stratifications simply social constructs, figments of a sociological imagination, or are they representations of actual divides that have real effects on people's lives and upon the way that society has developed? One answer to this was supplied by Weberian sociology: sociological categorizations of people in terms of gender, race or class were 'ideal types' – social constructs that serve as templates for empirical investigations (Davidson and Wyly, 2012: 401). In this view, people 'in the real world' do not absolutely conform to the divisions described by the ideal types – 'working class', 'man', 'Asian' and so forth, but these idealized constructs are sufficiently accurate to offer a broad insight into how the world is in terms of genders, races and classes.

For other sociologists, the aim was to model much more closely the 'reality' that their studies sought to reveal. Marx's historical materialism is a good example – the class categories in his analysis: proletariat (workers) and bourgeoisie (owners of capital), plus a few residual categories such as petty bourgeois (self-employed) or 'lumpen proletariat' (non-employed underclass) were not ideal types, they were descriptions of real classes that were defined by their relation to the capitalist economy (Marx, 1959: 70). This realism may also be seen in sociological perspectives upon social class that link class position to individuals' social attributes. The best-known example of this is the Goldthorpe class scale (Goldthorpe and McKnight, 2006), which categorized people into occupational grouping, from professional through to unskilled manual workers. More recently, efforts have been made to further refine class categorizations, drawing in determinants other than employment, such as access to 'social capital' and 'cultural capital' (Savage et al., 2013). We will have more to say about these developments later.

At the other extreme, post-structuralists and others have questioned any relation between ideas of class, race and gender and an underlying 'reality'. Instead, they have treated these categorizations as discursive formations serving particular power interests within societies. Along with feminist theorists, they revealed the social construction of gender as a binary divide that privileges male power by ascribing differing qualities to male and female, masculinity and femininity (Francis, 2002; Herdt, 2012) – male/female binarism is increasingly challenged as a simplistic social construction (Francis and Paechter, 2015: 9). Race has been exposed as a 19th century fabrication, developed by an unholy alliance of Christian missionaries, European colonialists, natural scientists and anthropologists, who differentiated humankind into a number of different racial types, based partly upon physical attributes and partly on cultural assumptions and prejudice (Smedley and Smedley, 2005; Winant, 2000: 174). When subsequent studies (later revealed to be flawed or even based on faked data) claimed to identify links between membership of a racial category and capacities such as intelligence, race became wholly discredited as a social division within sociology, and for a long time appeared within sociological texts only between quotation marks.

So constructionists and realists hold very different perspective on social stratifications. What then should a materialist 'sociology of associations' make of social stratification, and indeed with sociology's concern with social divisions? We want to approach this in two ways. First, to consider how a relational ontology requires a shift in how we understand classifications such as race and social class; and second, how social divisions may be analysed in terms of assemblages and affect economies. We will focus upon social class, with reference to other stratifications as appropriate.

A starting point for our reflection on social stratification begins by recalling that materialist ontology focuses on what bodies and things *do*, rather than what they are, addressing their capacities within particular event-assemblages. This focus is not simply a matter of choice, but a necessary consequence of a relational sociology of associations (Latour, 2005: 9) or assemblages (Deleuze and Guattari, 1988: 4) – as we discussed earlier in this chapter, these relational perspectives differ from functionalist and structuralist sociologies, in which the unit of analysis is a body, individual or other thing regarded as possessing pre-existing properties or attributes. A relational sociology focuses instead on capacities produced during interactions with other entities (Barad, 2003: 818; DeLanda, 2006: 10). Bodies and other material relations may be components in a potentially unlimited range of possible assemblages, and their capacities – what they can do, and consequently also what the assemblage produces – will depend entirely upon their interactions with other relations within a particular assemblage. (This is the distinction referred to earlier between relations of 'interiority' and 'exteriority'.)

This relational perspective poses foundational problems for any kind of classificatory effort by sociologists that depends upon fixed understandings of a body's characteristics, such as gender, racial and social class definitions of an individual (for instance, as 'masculine', 'Asian' or 'working class'). If instead a body possesses an indefinite repertoire of potential capacities, whose manifestations are entirely contingent upon the assemblages within which it is an element, it is not possible to ascribe fixed classificatory labels to that body. We simply do not know what a body can do until we observe it in a particular context (i.e. in a particular event-assemblage). Any attempt at classification thus must be regarded as an unwarranted sociological *aggregation* of bodies, which, though they may possess some similarities in terms of specific settings (assemblages), are just as likely to be distinct and disparate in others.

We have already noted that efforts in times past to differentiate people into distinct racial categories have been discredited as an exercise that sought to generalize from physical differences concerning skin colour and body shape, in order to support colonialist or racist views. As Colebrook (2013: 36) argues, it is only by *repressing* the multitude of differences between people and focusing on a specific characteristic (for instance, skin colour) that they may be aggregated into distinct 'races' (see also Thomas, 2014: 81–82). The same argument may be made concerning gender classifications of people as either 'men' and 'women' (Lorraine, 2008: 65) and of social position (social class), whether based on occupation, income or other variables. Such simplistic classifications aggregate together bodies that may be profoundly different from others in the *same* category, as well as from those in other categories.

This criticism extends to recent efforts to define people's membership of one social class or another in terms of more sophisticated criteria than occupational categories. Based upon statistical factor analysis of a large British dataset of people's social, cultural and economic circumstances, a team led by sociologist Mike Savage (Savage et al., 2013) have aggregated the UK population into seven classes, including a 'precariat' (a low income group often without a secure income), 'emergent service workers', 'technical middle class' and an 'elite' class (a privileged group with a range of social advantages). Membership of these classes is defined by a person's 'social capital' and 'cultural capital' – concepts deriving from the work of social theorist Pierre Bourdieu (1984: 114) – alongside their financial resources ('economic capital'). In Savage's model, social capital is a measure of the breadth and social value of a person's social networks (who and what occupational class of person they know), while cultural capital marks out their engagement with different cultural forms, from opera to sport to video games (Savage et al., 2013: 225–227). Economic resources include household income, property and savings. The authors argue that this model offers a more detailed analysis of contemporary social divisions and inequalities (2013: 246).

Despite the relative sophistication of this model of social class, we would argue that both the approach and the concepts used are inherently problematic from the perspective of the relational and materialist sociology we are pursuing in this book. Firstly – for the reasons outlined – rather than differentiating the inherently different, sociological classification systems serve to *aggregate diverse individuals into sociological categories*. This is the case whether the classes are top-down categorizations (as in the case of occupational groupings) or generated by methods such as factor analysis, as in the Savage model. Though no doubt undertaken for the best of intentions (to make sense of a social world that appears – because it is – chaotic and unfathomably complex), such aggregations are a denial of difference that constrains understandings of individual capacities, and may add to the very oppression that sociologists may be seeking both to expose and to overcome, by imposing assessments of what social variables (for instance, employment, tastes in music) are of social significance in people's lives.

We also need to interrogate critically (and suggest a different emphasis to) Bourdieusian concepts of social and cultural capital, at least as used in this recent study of social class. This latter treats these various capitals – along with financial resources – as things of which individual bodies possess a greater or lesser 'stock' (Savage et al., 2013: 223), which in turn enables or defines an individual's class position. From the perspective of Latour's sociology of associations, both these kinds of 'capital' require a relational re-interpretation. For instance, 'social capital' – which in Savage's model of social class describes the resources that an individual gains from its social connections and networks – may be re-thought in terms of the affective rela-tions that bodies have with an assemblage of other bodies and collectivities (such as membership of a profession or a trade). It is the affect economy of this assemblage that produces particular capacities in those bodies (in this case, capacities that establish certain 'class' positions or identities).

Cultural capital meanwhile, as Wetherell (2012: 108) notes, is not simply an abstract set of preferences, tastes or inclinations, but is objectified through the material goods that supply this 'capital' to an individual (for instance, works of art, bottles of wine, tastes in music or books), as well as the other members of a culture or sub-culture who acknowledge the symbolic significance of these goods (Bourdieu, 1990: 111). Once again, these may be differently interpreted as a material assemblage of bodies, things and ideas, that together produce the affective capacities in bodies that Bourdieu and followers have treated as a capital resource, and a marker of 'class' (Bourdieu, 1984: 2).

While a focus upon 'capitals' emphasizes these affective capacities (which include 'class identities') of individuals, it does this at the expense of exploring the broader assembling of materialities that are the contexts within which these capacities manifest. For both 'social capital' and 'cultural capital', there is a need to explore the relational assemblages within which capacities emerge, the affect economies that produce specific capacities, and perhaps most importantly, the *micropolitics* that these affect economies establish. This marks a shift from analys-ing 'class' (and for that matter, other stratifications) as a feature or attribute of an individual or category of individuals, focusing instead on the affect-economies of particular assemblages, as manifested in empirical data.

The micropolitics of social divisions

These critiques of sociological approaches to stratification do not mean that sociology must abandon altogether efforts to address the divisions and inequali-ties in contemporary societies. While efforts by sociologists and others to establish classifications such as social class and race must be considered as prob-lematic denials of difference, we can use this criticism as part of the basis for understanding the micropolitics that produce and sustain social divisions. Many of the social divisions that sociology has observed in contemporary societies are products of implicit or explicit aggregations that deny difference and shoe-horn dissimilar bodies and collectivities into arbitrary categories. The treatment of individuals aggregated into an ethnic grouping and then subjected to discrimina-tion (Isaki, 2013; Stringer, 2007); homo/bi/transphobic bullying of children who do not conform to normative models of masculinity and femininity (Renold, 2002; Ryan and Rivers, 2003); and differential access to material resources between urban districts and neighbourhoods with distinct class and ethnic mixes (Davidson and Wyly, 2012: 410) all reflect material processes that aggregate bodies into categories and then act differentially towards these categories.

So to conclude this chapter, we turn explicitly to a materialist consideration of social divisions, analysed not in terms of structures or systems, but at the level of assemblage micropolitics. We noted earlier that sociology has identified three processes in the production and maintenance of social divisions: classification of members of a population into groups, differential treatment of these in terms of attributed capacities or needs, and modes of exclusion based on this classification (Anthias, 1998: 506). To explore these processes, and how they are to be understood in the materialist sociology of association we have been exploring in this and earlier chapters, we will take as an illustration the intersections between social class, education and social mobility. We begin by recalling a classic of qualitative sociology: Paul Willis's (1977) sociological study *Learning to Labour*, a book that had the sub-title 'How working class kids get working class jobs'.

Social mobility: learning to labour?

Willis's study was conducted at a time when UK secondary education was transitioning from a model that incorporated a structural divide between those who passed or failed the '11-plus' examination at 10/11 years of age, to a system of non-stratified 'comprehensive' schools. In the old system, this exam entitled successful candidates to attend an academic 'grammar' school for their secondary schooling, while those who failed went to a more vocationally-oriented 'secondary modern' or technical school. Willis studied one such secondary modern school, in '*Hammertown*', an industrial town in central England, using a mix of ethnographic approaches – interviews, participant observation, and analysis of case studies. His main focus was a group of non-academic 'lads' from 'working-class' families who lived on the council estate (social housing) that surrounded the school, following them through the last two years of their school education and into their first jobs. He also conducted comparative studies with other 'working class' and 'middle class' boys who were more academically inclined ('conformists' in Willis's terminology) from the same school and from nearby secondary modern and grammar schools.

What Willis found was a 'form of cultural reproduction' (Willis, 1977: 185) that appeared to sustain social class divisions from generation to generation. School failed to inspire the core group of disaffected 'lads' towards academic interests. Instead, they espoused positive values linked to their working backgrounds, to masculinity, and to the manual labour that most of their families and social acquaintances undertook in Hammertown (1977: 150), considering non-manual labour as feminine or 'sissy' (Willis, 2004: 155). Teachers responded to these acts of resistance to educational values both by efforts to control and discipline the 'lads', and by progressively pointing school rejecters towards non-academic subjects. Willis concluded that this fundamental clash of cultures between the values of the educational system and the 'lads' had the unintended consequence that these boys left school without academic qualifications, or the academic skills or knowledge that might lead them into further education and 'white-collar' or professional careers. Indeed, when they left school in 1975, all his sample found manual jobs in building, factories or painting and decorating, though some were unemployed a year later (1977: 106).

What may we make of this study, and more generally of the important issue of social mobility (or lack of social mobility) in contemporary society? In the light of the earlier discussion of stratification it is worth beginning by problematizing the easy attribution of 'working-class' and 'middle-class' to the boys in Willis's study. This for Willis was defined in terms of parental occupation (1977: 6), with the consequently circular argument that working-class jobs (meaning predominantly manual labour in Hammertown) are what working-class people do. However, Willis's sociological aggregations (and his book's sub-title) disguised the fact that not all children followed in their parents' footsteps in terms of their work careers, not all 'working-class' boys, got 'working-class' jobs. In line with the analysis we set out earlier, we avoid this sociological aggregation, but instead seek to make visible those processes within the school and in Hammertown that produced social divisions in terms of employment prospects (and consequent financial and other opportunities).

A first step in understanding the micropolitics of social mobility entails identifying the range of relations, affects and consequent capacities involved. In terms of relations, these will include:

- human bodies (workers, students, teachers, managers etc.);

- collective organizations and institutions (for instance, work-based clubs, professional associations, informal social groupings);

- family, friends and acquaintances;

- physical structures (for instance, schools, factories, offices);

- jobs and careers;

- money and wages;

- products of work (goods, services, knowledge);

- social institutions (family, marriage, school curricula, examinations, qualifications);

- memories of events and actions;

- desires and expectations;

- beliefs, values and norms; and

- abstract ideas (for example, work, social class, masculinity).

Willis's study provides a sense of what relations were significant within the 'education-assemblage' of which his 'lads' were a part. This assemblage comprised, at least:

> boys –families – council estate – masculinity/femininity – working-class values – schools – 11-plus examination – teachers – lessons – educational theory – curriculum – academic subjects – non-academic subjects – careers advisors – local employers – jobs

Within this assemblage, we can see a number of affective movements. These include:

- the classification of children by an 11-plus examination that divided them objectively and subjectively into academic successes and failures;

- an affect-economy associated with the school's orientation towards academic achievement;

- an affect-economy that linked families, jobs, money and employers;

- a gendered divide between manual and non-manual work;

- community and familial values around work, masculinity and ethnicity;

- material activities and events by young people around music, sport, sex, crime, violence etc.;

- power relations between school students, mediated by violence and by attitudes to education, work, sex and race;

- struggles between teachers and students for authority and control within school;

- classist, racist and sexist aggregations based upon lay classifications;

- an economy of teaching employment and academic qualifications across the grammar/secondary modern divide;

- allocation of financial and educational resources between schools; and

- the needs of employers – both locally and nationally – for the next generation of appropriately-skilled workers.

There are no doubt additional affects that might be drawn from Willis's work, or from other studies of schools (for instance, Lacey's (1966) analysis of children entering grammar schools in the 1960s, or Alldred and David's (2007) study of resistance to sex education among educationally-disaffected teenage boys). It is these affective movements that enable a range of capacities to manifest in the students. For some, the particular affect economy surrounding them may produce 'academic' capacities; for others, the mix is such that the capacities that emerge are non-academic, or in the case of the 'lads', anti-academic and pro-manual labour.

However, the data in Willis's study reveal the sheer complexity of these affect economies, in which multiple material relations and affects are at work. The myriad affects within educational and work assemblages variously territorialize capacities and aggregate bodies, and disclose huge variability in the micropolitical workings of the different materialities we identified a moment ago, and consequent capacities of different school students. So, for instance, assessments of achievement and behaviour territorialize students as 'conformists' or 'dissenters'; financial needs and wages territorialize people as workers; violence, sexism and racism, music and 'style' aggregate students into 'in' and 'out' groups; while of course, the 11-plus examination sustained an early aggregation into academic successes and failures. These micropolitical processes have a variety of consequences, both materially and in terms of capacities. For example, in order to manage the potentially disruptive effects of school rejecters' behaviour on school routines and other students' learning, the 'lads' in Willis's study were progressively shifted to non-academic classes. This in turn meant they left school with few or no qualifications.

Yet these apparent processes of class-related sorting are continually undermined by other affects. For example, Willis documented a boy from a grammar school, who left school at 15 to become a golf professional. This boy was 'working class, rejects school, but has a total commitment to upward mobility through his chosen sport of golf' (Willis, 1977: 86). From our perspective, this boy's application of sporting capacities as a work-skill supplied the affective means for a 'line of flight' from his parental background, which he considered as low status, and to advance himself despite a lack of academic capacities. Another example quoted by Willis also indicated the complex affective interactions surrounding social mobility: 'Larry', a grammar school boy interviewed by Willis, rejected his school's ethos of education as a means to upward social mobility (1977: 57). He planned to drop out, and spend a few years travelling and 'dossing around', yet also aimed to leave school with the qualifications that would open up possibilities in the future.

To make sense of the myriad affects that influence social mobility, sociology needs detailed analysis of the complex affect-economies and micropolitics operating, not only in schools, but also in workplaces, households and wider communities. While Willis's study is rich in data that can contribute to these insights, his explanation of social mobility/stasis is located beyond immediate assemblages, affects and micropolitics, in the shape of 'culture' (1977: 185), an aggregating and unifying concept denoting the 'materially symbolic patterns and associated practices of human meaning-making' (Willis, 2004: 169) that (in his view) structure societies into classes and sub-cultures. While the different focus we have taken here to the material relations, affects and micropolitics of Hammertown and its young people is of course only partial and preliminary, new materialism supplies an alternative to this kind of structural 'explanation'.

The flat ontology that we have set out in this and earlier chapters seeks its understanding of class and social mobility within the micropolitics of affects and relations, rather than invoking top-down structures or systems to explain apparent patterns in social mobility. It is by mining this complexity and unpredictability in affect-economies that we may find the means both to explain why social mobility in 1975 was limited (and remains so into the present), but at the same time why there are so many exceptions to what appears a 'rule' in an apparently class-ridden contemporary society. By identifying some of these exceptions we are not seeking to romanticise individual success stories or distract from the failure of a supposed meritocracy to deliver class mobility. What we are pointing out is that processes of social mobility are necessarily complex, involving many contextual factors that operate at the everyday level.

Our analysis also offers a glimpse of the kinds of methodological approaches needed to enable this detailed micropolitical analysis, methods that we will use throughout the chapters that follow, and explore fully in Chapter 9 when we look at materialist research methodology.

Summary

In this chapter, we have used Latour's argument for a 'sociology of associations' and made connections to the Spinozist/Deleuzian ontology of assemblages, aggregations and affects that we have developed in earlier chapters. Together these materialist perspectives have required that we re-think some key concepts in conventional sociology, from social structures to social stratifications. We have revealed the extent to which materialist, monist ontology re-shapes the landscape of sociological theory, and presents both challenges and opportunities for a sociology that does not depend upon ideas of structures and systems and top-down notions of power. Instead we have set out the basis for a sociology that addresses the working of power and resistance at the level of events, and forces us to develop an understanding of social continuity and change as a feature of the unfolding fluxes, flows and intensities of the social world that surround us every minute of our lives.

We are coming to the end of the first section of this book, and we have used these opening chapters to establish the theory and concepts for a (new) materialist sociology from which to theorize and research the social world. In the next section, we apply these models and concepts, to explore what this new take on the sociological imagination offers when applied to key aspects of the social.

Note

1. This latter aspect of neoliberalism has been developed in the work of post-structuralist scholars such as Rose (1999) and Dean (2014), who have focused upon the production of a neoliberal subjectivity that emphasises individualism, self-governance and self-interest.

Further reading

Colebrook, C. (2013) Face race. In: Saldanha, A. and Adams, J.M. (eds.) *Deleuze and Race*. Edinburgh: Edinburgh University Press.

DeLanda, M. (2006) *A New Philosophy of Society*. London: Continuum. Ch. 1.

Dolphijn, R. and van der Tuin, I. (2013) A thousand tiny intersections. In: Saldanha, A. and Adams, J.M. (eds.) *Deleuze and Race*. Edinburgh: Edinburgh University Press, pp. 129–143.

Latour, B. (2005) *Reassembling the Social*. Oxford: Oxford University Press. Ch. 1 (Introduction).

Part 2

Applying New Materialism Sociologically

5

Creativity
Imagination, Social Production and Social Change

Creativity and production

Were there only one adjective to describe the material world that we are exploring in this book, it would be 'productive'. To quote the materialist geographer Nigel Thrift (2004: 61), production is the means by which lives, societies and history unfold, 'by adding capacities through interaction, in a world which is constantly becoming'. Minute by minute, year by year, the social/natural world assembles and disassembles; bodies and other physical and cultural relations affect and are affected; assemblages specify (territorialize) and generalize (de-territorialize) capacities, aggregate and dis-aggregate entities. In this fluid and fluctuating maelstrom of interacting bodies and things, ideas and social formations, an endless cascading stream of events produces the world; without these flows, there would be no societies, no cultures, indeed, no nature. Production may have a physical outcome – for instance, a foodstuff, or a piece of software (or a shower of rain or a clap of thunder). But there is also a vast quantity of production where the outcome is 'social' – an interaction, an emotion, a word, thought or idea, a new association or collectivity – the very stuff that makes up societies and cultures.

Not all production is novel, and though events are the means by which our lives and societies unfold, numerically speaking, few events lead us off in entirely new directions, on a 'line of flight'. Some production is actually destructive; think of our daily consumption of natural resources, or war, or the erosion of the landscape by rain and wind. In the social sphere, production is often repetitive or routine – work is a good example, or childcare, or cooking. But a portion of social production does break new ground, is innovative or creative in what is produced, does open up new possibilities for bodies and collectivities. This creative production is of central concern to materialist sociology, as it is the engine of social change and development and is thus the focus for this chapter, though we shall always keep one eye firmly on the rest of social production.

Creativity has been considered by social scientists as something extraordinary and remarkable (de Filippi et al., 2007: 512), or as frequent and common-place (Gauntlett, 2011: 15). The former perspective marks out a 'creator' as distinct from the mass of 'non-creative' people, and examples from the arts (Leonardo, Cézanne), science (Einstein, Marie Curie) and literature (Shakespeare, Jane Austen) bolster this perspective. Sociologists have preferred the latter position: for Marx, the creativity of human labour has fashioned history (1975: 328, 357) and objects of beauty (ibid: 329). From this perspective, creativity is key to human life, human progress and our capitalist economy (Sayers, 2003: 111–16; Thompson et al., 2007: 625).

Despite this assessment, generally contemporary sociology has shied away from trying to make sense of what creativity entails, limiting itself to assessing the social and economic relations surrounding creative production and reception (Becker, 1974; Bourdieu, 1983). Historically, sociology has not seen creativity as its business, considering that its characteristics can be left to psychologists, neurologists or complementary therapists, while any attempt to value specific creative outputs over others should be delegated to aesthetics and art criticism (Born, 2010: 172). Perhaps creativity is unworthy of sociological comment: it is simply the process by which humans interact (materially and symbolically) with the world, little more than the daily innovative production of things or ideas in media, business and educational workplaces (Osborne, 2003: 508). Imagination is not a topic for the sociological imagination!

In this chapter, we reject this view, and will aim to show why – from our materialist perspective – creativity is both ubiquitous *and* profoundly sociologically interesting. Creativity, we will suggest, plays a key part in much of what people do, and is the engine of change and development for bodies, and for social and cultural collectivities, from interpersonal relationships, through social action, politics and policy-making, to technological advances and the 'creative arts'. But it is also important for sociology for exactly this reason: for its ubiquity in how human bodies engage with, produce, and are produced by other bodies, things and ideas in the world. It is thus central to the production of human culture – from science and technology, to the arts, to the social forms and institutions that we explored towards the end of Chapter 2, and indeed to the moment-by-moment unfolding of life and history.

To establish a materialist understanding of creativity, we will elaborate a materialist ontology that fully engages with creative and cultural production, and with creativity's products. This ontology is founded on two propositions.

First, that creativity is inextricably a material process – the relationship between creativity, materiality and embodiment is critical to understanding how it manifests in fields of human endeavour as wide-ranging as science, sex and sculpture. Second, that creativity cannot be reduced to an individualized human 'spark', but is located within a broader network of bodies, things and ideas. Both of these propositions reject any notion that creativity is 'all in the mind' (the mind of a genius, or the mind of an innovative office-manager). Instead, we conceptualize creativity in terms of flows within a network of physical, psychological and cultural relations. The latter constitute a *creativity-assemblage* that establishes the limits of what a creative human body can do, feel and desire in artistic production, technological innovation and knowledge development.

With this focus, the key questions to ask about creativity are less about who is creative and who is not, or what activities should be considered as 'creative' and which simply routine or productive (a distinction between 'art' and 'craft', for instance) and more about how creative bodies are assembled and consequently what and how they produce. Because so much sociological writing on creativity has focused on the arts, we will use this as a familiar starting point. We begin by reviewing sociology's limited engagements with creativity, and then examine how the so-called 'new sociology of art' began to challenge these limits. This will lead us to a more formalized proposition concerning creativity, broadening our analysis to think about human cultural production in general. We will end by using this materialist model of the creativity-assemblage to examine the affectivity of creativity; what it does, and what this adds to a new materialist sociological analysis of change and continuity.

Creativity and the sociological imagination

Creativity has been an elusive or even mysterious concept within the social sciences (Klausen, 2010). As Ford (1996: 1112) points out, the *Academy of Management Review*'s subject index entry for 'creativity' read 'see innovation'. Psychological approaches have evaluated creativity as a human trait, present to a greater or lesser extent, and independent of other cognitive functions. According to this view, individual creativity may depend upon genetic predisposition or neurocognitive characteristics (Schweizer, 2006: 165), including unconventionality, imagination, and motivation (Klausen, 2010: 348); while the capacity for 'novel and personally meaningful interpretation of experiences, actions, and events' underpins creative potential (Kaufman and Beghetto, 2009). A desire to encompass both the creativity of 'the great' and the more mundane creativity of production and innovation within a single theory led Kaufman and Beghetto (ibid) to distinguish 'Big C' (or 'eminent' creativity), 'little c' ('everyday creativity) and 'mini c' (the genesis of creative expression).

Discomfort with this individualistic psychologism may have encouraged social scientists to focus upon the contexts within which creativity occurs, or has been judged to have occurred (Ford, 1996: 1112, Simonton, 1997). Studies of the workplace suggest that the extent to which individual creativity or innovation is fostered or acknowledged may depend upon a worker's position within an organization (De Fillippi et al., 2007: 512), the organizational culture or context (Kirton, 1994) and social evaluations of individuals' creative competencies (Fraser, 1998: 16). From an anthropological perspective, cultural production emphasizes the social relevance of material culture: lurking behind an arrow head, a totemic mask, or a potsherd is the material or symbolic purpose relating to (and perhaps mediating) the needs of a social group or people (Gell, 1998; Hodder, 1994: 394).

An emphasis on social contexts of production and consumption has dominated both the sociological study of creativity in general and the specific area of artistic creativity, at the expense of any study of the products themselves (Born, 2005: 15-16, De La Fuente, 2010: 4). In sociology, the concept of the creator has been displaced. Thus the interactionist sociologist Howard Becker (1974) asserted the dependence of the artist upon a network of human actors for creative production to occur, requiring a range of activities, including:

> conceiving the idea for the work, making the necessary physical artefacts, creating a conventional language of expression, training artistic personnel and audiences to use the conventional language to create and experience, and providing the necessary mixture of those ingredients for a particular work or performance. (Becker, 1974: 768)

Creativity, for Becker, was social through and through, and his interest in 'art worlds' focused on art and business networks, the conventions of work that bind them together and the resources deployed to achieve their goals (Becker, 1982). This approach has been used to analyse all kinds of creative production, artistic genres and art movements. So, for instance, analysis of the punk rock 'world' of the late 1970s – according to Bottero and Crossley (2011: 117) – revealed how networks, conventions and resources provided an underlying coherence to punk's creative production and consumption, in what might seem an anarchic and chaotic musical phenomenon.

Another well-known sociologist, Pierre Bourdieu, took a different sociological approach to artistic production, pointing to the social and economic power relations and struggles that surround and link art producers, consumers and markets. He suggested the existence of artistic 'fields' that were more structural than the kinds of interactional networks in Becker's analysis. These fields reflect forces and struggles over artistic capital (Bourdieu, 1983: 312–3), and situate the production, reception and consumption of art and culture. The artistic field extends well beyond the immediate site of creative production, meaning that familiarity or association with the arts and their performance may provide cultural capital to producers and consumers, reinforcing social position and status, or fuelling struggles between artistic movements (Born, 2005: 7; Bourdieu, 1984; Cheyne and Binder, 2010). This approach informed Bourdieu's analysis of fashions in the arts, and the institutionalization of the cult of the individual creator and the 'art work' as object of veneration (1983: 318), referring back continually to the social and power relations that shape the artistic field (1983: 322). From this perspective:

> it behoves the sociologist of art to shine a light into the murky waters of artistic fields to show what really guides them, to reveal the hidden depths of inequality in what appear to be disinterested practices and to demonstrate how power relations in such fields fulfil a grander role of hardening structures of social and cultural inequality at large. (Prior, 2011: 124–5)

Music and art sociologies drawing on Becker's and Bourdieu's positions have countered romantic and liberal-humanist notions of creativity (Fraser, 1998; Osborne, 2003: 508), and situated it firmly within social contexts. More recently, however, some have criticized these sociologies of art as reductionist (Born, 2010: 173–4), indicative of sociology's inability to treat art as 'anything more than a proxy for or pseudo-reflection of the social' (Prior, 2011: 123). We suggest that such criticisms of the sociological imagination in relation to the arts may be further generalized to all creative production. Creativity has been side-lined in sociology, either considered as a psychological characteristic opaque and alien to sociological insight, or as an ideological construct that obscures the social relations of production or (in the case of the arts) sustains privilege and social division. If the reason for this lacuna derives in part from a legitimate sociological rejection of essentialism and romanticism concerning creative production, we would argue it is also a consequence of an inadequate sociological ontology to address the task. The contemporary sociology of creativity reflects the kind of reasoning that we discussed in Chapter 4, in which phenomena such as creativity are supposedly 'explained' by social forces such as the market or patronage, whereas in fact it is the production of such forces in relation to creativity that need to be explained.

Our conclusion is that for sociology to adequately theorize the creative process, it requires an ontology that acknowledges creativity as simultaneously *materialist* and *social*. Creative production is necessarily mediated through material actions – from painting and making music to computer programming and engineering design, to the creative ideas and theories that are the product of an embodied cognition. Were this simply to internalize creativity as the outcome of a material body, we would be back to an essential and individualistic understanding. But from the materialist perspective we are using, bodies are unequivocally social – in the widest Latourian (2005: 5) sense – caught up in networks of both cultural and natural, organic and inorganic associations (see Chapter 4).

The artwork made me do it: materialist rumblings

We noted a moment ago that some sociologists criticized the sociology of art as theoretically impoverished, focusing either upon artistic agency (an 'under-socialized' account of creativity) or social structures and contexts (the 'over-socialized' alternative), failing to recognize confluences between micro-processes and the 'historical trajectories' and 'macro-dynamics' of art assemblages (Born, 2005: 34). While we in no way intend to confine our analysis of creativity to the arts, this critique provides a useful point of access from which we can develop and explore a materialist understanding of creativity.

The champions of the 'new sociology of art' (De La Fuente, 2007) have sought to engage more directly with creative products and their meanings (DeNora, 1999: 32; Prior, 2011: 125; Wolff, 2006: 144), to complement the more conventional sociological study of contexts of creative production and reception. As Born (2005: 16) put it:

> banal observations on the complex division of labour in modern media can obscure the more interesting point that ... all cultural production constructs and engages relations not only between persons, but also between persons and things, and it does so across both space and time.

For this group, the sociology of art should be reinvigorated by exploration of form, style and content in artistic production (De La Fuente, 2010: 6; Prior, 2011: 135). This has meant challenging conventional conceptions of the artist as agentic creator, and drawing on some of the materialist and posthuman understandings of agency that we looked at in Chapter 2. Prior (2011: 125) suggested that sociology might usefully apply Latour's Actor Network Theory (ANT) to attend more fully to how art objects are 'artfully present in the world [and to] the multifarious ways they resist and react'. For DeNora (1999: 34), the focus of research should change from what music means to what it actively does. Born (2005; 2010) found value in Alfred Gell's art anthropology (of which more below), which 'considers art objects as persons' (Gell, 1998: 9); while Strandvad (2011) has argued that the materiality of art objects actively contribute to the processes of their production – a proposition neatly captured in De La Fuente's (2010) paper title *'The artwork made me do it'*.

The most developed effort to develop a relational sociology of art may be found in Arthur Gell's (1998) anthropological analysis, as set out in his posthumously-published *Art and Agency*. Gell began by recognizing a range of actors in the production and consumption of art: artists, artworks (which he called 'indices'), art audiences ('recipients') and the models or other things represented in art ('prototypes'). All and any of these could act either as 'agents' or 'patients' (targets of agency) within their relationships (1998: 27). He theorized an 'art nexus' of interactions that could comprise just two components – such as an artwork and an artist, or an artwork and a recipient (audience); but which would typically involve an artist, an index, a prototype and a recipient, and might involve chains of interactions in which each element might be active or passive in their relation to other elements. As an example of a more complex nexus, Gell (1998: 62–5) used the example of the interactions surrounding Velasquez's painting *The Rokesby Venus,* which was slashed in 1914 by a suffragette artist protesting the imprisonment of Emmeline Pankhurst. Rather than simply treating this as an act of vandalism, some have suggested that the slashed painting is an artwork in its own right, a creative act superimposed upon Velasquez's original. Gell analysed this nexus, showing how multiple artists, artworks, political figures and audiences interacted across time and space.

Gell's analysis has been criticized for its aesthetic and anthropological limitations (Bowden, 2004: 319–23). Despite this, it provides us with a starting-point for a materialist sociology of art and creativity, and readers will recognize in it many elements congruent with the materialist perspectives on agency/affect that we developed earlier in this book. As formulated, however, it fails for various reasons. First, although Gell was willing to ascribe agency to inanimate objects such as paintings or sculptures, he remained constrained by a conventional notion of agency, in which non-human objects such as artworks possessed only a 'secondary' or 'second-class' agency, 'borrowed' from 'primary' human actors, who were the only agents possessing intentionality (Gell, 1998: 36). It thus retained a foundational anthropocentrism that privileged human action over a wider affectivity of matter.

Second, his analysis of possible interactions between elements produced what he saw as 'illegitimately-formed expressions' (1998: 36), in which an artwork played no part (for example, the power of an artist over a recipient, independent of an artwork), or in which an element had an agentic interaction with itself. For Gell, these were by definition not part of an *art* nexus, and were thereby excluded from discussion; yet a sociological imagination would recognize the potential significance of these wider material interactions (for instance between an artist and her public) for the practices and institutions of art and creativity.

Third and perhaps most critically, Gell's approach to power was top down. While he reflected at length upon the wider relations of power extrinsic to the creative process (for instance, social status), which art objects might indicate, reflect or refract (1998: 157), his analysis lacked any conception of power or resistance operating *within* the art nexuses he described. Despite the recognition of an active or passive role for all human and non-human elements in the nexus, we are left wondering about what this agency does, above and beyond simply producing an art object. How is power distributed within a nexus, and how might it be resisted? A final related criticism is that the approach does not take into account development or temporal change in the agency of elements, indeed the theory feels static and lacking in dynamic qualities.

For all these reasons, as it stands, Gell's approach does not supply an adequate basis for a materialist sociology of creativity. But might its relational underpinning and its openness to non-human action within creativity be developed without its residual anthropocentrism, and with a micropolitical understanding of power and resistance? We see as positives Gell's willingness to recognize that there are multiple agencies at work within an art nexus (or assemblage), the critical importance of relationality between these multiple elements to understanding what is entailed in creativity, and also an emphasis upon the transformative (or 'affective') power of the art object itself. We can take these aspects as the basis for a materialist perspective on creativity, drawing upon the new materialist scholarship that we have explored in the earlier chapters to develop the position.

Towards a materialist view of creativity

The Deleuzian/Spinozist toolkit of assemblages, affects and 'lines of flight' that we introduced in Chapter 2 has been applied by various writers on creativity (Hickey-Moody, 2013; Jeanes, 2006; Osborne, 2003; Thrift, 2004; Whitaker, 2012). Indeed Deleuze wrote at length about the different creativities underpinning philosophy, science and the arts (Deleuze and Guattari, 1994; Jeanes, 2006: 128). We will not here recapitulate at length the ontology that we established as a basis for materialist sociology in the first section of this book, but instead suggest how key concepts may be used to provide a materialist basis for understanding creativity; readers may refer back to earlier discussions for more background. At this point we retain a focus upon artistic creativity, before shifting back in the latter part of this chapter to consider creativity more generally.

First, a materialist sociology of creativity will treat the various human bodies (artist, model and so on) and other entities such as artworks or art materials involved in artistic production and consumption as possessing no essential existence or attributes, except in their relations with other (similarly contingent and ephemeral) bodies, things, ideas or social institutions. Rather they gain these identities only in *assemblage*. 'Creativity-assemblages' of such relations will develop in unpredictable ways around creative actions and events, and have an existence, a life even, independent of human bodies – as such, it is the assemblage that is the unit of analysis in a sociology of creativity. Applying this to artistic creativity, we might conjecture a minimal 'painting-assemblage', comprising, at least:

subject-matter – medium – canvas – paintbrush

although a creativity-assemblage will typically incorporate many more disparate relations, as we will see in the example that follows.

Second, in this creativity-assemblage, no single element (for instance, an 'artist') possesses primary agency; instead we apply the concept of *affect* (meaning the capacity to affect or be affected), to reflect the ways in which assembled relations interact. Affects may be physical, psychological, emotional or social – so within a creativity-assemblage all kinds of affects may be at work, including how artist and paint mark a canvas, how a model's image inspires an artist when drawing or painting, how artists develop a style or focus, and how audiences respond to artistic products such as music or film. Non-human materialities are affective – for example, the marks on a canvas will affect which next mark a painter makes; an artwork will affect its viewers in many differing ways, including how much a buyer might pay for it at auction.

Third, we can explore affect economies in terms of their micropolitical effects on the different relations in the creativity-assemblages – artists, subjects, art objects, audiences, and this is the means to differentiate creative and non-creative products. In Chapter 2, we distinguished between 'singular' and 'aggregative' affects, and this is important here. *Singular* affects or affect economies change relations in ways that 'represent nothing, signify nothing' (Deleuze and Guattari, 1984: 286) beyond the immediate – an example would be a single mark on a canvas, or a unique musical phrase. By contrast, *aggregating* affects or affect economies produce 'stable forms, unifying ... organizing the crowds' (ibid: 287–8). An example of the latter might be an artist's selection of a palette of colours that match her/his current style or portfolio of past work: this will affect not only the current work, but also contribute to a 'body of work' and perhaps a reputation.

Both singular and aggregative affects may be present in creativity-assemblages, but while the latter imposes order upon what bodies can and cannot do, the former has no consequences beyond the immediate, and may indeed dis-aggregate bodies or things in the assemblage, opening up possibilities for becoming other. For example, a bold treatment of a subject – for instance, the abstract expressionist technique of Jackson Pollock, or a discordant sequence in a piece of classical music – can displace an art object from conventions or traditions, with a consequent effect on its audience. Singular affects thus have the potential to generalize relations in the assemblage, and produce a *line of flight* (Deleuze and Guattari, 1988: 9) away from a stable state, identity, artistic style, genre or convention, shifting artists and art objects toward a more 'nomadic' space of possibilities for action or desire. This sounds a lot like how artists, innovators and inventors describe the creative process, both in terms of the creative act (Deleuze, 2003: 71) and the effect of a creative product upon its audience (Deleuze and Guattari, 1994: 175–6).

We would suggest that these three assertions supply the framework for a materialist sociology of creativity. In a nutshell, this focuses upon assemblages of human and non-human relations rather than creators and outputs; on flows of affect within assemblages rather than notions of creative agency; on the affect economies and micropolitics of assemblages and their effect (rather than social structures and deterministic fields); and upon the affective capacities of creative products themselves. This materialist sociology de-privileges the individual creator and her/his 'creativity' (Deleuze and Guattari, 1994: 164), and indeed creativity must no longer be considered as an agentic attribute of a body, but rather as an *affective flow* between assembled bodies, things and ideas. To recognize the potential of this approach, the following example explores an artistic creativity-assemblage in more detail.

Botticelli and Picasso: two art-assemblages

Using the ontology we have developed to explore artistic creativity, the simplest creativity-assemblage that could give rise to a painting may be summarized as:

painter – subject-matter – surface – medium (e.g. oil paint) – painting implement

However, for an artist other than a pre-school child or a chimp, we would expect an assemblage such as:

painter – subject-matter – surface – medium – painting implement – ideas – past events – technique

in which affects deriving from personal experiences, emotional responses, skills and creative ideas will create the conditions of possibility for what a painter can do, feel and desire, and the marks s/he makes on the painting surface.

Consider two very different representations of a female body, such as Botticelli's Renaissance work *The Birth of Venus* (1486) and Picasso's cubist *Crouching Nude* (1954). We may guess that both Botticelli and Picasso used female models as they painted, and that the light from their models cast similar images on these artists' retinas, yet their subsequent creative productions have little in common. In the materialist perspective, we would say that both artists were caught up in creativity-assemblages that produced their capacities to paint their subjects. But for each, these capacities were produced by unique flows of affect that derived from their very different psychological, social and cultural relations in the creativity-assemblage. For each artist, this assemblage might incorporate:

canvas – paint – model – beliefs about women – ideas of beauty – artist's sexual or other responses – artistic traditions and vogues

though these relations would be augmented by many other personal and social relations within the immediate contexts of artistic production. Botticelli's Renaissance sensibility harked back to classical times, but with a new focus on beauty influenced by humanism. For Picasso, those influences *plus* Botticelli and the Renaissance were necessarily part of the assemblage, along with the subsequent artistic canon of classicism, Impressionism, post-Impressionism and modernism, and refracted via a 20th century sensibility fractured and brutalized by ideologies and war. The differing Botticelli and Picasso creativity-assemblages – which resulted in their very different works – defined what their creative bodies could do. To produce a cubist nude would be as much beyond a Botticelli-assemblage's capacities as it would be impossible for a Picasso-assemblage to produce anything other than a self-conscious pastiche of a Renaissance painting.

This example illustrates the affectivities surrounding the creative production events that created these two different artworks. Key to the analysis of the differing creativity-assemblages that may be constituted around different creativity events is the focus upon the rhizomic flow of affect and desire that link relations, break those links, draw relations into new combinations, and fracture or renew assemblages. Contexts and traditions were only part of the flow that established Botticelli's and Picasso's capacities to paint: all the relations that accrete over a lifetime of work, social and sexual interactions, social and personal attitudes to women, their moods as they painted, plus physical characteristics of their materials and media also contributed to the creative-assemblages, both enabling and limiting the representations they could produce.

While this analysis frees us from any conception of creator as individual genius, it is crucial, however, to step back from the possible conclusion that creativity is simply *determined* by the assemblage of relations in which it takes place. Certainly, Botticelli's or Picasso's capacities were specified by the creativity-assemblages of which they were a part: for instance by relations and affects that derived from training and technique, knowledge and critical responses to art traditions, style, practice and repetition, or by the demands of their markets or patrons. But other relations in the mix contributed flows of affect that de-territorialized and produced lines of flight in these artists' capacities to do, feel and desire when they stood in front of a model and canvas. Botticelli's and Picasso's artistic capacities – what they could do – emerged *as* they worked, in the specific assemblages of subject-matter, canvas, media and much more that constituted these painting events. Similarly, the capacities of the products (the paintings) and their audiences also emerge within subsequent events with their own specific affective flows. (For more on this analysis of assemblages, see our discussion of 'relations of exteriority' in Chapter 4.) We would re-iterate that creativity, in this perspective, is not a human attribute, nor even a human capacity, but no more and no less than the unfolding flow of affect (or affect economy) that assembles both creative-production and creativity-reception events.

Four propositions for a sociology of creativity

Having dwelt at length upon the specific area of artistic creativity, we are now in a position to develop a more generalized analysis of creativity. We suggest that a materialist sociology of creativity may be founded upon four propositions.

The first proposition is that creativity is an open-ended flow of affect that produces innovative capacities to act, feel and desire in assembled human and non-human relations. This proposition de-centres creativity from a human prime mover, or as an attribute of a human mind, and recognizes instead the affectivity of all the physical, cognitive, emotional, cultural and social relations in an event. Creativity emerges from a complex ecology of relations between things, bodies, ideas, memories and social formations within an assemblage, and how these affect (or are affected). Furthermore, creativity cannot be tied to a single moment of 'creation', rather, the flow of affect that led up to that moment comprised a multitude of event-assemblages that began way back, and will continue far into the future as the creative product affects audiences and other subsequent creators.

As we saw in relation to artistic production, it is the affectivity within an assemblage that comprises artwork, artist, materials, audience, sponsors and other contexts that is productive. More generally, creative production (for example, development of a new scientific theory, a piece of software or a novel idea) is the outcome of the capacities of a multiplicity of assembled relations. These may include the physical properties of materials, the demands and needs of consumers, the physical and social infrastructure surrounding development, concepts and theories, and the skills, memories and experience of human bodies, drawn together by an affect economy within a creativity-assemblage. This flow is part of, and contiguous with, the on-going affect economies that produce the social and natural world, lives and human history (but see the third proposition below).

The second proposition is that *creative products are themselves affects, which will produce further capacities in both human and non-human*. This proposition recognizes the processual and unfinished character of creativity, and shifts attention to the rhizomic, processual flow of affectivity in the social and natural world that is productive of events, lives and history. It suggests it is mistaken to conceive of a painting, a theory or a new technology simply as an outcome or 'consequence' of a creative act. Rather, each of these outcomes may themselves be affective lines of flight that will carry off those with whom they assemble in new, unexpected directions.

Creativity should thus not be considered as an attribute, or even a 'potential' possessed by an individual or group of humans (this would be to fall back into an essentialist and anthropocentric conceptualization), but rather in terms of the capacities of its products. Creative products are defined by their *own* capacity to affect, and in turn enable capacities to emerge in human and non-human relations. So, for example, in the arts, 'creativity' is contingent upon the effects that art objects (paintings, performances) have as they emotionally, cognitively, spiritually or even physically affect their audiences (and those who produced them). More generally, creative or innovative products are those that open up new opportunities for action or interaction (for instance, a new software interface that enhances communication or commerce, or a theory that enhances understanding of a phenomenon or promotes positive social change).

The third proposition is that *we can differentiate creativity from other social or natural production in terms of the qualities of what is produced*. This proposition builds on the previous one, to provide a way both to recognize creativity, and to establish a means to evaluate creativity and creative products.

All affect economies are 'productive' in the broadest sense (for instance, the affects in a doctor – patient – disease assemblage may produce a diagnosis and a treatment plan – see Chapter 8), and a few may be 'anti-creative' or destructive (for example, a robber – victim – weapon assemblage, that produces injury or death). As stated in the second proposition, for an assemblage to be *creative* will depend simply upon what its products can do, and this can be revealed by looking at the micropolitics of event-assemblages in which these products play a part. Based on our earlier analysis of aggregation and dis-aggregation, a product's creative capacity may be assessed in terms of the extent to which it produces a rich and rhizomic flow of affect, increasing the frequency, strength and complexity of affects, branching and going off at tangents, rupturing and reaching dead-ends (Deleuze and Guattari, 1994: 165). The generation of affective flows makes a 'creative' product a potent generator of capacities in those that it affects. We can see this in both 'grand' creative products such as the theory of evolution or a moon rocket, and in something as prosaic as a new children's game that inspires and engages them in de-territorializing, becoming-other play.

This understanding provides a means to assess creativity sociologically, in terms of the material outcomes of creatively-productive events, and can be used both to explore artistic creativity and creativity in other arenas. Products may be explored through the assemblages in which they are invested, and the richness and strength of the affects they generate, including their capacities to generate further creative events and affect economies. This counters the argument that almost any kind of productive event might be described as creative, degrading the meaning of the word (Osborne, 2003). It also allows for the potential for entirely 'natural' products (for instance a shell, a landscape feature eroded by wind and rain, or a fractal pattern) to be assessed as creative, because of the affects they produce in observers.

The final proposition is that *the creative power of a product is not fixed and final, but is entirely contingent upon how it assembles with other relations.* This recognizes that a product's affectivity is not an essential attribute, but will emerge in the relations it forms with human and non-human elements subsequent to its production.

Consider, for instance, 'Stonehenge', a massive product of engineering and human vision that for those who built it may have had immense religious, ritual or empirical value (as a cosmic calculator, perhaps), now lost to a modern sensibility. For a small minority of contemporary humans such as the Druids and 'new-agers', the monument still supplies lines of spiritual flight; for the rest of us it is affective in quite limited though possibly still de-territorializing ways: as an object of wonder, a disconcerting but evocative link to our past, or as a basis for historical or scientific investigation. We can still speculate about the mysterious 'creativity' of Stonehenge's architects, but our enthusiasm over its production is tempered by doubts over what it can or could actually do. Like a dog with a book, some crucial affectivity seems to have gone missing from the assemblage. More generally, what may be deemed creative in one setting may be run-of-the-mill or trivial in another.

Is 'creativity' special?

The four propositions above set out a basis from which to think about creativity from a materialist perspective, and move the sociology of creativity from the narrow confines of the arts (that we used earlier as a way into the analysis) to address creativity more generally. We have shown how materialism de-centres creativity from any notion of a human creator, to focus on two associated aspects: the affect economy that surrounds creative production, and the affect economies of events within which creative products subsequently play a part. However, by situating our analysis of both of these aspects within the materialist ontology that we have been using to explore social production, a critical question has to be posed: What value is there, sociologically, in distinguishing between creative and other forms of material production?

We have asserted from the start of this chapter that creative production shares the same ontology (assemblages and affects) as the general processes of production that are foundational to the world, social and natural. Production is a moment-to-moment 'becoming-other' (Ballantyne, 2007: 97), as the affects in an assemblage change relations' capacities: what they can do. For example, in manufacturing, the worker and her tools change raw materials into an output product with specific capacities; in a classroom, a teacher's explanation changes a student's understanding, in turn producing new capacities to use knowledge to solve a problem.

Our four propositions for a materialist sociology of creativity have acknowledged this continuity between production and creativity, but can we differentiate creative production in terms of the micropolitics of creativity-assemblages, both during creative production and during 'creative reception': the subsequent events involving creative products? In Chapter 2, we described two dynamics within which affects can alter the state of a relation in an assemblage. The first of these concerns the ways affects specify or generalize (territorialize and de-territorialize) a relation's capacities. Specification is the means by which capacities are enabled or disabled by an affect – for instance, an affect in which a hand picks up a stone and thereby turns it into a tool for hammering; once cast aside the tool regains its generalized state as 'stone'. We touched upon the second of these earlier – whether or not affects aggregate relations. Aggregation occurs when an affect draws relations into combination physically, psychologically or conceptually – categorizing an individual body as female, for instance. Other affects, however, are singular, and do not aggregate; on occasions they may dis-aggregate individual relations from previously aggregated collectivities. Production will entail various mixes of these movements of specification and generalization, aggregation and disaggregation.

To explore how creative production may diverge from generalized production, consider the following event:

> Sarah calls her bank. She speaks to Joseph and asks him to transfer a specific sum of money to the account of Indira, to pay for the car that Sarah is buying from her. Joseph undertakes this transfer for Sarah.

We may analyse this as an assemblage, containing at least these relations:

> Sarah – bank – money – bank account – telephone – Joseph – Indira – car

Various affects link these relations, and this event produces outcomes: a financial transaction occurs; Sarah has less cash in her account but gains the capacity to buy a car; Indira is rid of her car, and gains the capacity to spend or save the money; Joseph performs a banking work-task. This event contributes to social production (both locally in terms of car buying and more broadly in terms of sustaining a market economy and a banking system), and may set in train a rhizome of many subsequent events that lead off in many directions.

We can contrast this example of social production with an event in which both the processes of creative production and the capacities of the product (what it can do) may be considered novel. Innovation is often highly valued in organizations, but as Kirton (1994) has pointed out, sometimes adaptation can be equally creative. Consider the application of a pharmaceutical drug (licensed for one use) to an entirely new and distinct purpose, with valued and sought-after results for those using it (for instance, the medicine *norethisterone* – originally developed to treat breast cancer, but which is now also used to delay menstruation for lifestyle reasons). The event-assemblage that led to this adaptive use comprised: the drug, the manufacturers, the original biochemists, women using the drug, the menstrual cycle, and so forth. Its innovative re-application supplied female users with a means to delay onset of a menstrual period until they ceased the drug, once a holiday or other event had occurred.

Micropolitically, there is a qualitative difference between these events. In the first case, the event produces a routine financial transaction which simply has the effect of re-specifying the money as now belonging to Indira. Nor does the product (the transaction) – while highly useful to Sarah and Indira (and to Joseph in keeping him employed) – have any novel or extraordinary consequences: it allows the car to be re-specified as belonging to Sarah, and it further aggregates all these elements of the assemblage into wider market and banking assemblages. We would argue that on both counts, this is not a 'creative' act of production.

In the second case, the affects in this assemblage produced a generalization of the drug from a specified patient group and specification to a new user group. For the users the drug provided a radical line of flight from the menstrual cycle, opening up new capacities by delaying menstruation, and a dis-aggregation of an individual user from the hormonal cycle that affects most women between menarche and menopause. For women suffering debilitating and painful or inconveniently-timed periods, use of the drug might provide a line of flight providing new opportunities for action. On both counts, we would argue that this event is qualitatively distinct from the first, and might be considered an example of creative production.

This offers a means to define creative production in terms of the kinds of affectivity that it produces, opening up possibilities for bodies, collectivities and things to become-other – to launch them upon a line of flight to other states or intensities. This would suggest that assemblages containing creative products will tend to have affect economies that generalize rather than specify, and dis-aggregate rather than aggregate. This would not necessarily be the case with assemblages not involving creative products. This provides sociology with a means both to mark out 'the creative' from other production, and to evaluate the 'creativity' that a product displays. As such it addresses the requirement set out by the sociologists of the arts, such as Born and Prior reviewed earlier. However, we want to conclude our discussion of creativity by looking at its contribution to a key feature of sociology: change and continuity.

Creativity and social change

We began this chapter by recognizing the ubiquity of production, whether that involves 'natural' or 'social' processes (in new materialist ontology, there is no distinction between these realms). In the previous section we established a mic-ropolitical differentiation between creative and non-creative, although rather than setting up a binary opposition, it is perhaps more appropriate to regard production as a continuum, with creative production marked out by its capaci-ties to produce de-territorialization (generalization) and lines of flight. We want to look now at the sociological consequences of events that have such effects on bodies and social formations, and consider the part that creative production plays in fostering change.

Though it might seem almost too obvious to be worth asserting that novelty contributes to change, it is important to recognize that in materialism's flat ontol-ogy there can be no recourse to ideas of social structures, systems or mechanisms to explain how change occurs (see Chapter 4). The micropolitical analysis we have conducted reveals how innovation and creativity can contribute to change, at every level from personal identity (DeLanda, 2006: 50) to the broad shape of societies and cultures. We would suggest that the de-territorializing and/or dis-aggregating affect economies associated with creativity generate new capacities and assemblages that can have rhizomic and far-reaching consequences. Creative, innovative or simply novel events have the capacity to de-stabilize the habitual or routine, to open up possibilities that things could be otherwise, and to bring relations into new or unexpected associations.

While physical creative products (everything from a new phone app to an assistive technology such as a wheelchair) may be particularly productive at changing physical capacities, novel ideas and theories have a similar capacity in terms of generalizing and dis-aggregating social and cultural constructs and formations. Deleuze and Guattari (1994: 18) argued that concepts are 'becomings' that disconnect habitual relationships and make new connec-tions; as such they are the contribution that philosophy (and we would add, social theory) makes to the material transformation of the world. This, in part, provides a justification for the new materialist assertion that social constructs are part of materiality.

However, ranged against these physical, psychological and social consequences of creative products are powerful affects (operating in all these realms) that do the opposite, that tend to establish habituated capacities that sustain continuities and established formations and traditions. These latter forces produce and reproduce those aggregating affect economies that sociology conventionally has called nationalism, imperialism, institutional racism, patriarchy and so on, and sustain the organizations and institutions operating within these contexts. They also include the cultural formations that Deleuze and Guattari (1988: 373) termed 'royal', 'State' or 'major' forms in science, in art and in philosophy (see also Massumi 1992: 4–50, Osborne 2003: 511). These 'State' forms specify and aggregate what may be done, and what may be thought; in science the objective is to establish reproducible laws that define and organize matter, these laws institutionalize and capture the very creative spark upon which science depends (Jeanes, 2006: 130); the same can happen in the arts when institutionalization means that imitation and profitability replace passion (Fox, 2015a).

We will have more to say about this in the final section of this book when we consider sociological research, activism and policy. For now, suffice it to say that – based upon the materialist analysis in this chapter – creativity has a contribution to make to an alternative 'minor' or 'nomadic' form of science, art or philosophy (Deleuze and Guattari, 1986; 1988: 369; 1994: 113) that rejects the aim of 'reproducing', favouring instead a commitment to 'following' the singular interconnections between relations, and the lines of flight that these produce. As a subject that straddles these three areas, sociology must ensure that creative thought and actions are central to a sociological imagination.

Summary

In this chapter we have set out a materialist approach to studying creativity sociologically, shifting from an anthropocentric focus on human creators, toward a creativity assemblage that recognizes it as the product of an affective flow between human and non-human relations. We have used the materialist toolkit developed in earlier chapters to explore the micropolitics of creative production and make sense of what creative products do, and the capacities they produce. By linking creativity to broader social production, we have acknowledged the intense sociological significance of creativity as both a way to enrich life and human history, but also as a motor for change and renewal. Sociology can use understanding of the micropolitics of creativity to suggest which kinds of material, psychological and social relations (confluent within an assemblage) might lead to what kinds of production; what is conducive to creativity and what limits its manifestation. Creativity becomes not just a prized feature of social life, but a force that may be used proactively to facilitate social change and challenge oppression or inequality. It is both social and material, and in both aspects is fully amenable to, and ripe for, sociological exploration.

Further reading

Hickey-Moody, A. (2013) *Youth, Arts and Education: Reassembling Subjectivity Through Affect*. London: Routledge, Chapter 5.

Jeanes, E.L. (2006) Resisting creativity, creating the new. A Deleuzian perspective on creativity. *Creativity and Innovation Management, 15*(2): 127–134.

Osborne, T. (2003) Against 'creativity', a philistine rant. *Economy and Society, 32*(4): 507–525.

Prior, N. (2011) Critique and renewal in the sociology of music, Bourdieu and beyond. *Cultural Sociology, 5*(1): 121–138.

6

Sexuality
Desire, Intensification, Becoming

Introduction

In this chapter, we consider how sexuality may be understood from within a materialist perspective, and take issue with some of the conventional perspectives on sexuality, drawing on two ontological issues raised in the first section of this book. First, we question (and reject) the anthropocentric privileging of the human body and subject as the locus of sexuality, posing a profound challenge to the Western (liberal, humanist) understanding of sexuality. Second, we dissolve the traditional mind/matter dualism in social theory (Braidotti, 2013: 4–5), to explore sexuality – and the micropolitics that surround it – from within an ontology that asserts a central role for matter (Coole and Frost, 2010: 19).

To explore sexuality from a materialist perspective, we shall ask some new questions. How do we understand desire? How do we theorize sexuality as a site of intensification of experience and also of intense political contestations, globally and at home? Central to our analysis will be our proposition of the 'sexuality-assemblage' (Alldred and Fox, 2015b; Fox and Alldred, 2013), that shifts the location of sexuality from individual bodies or subjectivities.

Sexuality from biomedicine and religion to the cultural turn

Sexual desire, sexual arousal and sexual pleasure seem amongst the most personal, interior aspects of the experience of having a body, and so frequently focused 'outwards', on to external objects of desire. Perhaps unsurprisingly – as a consequence – it has appeared self-evident to many (including biologists, psychologists, doctors and therapists) that sexuality is an integral attribute of an organism, be it plant, animal or human. Sexuality has served as a marker of individuality, and sexual identities have been used positively and negatively to assert social position. Historically, those whose sexualities have diverged from normative practices (heterosexual, monogamous, non-promiscuous, consensual) have been labelled bad, mad or ill, and punished/analysed/treated accordingly by religions, the law, medicine, psychotherapy and other social agents (Alldred and Fox, 2015a). Contemporary claims that culture or religions have repressed sexuality are similarly founded in a view of individuals whose true (sexual) natures have been suppressed, but whose sexualities may be released or emancipated by Western liberalism or secularization (Rasmussen, 2012).

These perspectives on sexualities are founded in 'essentialism', and upon 'relations of interiority' (DeLanda, 2006: 9) that ascribe fixed or at least stable properties or attributes to bodies and things (see Chapter 4). As such these views have come in for criticism by anti-essentialist social scientists, in particular from strands within post-structuralism, post-colonial studies, feminist and queer theory, later psychoanalytic approaches and critical psychology (Flax, 1990; Henriques et al., 1998; Jagose, 1996; Sedgwick, 1990; Spivak, 1988). Foucault's (1981, 1987, 1990) historical studies undermined a view of sexuality as prior, unproblematic and apolitical, and revealed how an individualized understanding of sexuality was differently understood at various points throughout history.

So, for instance, from the 18th century until quite recently, specific discourses on female and childhood sexualities, human reproduction and the nature of sexual instincts together shaped a view of sexuality as potentially disruptive to the social order (Foucault, 1981: 103–5), whereas in the pre-Christian era, sexual activity was itself regarded as potentially physically and mentally harmful and debilitating, particularly for men (Foucault, 1987: 118). Queer theory has built on post-structuralist analyses (Butler, 1990, 1999; Eng et al., 2005; Grosz, 1994; Puar, 2007), replacing an emphasis on desire (which may constrain or regulate identity) with 'pleasure', which is diffuse, intense and opens up possibilities (Allen and Carmody, 2012: 462; Butler, 1999: 11; Jagose, 2010: 523–4), and highlighting how gender identity and a notion of an essential sexual subject are 'performatively' fabricated from acts, gestures and desires (Butler, 1990: 136).

These more critical readings of sexual ontology displace focus from physiology and psychology, and establish a 'sexual subject' socially constituted by forces in a body's immediate and general contexts. However, they do not in themselves counter the human-centredness or anthropocentrism that sustains a view of the human body as the location of sexuality, as manifested by sexual desires, attractions, embodied responses and experiences. Thus psychology and sexology have made links between physiology, neurology and sexual experiences (Diamond, 2004; Hines, 2006: 119; Hird, 2000: 356), while commentaries upon the 'human sexual response' and the medicalization of sexual 'disorders' have established sexuality as an attribute of the human body (Garfinkel, 1984: 123; Gatens, 1996a: 5ff.; Gordo-López, 1996: 171; Potts, 2004: 21). Sociologists have been more circumspect concerning sexual ontology, although Giddens (1992: 31) stated bluntly that the body is 'plainly enough ... the domain of sexuality'.

Another outcome of sexual anthropocentrism has been to define quite narrowly what counts as sexuality and sexual identity, for instance through the simplistic classification of sexualities in terms of their gendered objects of desire as hetero, homo or bi-sexual (Lambevski, 2004: 306). Meanwhile the sciences and social sciences have reified Foucault's (1981) societal problematizations of sexuality, establishing individualistic norms for gender roles, child sexuality, sexual identity, monogamy and gendered mental health. Biomedicine and health technologies have also contributed to a narrow view of sexuality, for example in the development of treatments for 'erectile dysfunction' (Potts, 2004) and aesthetic plastic surgery, while consumerism and communication technologies have added to the commodification of pornified bodies and body-parts (Gordo-López and Cleminson, 2004: 106).

For these reasons, the sociology of sexualities is ripe for re-thinking in terms of the post-anthropocentric and posthuman materialist ontology that we developed in the earlier chapters of the book. In the next section we will explore this materialist take on sexuality, and consider how this may translate into a strategy for empirical research that produces novel sociological insights into sexualities, untrammelled by either anthropocentric or deterministic biases. Later in the chapter we will ask what this perspective means for how we understand human sexualities more generally.

Materialism and the 'sexuality-assemblage'

Some but not all of the materialist authors we have focused upon in this book have specifically addressed sexuality. Braidotti's (2011, 2013) posthuman philosophy and ethics of engagement steps beyond the dualisms of nature/culture, man/woman, and human/non-human, to recognize the inherent self-organizing properties of matter itself (Braidotti, 2013: 35), opening up all kinds of possibilities for 'becoming' (2013: 190), including possible sexualities. In this posthuman vein, sexuality is a 'complex, multi-layered force that produces encounters, resonances and relations of all sorts' (2011: 148). Sexuality is a central element in Deleuze and Guattari's (1984) collaboration *Anti-Oedipus*, which claims that 'sexuality is everywhere' (1984: 293) – in a wide range of interactions between bodies and what affects them physically, cognitively or emotionally, in fields as disparate as finance, law and social movements.

The materialist perspectives that underpin these assessments situate sexuality not as an attribute of a body (albeit one that is consistently trammelled by social forces) but as relational and posthuman. In what follows we draw upon the discussion of sexuality in Deleuze and Guattari's work (1984: 291–4), and recent theoretical and research-oriented studies of sexuality informed by materialist ontology (Beckman, 2011; Fox and Alldred, 2013; Gatens, 1996a; Grace, 2009; Grosz, 1994; Lambevski, 2005; Renold and Ringrose, 2008, 2011; Ringrose, 2011). We shall begin our effort to develop a materialist sociology of sexualities using the now-familiar conceptual toolkit of assemblages, affects, capacities and micropolitics that we developed in Chapter 2.

An 'assemblage' approach to sexuality requires that we attend to 'the relations between bodies, their configurations within specific assemblages and the dynamic of the interrelations of their intensive capacities' (Gatens, 1996b: 170). Assemblages connect multitudinous relations from physical, biological, cultural and abstract realms, while the flows of affect between and among these relations produce bodily desires and capacities. Thus, a sexuality-assemblage comprises not just human bodies but the whole range of non-human – physical, biological, social and cultural, economic, political or abstract – relations with which they interact (Lambert, 2011: 138): as such sexuality-assemblages bridge 'micro' and 'macro', private and public, intimacy and polity.

In this view it is not an individual body but the sexuality-assemblage that is productive of phenomena associated with the physical and social manifestations of sex and sexuality, and that establishes the capacities of individual bodies to do, feel and desire. Consequently, sexuality-assemblages can be understood as the machines that produce all aspects of sexualities, including sexual desires, sexual identities and sexual conduct. It is the sexuality-assemblage that creates the conditions of possibility for sexual desire and sexual responses, and shapes the eroticism, sexual codes, customs and conduct of a society's members (Fox and Alldred, 2013), as well as the identity categories of sexuality such as 'hetero', 'homo' and so forth (Linstead and Pullen, 2006: 1299). All the capacities of bodies to do and feel in relation to sexualities (to be attracted or aroused, to kiss or fuck or come; to fall in love or leave before morning, to be hetero or homo, camp or butch, and so forth) are products of flows of affect within sexuality-assemblages.

We can begin this analysis of sexuality as assemblage, to illustrate its relationality and the flows of affect between the multitude of psychological, emotional and social relations it may comprise, using the example of a sexual kiss.

Assembling a kiss

Consider a 'kissing event' involving two bodies: 'A' and 'B'. At its simplest, we could represent this as:

A's lips – B's lips

While the affects within this assemblage are in part physical, sensually stimulating the tissues of lips and mouths, perhaps producing arousal and pleasure, there are typically many more relations in the kissing-assemblage than just two sets of lips. The flow of affect may link the physical event (the kiss) to many other relations: personal and cultural contexts; past events, memories and experiences; codes of conduct and so forth. So a kissing-assemblage could comprise (at least):

A's lips – B's lips – past experiences and circumstances – social and sexual norms – A and B's personal attributes (e.g. physical characteristics, personality, job, smells and tastes) – dating conventions – immediate material contexts

The affective flow associated with a kiss links these relations rhizomically (for instance, between some characteristic of A or B, a memory of a past lover and a stereotype of masculinity or femininity), producing capacities in A and B to do, to think, to feel and to desire. These capacities and desires in turn produce further affects that may lead to sexual arousal, mutual attraction, desires for intimacy, and positive or perhaps negative emotional reactions in one or both parties. Such capacities may extend the sexual encounter beyond a mere kiss to other sexual interactions that draw into the assemblage all kinds of relations, including previous sexual and non-sexual events, cultural codes of sexual conduct, physical relations of arousal and orgasm, public decency laws and so on. These affective flows may eventually assemble A and B within a sexual relationship, in which the assemblage might comprise all the accumulated interactions, emotions, experiences – from commitment to rejection, social networks, cultural norms and epiphenomena of sexuality; perhaps also family-life and child-rearing. In this way a kiss is profoundly productive, not only of desires or intimacies, but also of the social world.

We can use this brief illustration to set out more formally what this assemblage perspective on sexualities means. First, the sexuality-assemblage asserts the fundamental *relationality* of sexualities. Rather than taking a body as the 'possessor' of a sexuality, a multiplicity of relations coalesce around even the simplest of sexual events, as we have just seen in the kiss illustration. An erotic kiss draws together not just two pairs of lips but also physiological processes, personal and cultural contexts, aspects of the setting, memories and experiences, sexual codes and norms of conduct, and potentially many other relations particular to that event. Louis Armstrong may have sung that 'a kiss is just a kiss' (in the song '*As Time Goes By*'), but for the materialist sociologist, this is certainly not the case.

Second, a sexuality-assemblage must be analysed not in terms of human or other agency, but by considering the assembled relations' ability to *affect* or *be affected* (Deleuze, 1988: 101). Within a sexuality-assemblage, human and non-human relations affect (and are affected by) each other to produce material effects, including sexual capacities and desires, sexual identities and the many 'discourses' on sexualities; these affects are qualitatively equivalent regardless of whether a relation is human or non-human.

A theory of sexuality clearly needs to address issues of *desire*. Desire has been conventionally understood as a gap, lack or void waiting to be filled by the acquisition of a desired object, be that a lover, a tasty meal or a new purchase (Deleuze and Guattari, 1984: 25–6). However, some of the materialist scholars we have been employing in this book are strongly critical of this view of desire, and how it has been used in psychology and psychoanalysis to normalize certain sexual behaviours (for instance, heterosexuality, monogamy) and pathologize others. While Deleuze and Guattari acknowledged that desire *can* be a lack, their 'positive desire' (Bogue, 1989: 89) was not acquisitive but instead *productive* of action, ideas, interactions, and thence reality (Deleuze and Guattari, 1984: 26–7).

Importantly for the study of sexuality, in this ontology, desire is itself an affect (rather than some essential or culturally-shaped quality of a body). Desire produces specific capacities to act or feel in a body or bodies, be it arousal, attraction, sexual activity, rejection or whatever. It makes other affects flow in assemblages (Deleuze and Guattari, 1988: 399); it is the creative capacity of a body to act, feel or otherwise engage with other bodies and the physical and social world (Jordan, 1995: 127), and consequently the force that drives becoming-other (Braidotti, 2013: 134). This way of thinking about desire turns sexual desiring from a yearning for an 'object of desire' (whether a human body, a 'fetish' object such as a silk stocking or shoe, or an abstraction such as 'love' or 'faithfulness') into a productive force capable of transforming bodies, social formations and ideas.

The micropolitics of sex and sexualities

This emphasis on affect economies (Clough, 2004) and the changes they produce in relations and assemblages, provides a dynamic focus for the study of sexuality-assemblages. We may ask what a body can do within its relational assemblage, what it cannot do, and what it can become. To study the micropolitics of the sexuality-assemblage, we can use the two affective movements we have discussed in earlier chapters: 'specification/generalization' (territorialization/ de-territorialization) and 'aggregation/non-aggregation'. Sexual arousal, attraction, preferences and conduct can be understood in terms of these micropolitical effects on bodies within sexuality-assemblages, though we can never be certain what may be the outcome of a particular sexuality event/ assemblage. So an erotic kiss from an established partner might lead to physiological, cognitive and emotional specification of their relationship (as a passion still burning, perhaps as commitment, perhaps monogamous and so on). Yet that same kiss – say from a new lover, might open up a radically de-territorializing (generalizing) 'line of flight' (Deleuze and Guattari, 1988: 277), propelling a body into possibilities such as polyamory, a 'new' sexual identification or a new life begun elsewhere.

Aggregating affects act similarly on multiple bodies, organizing or categorizing them to create converging identities or capacities. As an aspect of human existence, sexuality seems replete with aggregations. Ideas and concepts such as love, monogamy, chastity or sexual liberation, prejudices and biases, conceptual categories such as 'women', 'heterosexual', 'perverted' or 'Masochist', along with the discourses on human sexuality documented by Foucault (1981: 103–5) all aggregate bodies. These micropolitical aggregations produce (among other outputs) the social relations between bodies traditionally summarized and problematized as 'patriarchy', 'heteronormativity' and 'hegemonic masculinity'. By contrast, non-aggregative or 'singular' affects (for instance, a gift from a lover, or a smile from a stranger) produce a one-off outcome or capacity in just one body, with no significance beyond itself, and without aggregating consequences. Singular affects may be micropolitical drivers of de-territorialization, enabling bodies to resist aggregating or constraining forces, and opening up new capacities to act, feel or desire.

Together, these micropolitical processes provide the basis for a materialist exploration of sexuality. In this perspective, how sexuality manifests has little to do with personal preferences or dispositions, and everything to do with how bodies, things, ideas and social institutions assemble. Sexuality is hence 'an impersonal affective flow within assemblages of bodies, things, ideas and social institutions, which produces sexual (and other) capacities in bodies' (Fox and Alldred, 2013: 769). Territorializing forces produce body comportments, identities and subjectivities, 'masculinity' and 'femininity'; and shape sexual desires, attractions, preferences and proclivities according to the particular mix of relations and affects in an assemblage. Sexual codes are culture-specific aggregating affects that establish the limits of what individual bodies can do, feel and desire in specific sociocultural settings, and shape the eroticism, sexual codes, customs and conduct of a society's members, and into specific categories of sexual identity (Barker, 2005, Linstead and Pullen, 2006: 1299). Sexual development may be seen as the progressive complexification of a sexuality-assemblage during childhood and adolescence, shaped by these micropolitical forces (cf. Duff, 2010).

This micropolitics of sexuality is the main focus for a new sociological research focus, for example, offering a new take on ideas such as sexual 'repression' or 'liberation'. In anthropocentric social theory, sexuality has often been regarded as an attribute of a body or an identity such as 'heterosexual', 'homosexual' or 'bisexual' based on gendered sexual preferences (Lambevski, 2005). Within the materialist perspective developed here, sexuality must be both understood and researched differently, at the level of the assemblage. As has been noted, a sexuality-assemblage is not a stable entity, but one that is constantly in flux, awash with flows of affect that aggregate and dis-aggregate relations, that territorialize bodies this or that way, but may conceivably also release them into a singular, de-territorializing sexual line of flight.

Table 6.1 offers a comparison between the conventional anthropocentric view of sexualities and this relational and post-anthropocentric model.

Table 6.1 A comparison of anthropocentric and materialist conceptualizations of the sexual

	Anthropocentric sociology	**Materialist sociology**
Sexual arousal/ response	Innate, learnt or conditioned physiological/cognitive body response.	Body capacity to affect or be affected sexually.
Sexual attraction	Culturally-conditioned physiological/ psychological response to a sexual stimulus.	Body capacity to affect/be affected sexually, often specified and aggregated by social relations.
Sexual preferences	Innate or learned choices concerning sexual behaviour or pleasure.	Capacities to desire shaped by the sexuality-assemblage.
Sexual conduct	Behaviours constrained by personal, societal and cultural codes/systems of thought.	Capacities to act, feel or desire specified by affect-economy of the sexuality-assemblage.
Sexual codes	Culturally-defined moralities.	Aggregative cultural relations that may become part of a sexuality-assemblage.
Sexual identity	A relatively stable formation deriving from a mix of biological, learnt and socialized factors.	Reflexive capacity produced by affect-economy of the sexuality-assemblage.
Sexuality assemblage	–	Fluctuating mix of physical, social and cultural relations that assemble around sexual events.
Sexuality	A formation of preferences, desires, behaviours, dispositions and identity.	Rhizomic flow of affect, typically highly specified, but continually fracturing to produce specific desires, attractions and identities.

We radically re-conceptualize sexuality, following Deleuze and Guattari (1984: 294) as *the flow of affect in a sexuality-assemblage*. Sexuality, as a powerful affective force, consequently has two manifestations. First, it is a de-territorializing (generalizing), multiplying, branching flow of affect between and around bodies and other relations. As such it has the potential to produce any and all capacities in bodies: different sexual desires, attractions and identities, and those not normally considered sexual at all: this 'nomadic' and 'rhizomic' sexuality has nothing to do with reproduction or even genitality (Bogue, 2011: 34), and consequently may produce 'subversive and unforeseeable expressions of sexuality' (Beckman, 2011: 11).

However, as manifested in actual daily events, the flow of affect in the sexuality-assemblage is continuously subject to restrictions and blockages (Deleuze and Guattari, 1984: 293), often produced by aggregating affects that codify, categorize and organize the assemblage and its relations. Channelled in this way, sexuality loses its 'nomadic' potential, producing a relatively narrow range of sexual capacities linked to conventional and normative desires. Despite this, new affects still have the capacity to re-establish a rhizomic flow, creating possibilities for a line of flight. It follows that the sexualities thus produced in most cultures are conventional and prescriptive (Beckman, 2011: 9; Deleuze and Guattari, 1984: 294). While flows of affect in the sexuality assemblage can produce an endless variety of sexual capacities in bodies, aggregating forces may constrain sexuality into very limited manifestations. We will return to consider the significance of this later in this chapter, but for now, we will illustrate the application of this materialist sociology of sexuality-assemblages to research young men's sexualities.

The sexualities of young men

The sexualities of adolescent boys and young men have been a focus for a range of sociological studies. According to interactionist sociology, sexualities are 'learnt' progressively via a repertoire of socially-mediated attitudes, values, sexual scripts and behaviours that are transmitted to the bodies and minds of young men and women (Connell, 1987: 161; Frosh et al., 2002: 4, Schalet, 2011: 2). In Mac an Ghaill's (1994: 91) study of the socialization of sexuality among teen boys, an imperative to act like heterosexual men circumscribed both their everyday behaviour and conversational topics (which included penis size, uncontrollable urges and sexual potency). Frosh et al. (2002: 50–52) found that boys were active, interpretive and critical subjects, who continually re-invented their sexual and gendered identities as they interacted with peers and others, while Bale (2011) noted that masturbation, accessing online pornography and interactions with a peer group actively influenced the development of teen boys' sexualities.

Post-structuralist concerns with institutional power relations and associated systems of thought/discourses provide further insights into young men and sexuality. Pascoe's (2005) ethnography of a high school noted a 'fag discourse' that served to structure the social and power relations between boys. Nayak and Kehily (2006: 465) argued that teen boys aimed performatively to reproduce an idealized 'perfect boy' manifesting a straight masculinity, while Moscheta et al. (2013) found that young men who traded sex sought either to subvert or conserve normative sexuality discourses.

In many of these studies, a 'hegemonic' (or dominant) masculinity (Connell, 1987) has been discerned, reflected in 'compulsory heterosexuality, misogyny and homophobia' (Frosh et al., 2002: 76; Mac an Ghaill, 1994: 96). It manifests within a culture that regards male violence and competitiveness as normal, appropriate and acceptable (Holland et al., 1998: 151; Kimmel, 2008: 217ff.), and denies attributes of dependency, nurturing and feeling associated with femininity (Lees, 1993: 306; see also Holland et al. (1998: 160), and our discussion of Paul Willis' (1977) 'lads' in Chapter 4). More recent formulations have developed this analysis, recognizing the complex power relations that surround masculinity (Connell and Messerschmidt, 2005: 847–8).

This focus upon masculinity (understood as the concatenation of individual and collective behaviours, attitudes and subjectivities associated with 'being a man') has relegated sexuality, sexual desire and the physicality of sexual practices to the status of largely-unexamined backcloths to processes of socialization and/or identity-construction (Beasley, 2015: 570). Desires, attractions and sexual behaviours are individualized, to be studied as attributes of specific human bodies, and constitutive of (individual) human subjects (Foucault, 1981: 157).

To develop a materialist sociology of young men's sexualities, we sought (Alldred and Fox, 2015b) to focus upon the material aspects of sexuality. We analysed data from two studies – the first a multi-methods study of sex and relationship education (SRE) in UK secondary schools conducted by Alldred and David (2007), which included individual and group interviews with teenage boys in school and alternative educational settings; the other a secondary analysis of a dataset of 31 interviews with male students, employed and unemployed young men living in London, originally collected by de Visser and Smith (2007) as part of a study of masculinity.

We began by trawling the datasets to mine the relations in these sexuality-assemblages. The ethnographic observation of teen boys' sex and relationship education classes revealed a sexuality-assemblage that incorporated peers, girls, siblings, teachers, condoms, second-hand cars, the school's SRE curriculum, the Teenage Pregnancy Strategy (a policy in England and Wales at that time) and the school environment as affective relations. The second dataset provided insights into sexuality-assemblages when young men were at university, at work or unemployed, with many being sexually active, ranging from occasional sexual encounters to steady relationships, and for one respondent, marriage. For 'Najib', a 20 year old student, relations in the assemblage included women, men in his peer group, his self-image, physical attractiveness, his ethnicity, marriage, past sexual experiences and concerns with hygiene. Another student 'Neil' was in a steady relationship, and his sexuality-assemblage included not only his girl-friend, but also his family, male friends, past girlfriends, the university, music, the gym, his body shape, alcohol, pubs, male and female sexuality.

However, of more interest than simply listing these relations in sexuality-assemblages are the fluxes, stabilities and instabilities produced by the affect economies within them. The second phase of our analysis focused upon these movements, and the micropolitics of assemblage intra-action they reveal. We sought out the specifications (territorializations) that produced relatively stable capacities in young men, the generalizations (de-territorializations) that under-mined these and established different sexual or other capabilities, the aggregations that grouped or unified aspects of young men and sexuality, and the singular affects that occasionally offered new capacities and possibilities for sexuality or subjectivity.

Data from both sources provide examples of capacity specification by physical/biological, psychological and sociocultural affects in the sexuality-assemblages. For the teenage boys, physical relations such as bodily maturation, height, voices that had 'broken' and facial hair territorialized childish bodies into adolescence and adulthood. These physical affects combined with com-petitive and hierarchical displays of machismo or intimidation within the peer group to further territorialize and effectively rank their bodies (and their girl-friends and their cars) in terms of physical capacities.

For the older group, a similar specification occurred, though produced from the differing affect economies assembled in university and workplace settings. The social assemblages these young men inhabited comprised same-sex friend-ship groups, sporting activities, clubs and bars, alcohol, and social events where the main objective appeared to be for heterosexual men to 'pull' women, and vice versa. Micropolitically, these interactions produced limited sexualities in the young men, focused more upon competition between male peers than upon interaction with sexual partners. One student, 'Scott', described his efforts to be 'the person who's had a lot of sexual partners ... who attracts the best looking girl in the bar'. Like the teenage boys, their own bodies and those of the women they encountered were ranked in terms of physical looks, to produce informal hierarchies of who might have sex with whom.

These specifications of sexuality interacted with aggregating and non-aggregating affects in the two studies. Aggregative specifications drew both the teenage boys and the older group into narrow sexuality-assemblages. For exam-ple, the school-excluded teen boys were aggregated by the physical and social affects into a masculinist sexuality-assemblage that valorized heterosexuality, homophobia and misogyny, as reflected in the 'banter' and horseplay witnessed during the study. Physical maturation, actual or purported heterosexual experience, competitive homophobic posturing and (hetero)sexualized joking sustained them within this assemblage, aggregating their sexuality into what some scholars describe as 'compulsory heterosexuality' and 'hegemonic masculinity' (Holland et al., 1998: 149; Mac an Ghaill, 1994: 96; Rich, 1980).

Similarly, the physical and social specifications in the older group were often powerfully aggregative, and the data offered examples of aggregation into a specific sexual orientation, an attraction to a specific physical body-type or ethnicity, or into close monogamous relationships. 'Paul', a student and keen sportsman described how his physical, psychological and emotional needs were aggregated within a monogamous heterosexual relationship, and acknowledged he played rugby for reasons of body-appearance and to 'keep his girlfriend happy'. 'Lester', an unemployed 18-year old, expressed the pressures to find a girlfriend he had felt, both from his peers and his own expectations for his life. The transitions these sexual encounters represented territorialized him as both adult and man.

> I suppose it is quite an important marker your first girlfriend, or your first pull, or the first time you get laid. I suppose it is quite important as, like, a yeah 'Now I am ... more than I was yesterday', just because of that. It's kind of a rite of passage, maybe.

Not all sexual specifications were aggregative, however. Sometimes singular affects deriving from sexual encounters produced unique capacities in particular bodies, including emotions, personal perspectives on sexuality and opportunities for nurturing others. Nineteen-year old student 'Ross' found new capacities for sexual intimacy from a relationship:

> I'm always looking for, um, you know, someone who I, sort of, could completely fall for ... and spend a lot of time with ... Ah, it's nice to just have someone there. You know, I mean ... someone who's, sort of, not going to judge you and, sort of, who knows you really well. And who, ah, sort of, accepts you for who you are I suppose. ... I sort of find that if you're really head over heels with someone and you're sleeping with them, there's this, sort of, like a really, really intimate feeling.

Some of these singular affects were not only non-aggregative, but produced capacity generalization, opening up new possibilities for action and interaction in both groups we studied. School is a place where children's bodies (including or perhaps especially their sexualities) are sidelined or even erased as part of the disciplinary regime (Paechter, 2006: 122), so SRE classes are unusual as – instead of ignoring bodies – sexual desire and arousal become the topic for education (Alldred and David, 2007: 96). Our analysis suggested that in these situations, sexual bodies also supplied a resource for resisting, whereby educational agendas might be disrupted by displays of pubescent male sexuality, banter, sexist and homophobic jokes and horseplay. For disaffected adolescent boys excluded from school, the embodied pleasures of male sexual desire and arousal were an alternative both to the tedium of the classroom and to the values and educational discourses that had produced them as outcasts, excluded pupils, and sometimes failed educational subjects. While this behaviour was a specification into limited sexualities, it was at the same time a generalizing line of flight away from their unsuccessful educational identities into alternative 'adult' sexual identities.

Amongst the older group, the data also revealed occasional generalization of capacities. Student 'Neil' hesitantly revealed how a sexual relationship had produced for him new capacities that mitigated threats and risks in his daily life.

> You can talk to your girlfriend unlike the way you can talk to pretty much any other person. Like, there's just ... there's a bond that forms ... like you can literally just say what's, whatever is on your mind. And, ah ... and just, I don't know, that feeling of trust as well, that someone actually is thinking about you all the time ... and you're thinking about them.

We have summarized here some of the complex mix of animate and inanimate relations that assemble around sexual behaviours, regimes and identities, as analysed by Alldred and Fox (2015b). For young men, body and sexuality capacities are specified by myriad affects in the sexuality-assemblage deriving variously from physiology, from social interactions with peers or sexual partners, with institutions such as schools or clubs, and by things such as cars, condoms and alcohol. At the same time, we have seen how, on occasions, sexual capacities and sexual behaviour can be the means to instigate a line of flight. A materialist analysis of the relations in sexuality-assemblages, of the affects between these relations, and of the micropolitics these produce in bodies has supplied new insights into the micropolitics of young men's sexualities. However, it also poses some more fundamental issues concerning what is understood as 'sexuality', which we shall now consider.

'Sexuality is everywhere'?

As we have seen throughout this book, specification/territorialization and generalization/de-territorialization of bodies and other things are ubiquitous and inevitable features of social life, a consequence of the endless interactions between relations that take place in events, moment by moment. However, in the light of the analysis of young men's sexualities, we want to spend a little more time considering the significance of aggregating and singular affects upon human sexuality.

Sexualities seem to be peculiarly prone to aggregations. Bodies may be aggregated by psychological, social and cultural inscription into a hetero, bi or homosexual orientation; into a structured social formation such as monogamy, celibacy or promiscuity; by cultural codes surrounding sexual conduct (Foucault, 1981: 103–5); by popular media and pornographic representations of men and women (Bale, 2011); or by systems of 'knowledge' that define sexualities according to medical, legal, scientific or psychological concepts (Alldred and Fox, 2015a). We saw these aggregations at work in the case study of young men's sexualities (Alldred and Fox, 2015b) – our analysis revealed sexualities that were highly conventional and narrowly defined; everywhere aggregated and specified by cultural norms of sexual behaviour and expectations imbued with patriarchal and heteronormative biases; by daily interactions between the sexes (be this a misogynistic teen peer group or a ritualized dating game); and by the genitalization of sexuality.

However, a materialist analysis also enables us to recognize in sexualities and sexual encounters a means to harness powerful singular affects. Even among the many aggregating forces in young men's sexuality-assemblages there were singular affects that had the capacity to break bodies and subjectivities free from those aggregations. More broadly, singular affects may derive from physical or emotional intimacy, from embodied and psychological pleasures, or by transgressing the aggregating social codes of sexual conduct mentioned a moment ago. These singular affects can stand not only in place of aggregation but may even disrupt an aggregated affect economy, radically generalizing body capacities into a sexual line of flight (Renold and Ringrose, 2008: 316).

This micropolitical analysis offers a more optimistic perspective on sexualities than often found in sociology, either in perspectives that emphasize the dominance of forms of masculinity characterized by homophobia, misogyny and compulsory heterosexuality, or in the work of Foucault and followers, which has regarded sexual pleasure as progressively encircled by power and systems of knowledge – 'discourses' (Foucault, 1981; Kitzinger, 1987). Though we must conclude from empirical studies that sexuality is typically highly constrained, in our materialist reading there is always the possibility for it to become other.

The value of a materialist approach rests in its understanding of sexuality as an impersonal, micropolitical flux of multiple desires and intensifications within which bodies and subjectivities are assembled. It is this flow that produces the capacities in bodies that are described as 'sexual', but that also supplies endless possibilities for becoming. According to this analysis, beyond the depleted sexualities that we disclosed earlier among adolescent boys and young men (and we have no reason to suppose it is not also a feature of other groups), there always lurks another side to sexuality. It suggests the possibility for new desires, pleasures and capacities, ruptures and resistances that shift bodies way beyond the kinds of conceptions of sexes, genders and sexualities that inform many contemporary sexualities in the West.

Some of the materialist scholars whose work we have followed in this book have commented upon this micropolitics of sexuality. Braidotti (2013: 98–99) has seen in sexuality a vital and powerful force of de-territorialization that must be explored in all its multiple and 'perverse' forms. Deleuze and Guattari (1984: 49) argued that sexuality is not a 'dirty little secret' but a 'fantastic factory of Nature and production'; consequently 'sexuality is everywhere': a productive force to be seen operating in political movements, business, the law, indeed in all social relations (1984: 293). As such, sexuality has the potential to produce any and all capacities in bodies: different sexual desires, attractions and identities, and those not normally considered sexual at all. This 'nomadic sexuality' (Bogue, 2011: 40) has nothing to do with reproduction or even genitality, but with the 'proliferating, destabilizing connections and lines of flight' (2011: 32), that may produce 'subversive and unforeseeable expressions of sexuality' (Beckman, 2011: 11).

We alluded to this nomadic and 'rhizomic' understanding of sexuality earlier – a non-human sexuality that is not possessed by a body but is an affective flow between affected relations. But while such propositions offer a novel philosophical perspective, they also pose a challenge for a materialist sociology of sexualities. What does it mean to say that sexuality is everywhere? If sexuality has been drawn too narrowly, and extends beyond the conventional associations with sexual arousal and release, or with reproduction or a limited number of specific sexualities defined by gendered desires, what then is 'sexual', what 'non-sexual'? Or if the distinction is entirely arbitrary, then why speak of 'sexualities' at all?

One resolution might be to seek out features that could be considered 'sexual' in events and assemblages that are usually not regarded as sexual. The *intensifications* (arousal, orgasm, passion) associated with 'sexual' affects exist alongside a multiplicity of other body intensifications, which may derive from events ranging from yoga stretches, watching a sunset, or even an 'ah-ha' moment when reading a poem or a sociology text. Suitable candidates for such a re-designation of events from 'non-sexual' to 'sexual' might be interactive physical activities such as dancing or massage; shopping for a new dress or a new car; sports (doing or watching); alcohol, drugs or chocolate that produce a bodily 'hit'; climbing a hill on a sunny day; a promotion or other work achievement. All of these, and many other activities (including some of a distinctly darker hue) might be considered for inclusion in a re-drawing of sexuality's boundaries, as they all – to greater or lesser extents – mediate bodily intensifications between human and human, human and non-human.

An interesting and relevant example is Josie Austin's (2016) materialist exploration of how one young woman experienced her sexuality through the embodied pleasures of dancing. Austin's 17-year-old respondent 'Sarah' had made a decision to abstain from conventional sexual activity because of her and her family's religious views, which strongly opposed sex outside marriage. However, this personal commitment conflicted with the sexualized culture among her peer-group, leading Sarah to seek alternative outlets for her sexuality. This manifested in a consuming enthusiasm for dance, to the extent that she filmed herself dancing alone in her bedroom, and also performed sensual and rhythmic dance routines to popular music in front of her classmates. Dance, Austin argued (2016: 283), provided Sarah with a capacity to embrace her sexuality as a positive rather than a negative, de-territorializing her body from the forces of her religious upbringing, and enabling her to feel 'sexy' and 'naughty'. Sarah described dancing with others as follows:

> when you're dancing you feel like you are [laughs] [...] it is like sex in a way [...] you're kind of feeling sexy, I don't know, it's hard to explain. [...] it kind of like gives you that like vibe and that pleasure of like of knowing that you're both enjoying it, you're both enjoying dancing to the music and moving and stuff, you're touching each other and like the sweat and everything.

Some of the intensifications that dancing in private produced in Sarah's body (as documented by Austin) were of a quite conventional sexual character, as the sensuality of dance movements, the beat of the music and the sight of her own reflection together provided a route to mild arousal or a backcloth to sexual fantasies (2016: 286). However, other body intensifications occupied a different register from the usual sexual capacities of attraction, arousal or release. Sarah talked of her dancing-body being 'fully connected' to the music or to other dancers, with conventional notions of 'sexiness' fading, to be replaced with a transcendent sense of becoming (2016: 288). Emotionally she became one with the music, feeling lost in the dance and capable of doing anything in that moment.

Much of how Sarah described these embodied intensifications seems qualitatively similar to the intensifications associated with sexual encounters. We are reminded too of descriptions of the powerful intensifications associated with music in the Jamaican dancehall scene (Henriques, 2010), or with recreational drug use (Fitzgerald, 1998: 52). Yet while this similarity suggests that – for Sarah – events involving dance (and filming herself dancing in a sensual way) produced body intensifications not dissimilar from more conventional sexual intensifications, it would require an (aggregative) analytical leap to make the claim that dance is more generally part of 'the sexual'.

While acknowledging the continuities between sexual and non-sexual intensifications, we would argue that simply re-defining the boundaries of the sexual misses the full potential for a materialist sociology of sexualities. A focus upon sexuality-assemblages (rather than individual bodies) establishes a basis for re-thinking sexuality as post-anthropocentric and posthuman, to step beyond the confines that physical, social, cultural and political aggregations impose upon what bodies can do, feel and desire. The point is not to simply shift the basis for these aggregations, but rather to assert that we have absolutely no idea what a human body can do sexually, no way of knowing what are the limits of sexualities.

We can indeed conjecture that sexuality is everywhere, integral in the encounters between humans and between human and non-human stuff. But perhaps the task for the materialist sociologist is instead to use empirical data and micropolitical analysis to disclose the affect economies that produce the limited and impoverished sexualities that exist, and the processes that establish these limits. So for example, Fox and Bale (forthcoming) argue that the repetitive and stereotypical sexual practices portrayed in pornography and sexualized media imposed narrow and circumscribed definitions of what sex and sexuality comprise, 'grooming' young and old alike into unimaginative sexualities (for more on this, see Chapter 10). But such sociological analysis also has the potential to reveal the possibilities for dis-aggregations and generalizations of sexualities, sexual identities and sexual stereotypes and norms; to open bodies up to nomadic and rhizomic intensifications of desire, whether in events conventionally regarded as sexual or non-sexual; and to 'embrace an ethics of experiment with intensities' (Braidotti, 2013: 190) in relation to sexualities.

Summary

The materialist perspective on sexuality that we developed in this chapter offers an understanding of what seems (in anthropocentric sociology) to be an attribute and an identity of an individual body or human subject, as instead an impersonal, nomadic flux of multiple desires and materialities. While this sexual flux produces intensities, flows and desires in bodies, the latter are also progressively specified, aggregated and restricted by many other affectivities in the sexuality-assemblage, often deriving from the sociocultural baggage that surrounds contemporary sexualities. This should not, however, be taken as a re-statement of a 'repressive hypothesis' of sexuality (Foucault, 1981), in which a once-free body has been ground into submission by the forces of culture: in this ontology body capacities are always relational and contextual.

The value of a non-anthropocentric approach to the sociological study of sexualities lies in the opportunity to shift attention away from accounts of sexual identities. Instead the focus turns to the micropolitics of sexualities. The objective now is to explore the human and non-human elements and affective flows in sexuality assemblages, the aggregative and the singular affects, and the capacities for action, feeling and desire that affective flows produce. We have shown how this may be done for something as simple as a kiss, or as complex as the sexualities of young men.

Materialist sociology thus offers a new politics of sexualities, in which the aggregative actions of power can be challenged and dis-aggregating possibilities fostered. It poses challenges to foundational assumptions that link sexualities to families and reproduction, to fixed sexual identities and even to specific parts of the body – an out-dated sexual landscape (Braidotti, 2013: 189) that needs to move on. If sexuality and sexual pleasure are to become parts of human existence that are neither continually suppressed nor mired in innuendo, humour or phobias, then they must do so in all their transgressive rawness, recognizing the possibilities for sexuality, for embodied and interpersonal pleasures, and for sexual lines of flight that do not aggregate bodies and individuals into narrow and limited manifestations and from the constraints of particular sexual identities.

Further reading

Alldred, P. and Fox, N.J. (2015b) The sexuality assemblages of young men: a new materialist analysis. *Sexualities, 18*(8): 905–920.

Holmes, D., O'Byrne, P. and Murray, S.J. (2010) Faceless sex: glory holes and sexual assemblages. *Nursing Philosophy, 11*(4): 250–259.

Lambevski, S.A. (2005) Bodies, schizo vibes and hallucinatory desires – sexualities in movement. *Sexualities, 8*(5): 570–586.

7

Emotions
Embodiment, Continuity and Change

Introduction

In the previous chapters we examined two aspects of social life that have often been treated in the social sciences as individual attributes of humans: their creativity and their sexuality. In both cases, we have shown how a materialist assessment provides an alternative reading, in which the relationality of these phenomena is revealed. This analysis has led us to radically re-think creativity and sexuality, addressing the former in terms of the capacities of creative products to produce lines of flight, and the latter as part of an affective flow between bodies and the environment productive of particular bodily intensifications. We now want to turn to another topic that is often conceptualized as personal and 'internal' to the body – emotions. This is a topic that has exercised the sociological imagination because of their supposedly unique linking of mind (culture) and body (biology) to produce what might be called 'felt thoughts'.

We think that emotions warrant a chapter in this book on materialist sociology for two reasons. The first concerns the connections that emotions make between the worlds of nature and culture, which (as we considered in Chapter 3 when we looked at environment) have so often been regarded in social theory as distinct and mutually exclusive. The second reason is because until recently, sociology has underplayed the part emotions play in social production and social change, a lack of attention now being addressed by scholars of the so-called 'affective turn' in social theory (for instance, Blackman, 2012; Blackman and Venn, 2010; Clough, 2008; Jasper, 2011). These writers suggested that, alongside reasoned choices and decisions, what humans feel has a part to play in producing the world, from the progression of a conversation to the shaping of global politics and economics. Emotions, in short, are all around us. As Jasper (1998: 398) has argued:

> Emotions pervade all social life, social movements included. The most prosaic daily routines, seemingly neutral, can provoke violent emotional responses when interrupted. ... Not only are emotions part of our responses to events, but they also – in the form of deep affective attachments – shape the goals of our actions.

Our aim is to offer a balanced view of emotions, neither to sideline them as an evolutionary oddity that in contemporary rationalist human culture is increasingly irrelevant, nor to assert that emotions are in some ways 'special' because they appear to 'transcend' mind/body dualism (Bendelow and Williams, 1998: xiii). We are interested in how emotions contribute to social production, certainly, and we will examine this from within the materialist ontology we have developed in this book. But unlike some sociological commentaries that have seen emotions as remarkable because of a confluence between biology and culture that produces 'felt' or 'embodied' thoughts, we will explore them as part of a continuum of affectivity that links human bodies to their physical and social environment. We will begin this re-assessment of emotions by making a connection between emotion and 'affect' (used in our Spinozist conception as 'something that affects or is affected'), to advance a sociology of embodied affectivity that acknowledges emotions as a part, but only a part, of a more generalized interaction between humans and the environment.

So we will look not at what emotions are, but what they *do* (Ahmed, 2004: 4), shifting analytic focus away from fascination with minds and bodies interacting, to a fundamentally sociological (and research-amenable) exploration of emotions in terms of how bodies, things, social institutions and abstractions affect and are affected by each other. This will provide a materialist sociology that regards emotions not as distinctive in connecting mind and body, but part of a continuum of affectivity that links human bodies to their physical and social environment (Tamboukou, 2003: 211; Youdell and Armstrong, 2011: 145). This affectivity, as we have argued at some length earlier in the book, produces unfolding lives, societies and history, and we will explore how emotions are caught up in both social continuity and social change later in the chapter.

Sociology and the study of emotions

Emotions have long been of interest to sociologists. Psychology and neurology focused on the 'what' and the 'why' of emotions, suggesting variously that they are a motivational force, that they trigger or guide reasoning, and that they underpin behaviour, personality and social relationships (Izard, 1991: 1–3). Sociology, by contrast has been more concerned with the 'how' of emotions, and has explored the interplay between social environment, mind and body (Hochschild, 1983: 220; Turner, 2001), with various accounts of the relative importance of these dimensions (Belli et al., 2010). One hundred years ago, Durkheim's description of 'collective effervescence' during both religious and everyday gatherings established emotions as a social phenomenon that contributed to the shaping of human social action (Durkheim, 1976: 218). Some of the few sociological concepts to have translated successfully into mainstream usage notably concern emotions: 'stigma' (Goffman, 1968) – the social shaming of those regarded as deviant because of some personal characteristic, and 'moral panic' (Cohen, 1973, 2002; McRobbie and Thornton, 1995: 559) – a population-level emotional response to a perceived threat to social order (which we explore later in this chapter).

However, more generally, the trend within sociology and social policy to establish a scientific and rationalist understanding of society has tended to sideline the significance of emotions for social order and disorder (Fish, 2005; Jasper, 1998: 397–8; Shilling, 2002; Tamboukou, 2003: 210). The eventual 're-discovery' of emotions focused upon how emotions were managed socially, and to what ends (Hochschild, 1983; Williams and Bendelow, 1998a). For instance, studies of flight attendants (Hochschild, 1983) and nurses (James, 1989) revealed the 'emotional labour' at the heart of these workers' daily skill-set – skills that were exploited to support their respective clients.

Conventional sociological wisdom suggests that emotions are responses to cues in the social or physical environment (for instance, an event, an interaction or a person), that have a particular meaning or value to an individual or group (Barbalet, 2002: 3; Hochschild, 1983: 220; Jaggar, 1992: 153; Williams and Bendelow, 1998a: 137). So, for example, an item in the news may provoke a physical emotion such as anger, fear or distress in a reader/viewer, because its content has particular significance or relevance for that person. The challenge for sociology has been to offer a perspective that moves beyond psychology, to address satisfactorily both physiological and social aspects of emotion (Williams and Bendelow, 1996: 34).

One solution – usually typified as 'social constructionist' – was to explore empirically the social organization, manifestation and management of emotions and emotionality, side-stepping issues concerning the physiology of emotional responses. Because emotions vary culturally and socially in how they are expressed, constructionists argue that sociological focus should be upon relationships between emotions and the moral order, discourses about emotions and 'how various emotion vocabularies are used' (Freund, 1990: 453).

From a constructionist view, emotions are bodily experiences whose expression is tied to cultural contexts (Belli et al., 2010: 261) or to socialization (Turner and Stets, 2005: 2–3). For example, constructionists explain emotional differences between men and women in terms of their different socializations into gendered roles (Duncombe and Marsden, 1993; Jaggar, 1992: 159–60). Because of this link to cultural contexts, emotions may be manipulated to achieve particular social goals, for instance in social movements (Bensimon, 2012; Jasper, 1998) or the workplace (Lee-Treweek, 1996; Niven et al., 2009). Hochschild's studies of emotion management among workers such as flight attendants (1983) and in working parents (1989) are the best-known applications of this constructionist model.

A second perspective upon the sociology of emotions has been informed by approaches including interactionism, phenomenology and existentialism, and by a growth of sociological interest in embodiment (Freund, 1990; Williams and Bendelow, 1996). This thread sought to make sense of why and how certain environmental or social circumstances lead to emotional responses. Advocates focused their data upon 'a conception of the human body as a lived structure of ongoing experience' (Williams and Bendelow, 1998a: 137), with an 'actively feeling, embodied person as its control focus' (Freund, 1990: 470). These theorists have often drawn (explicitly or implicitly) upon individualistic approaches in biology, psychology, psychoanalysis and phenomenology, including cognitive, evolutionary and biopsychosocial theory to substantiate their models (Bendelow, 2009; Berezin, 2002: 37; James and Gabe, 1996: 8; Williams and Bendelow, 1996: 30).

In such accounts, biology, psychology and social context are inextricably intertwined, not least by an assumption that emotionality has some benefit for individuals or for the human species, for instance, to create social solidarity, signal danger, or protect individuals or groups against threats (Hochschild, 1983: 220; Lyon, 1996: 69–70; Massey, 2002; Williams and Bendelow, 1998b: 138). Most models assert that a discrepancy or dissonance between 'what we see and what we expect to see' (Hoschchild, 1983: 221; Turner, 2001: 134) produces corporeal or cognitive discomfort (or feelings of pleasure where there is congruity), or suggest that emotional responses indicate that the body is suffering distress (Bendelow, 2009), powerlessness (Freund, 1990: 466) or anxiety that others perceive the self negatively (Goffman, 1969: 246; Scheff, 2005: 147).

While constructionist accounts of emotions may be criticized for downplaying biology, interactionist perspectives suffer from a contrary weakness, biological or psychological reductionism. Yet there is a fundamental similarity between these sociological perspectives: both tie conceptions of emotions to the individual human body and human subject (Navaro-Yashin, 2009: 9; Tamboukou, 2003: 211). This anthropocentrism is clear from how these accounts describe emotions; hence, emotions are a 'bodily experience' (Belli et al., 2010: 261) or 'the most personal realms of an individual's experiences' (Freund, 1990: 453). As Sara Ahmed (2004: 8–10) puts it, emotions are conceived in these individualistic approaches either as something escaping from the interior of a body, or the product of exterior forces seeping in. This conception of emotions, Tamboukou (2003: 211) argues, was historically and culturally constituted as part of 'the emergence of "the man" as the object of psycho-scientific discourses'.

With these critiques in mind, we want to set out a materialist and posthuman analysis of emotions, which will question both the emphasis in sociological accounts of emotions as bodily phenomena, and their supposed 'uniqueness' as a link between the social environment and human biology (Williams and Bendelow, 1998a: 137). We will start this re-evaluation by looking at the ways that emotions have been linked to affects in the humanities, cultural theory and certain social sciences.

Emotions and affect

In recent years, some social scientists and arts and humanities scholars have suggested that we are in the midst of an 'affective turn' (Anderson, 2009: 78; Clough, 2008; Leys, 2011; Papoulias and Callard, 2010; Thrift, 2004). This move has been both a challenge to a dominant post-structuralist trend in the humanities and social sciences that has elevated language and social structure over biology (Papoulias and Callard, 2010: 30–1), and a means to promote 'a common ontology linking the social and the natural, the mind and body, the cognitive and affective' (Blackman and Venn 2010: 7). So, for example, Nigel Thrift (2004) has set out the agenda for a 'spatial politics' of affects and emotions in geography that explores how affectivity contributes to politics and citizenship. For the philosopher Brian Massumi (2002), affect links human bodies and brains to their environments in ways not reducible to language and reason, challenging contemporary views about consciousness and human intentionality. Ahmed (2004: 4) has suggested that we should look at emotions affectively, to ask what actions they perform and what effects follow from them.

This latter proposition is closely associated with the materialist approaches that we are using in this book, which has sought to shift from essentialism to this kind of focus on production and capacities. If anthropocentric perspectives in the sociology of emotions have been predicated upon the centrality of human action, a materialist ontology that steps back from a conventional agency/structure distinction can supply traction for a sociology of what emotions do. It suggests a sociological project to look at how emotions affect bodies, but also inspires a wider exploration of what they do within collectivities, social processes and social institutions, and the interactivity (in both material and interpretive registers) between human bodies and other physical, social and abstract entities in their physical and social environment (Tamboukou, 2003: 211; Youdell and Armstrong, 2011: 145), an interactivity that produces lives, societies and history. Accordingly, as we look at emotions and what they do, we shall apply the materialist concepts of assemblages, affects, specification/territorialization and lines of flight that we developed in earlier chapters.

An ontology that explores affectivity seems peculiarly appropriate to this task, as sometimes (mostly in psychology and related disciplines) the terms 'emotion' and 'affect' have been used synonymously (Wetherell, 2012: 3). However, foundational to our analysis is the broader sense of affect we have developed – as something that affects or is affected – rather than any kind of one-to-one equating of emotions and affects. And we will focus upon assemblages of human and non-human relations rather than upon individual 'emotional' bodies; on flows of affect within assemblages rather than notions of agency attached to humans; and on specifications and generalizations of capacities to do and feel rather than deterministic social structures and fields.

Affects, as we noted in Chapter 2, can be understood as 'becomings' (Deleuze and Guattari, 1988: 256) that augment or diminish the capacities of relations (for instance, for Jane to *love* Amy, or anger to *mobilize* citizens). But Deleuze and Guattari (1988: 400) also described affects as 'projectiles', which produce further affects within assemblages – as one affect produces capacities of relations to do, desire or (importantly, in a discussion of emotions) feel, these capacities in turn create subsequent affective flows. For example, watching a film about injustice may produce anger (an 'emotional' capacity), a desire to donate money or time to a campaign, and an identity as a campaigner, all of which in turn will lead to further affects, *ad infinitum*.

This dynamic understanding of affects and how they produce capacities is key to how we will theorize emotions. While emotions may be the product or outcomes of affects (for instance, a person feeling shame following a real or perceived shortcoming such as a failed examination), they may also be affects in their own rights, which produce capacities in bodies (such as 'love' for family or friends producing capacities for heroic action to protect them from danger). This dual character connects emotions firmly into affective flows in event-assemblages (Deleuze, 1988: 50–1), but also supplies the means to theorize how emotions may be 'becomings' that contribute to unfolding lives, societies and history (Thrift, 2004: 61).

Readers will recall that within an assemblage (for instance, a 'sexuality-assemblage' such as we explored in Chapter 6), there will be multiple flows of affects; however, only part of this flow will concern what a body can feel and how it affects other bodies or objects as a consequence of feelings or emotions (Deleuze and Guattari, 1988: 400). So while 'emotions' may be both outcomes and producers of affects, the broader conceptualization of affects in materialist sociology requires that emotions be understood as a sub-category of affects. *Consequently, while emotions and feelings may be affects (that produce states of bodies or minds), only a minority of affects are emotions or feelings.* This formulation recognizes that emotions may contribute to the affect economies of many assemblages, but does not require them as necessary elements of an affective flow. That said, emotions may be very important in producing changes in states of bodies, collectivities, or social organizations. The intense affective capacity of emotions (Massumi, 1996: 228) may implicate them in many lines of flight, from 'falling in love' to engagement in social protest against injustice. We will address this in more detail later, when we explore the part emotion can play in social change.

To explore and develop this sociology of emotions in terms of this understanding of the relationship between emotions and affects, let us consider a couple of examples of how emotions contribute to social production. The first example addresses the subject of romantic love; the second examines the potentially related topic of erectile dysfunction!

The love – assemblage

Love is a social form, phenomenon and emotion that has been subjected to much social scientific analysis and debate (Belli et al., 2010; Jackson, 1993). However, our approach to a sociology of love will not – as a conventional sociology might – look to experiential data, discourses or social structures for insights, but instead will consider the 'love-assemblage'.

A love-assemblage comprises those human and non-human relations that assemble as a consequence of the affective flows between them, and from which emerges the specifications and lines of flight that *inter alia* produce 'love' and other social, psychological and physical consequences. Here are some of the relations in a love-assemblage, as revealed in an extract from an interview with the young philosophy student Neil (whom we also encountered in Chapter 6), from our study of young men's sexualities (Alldred and Fox, 2015). He said:

> ... I fell in love with this girl. It was like our first love kind of thing. ... It's like, it's like a, it's like a kind of bubble amongst the ah ... I don't know, because the world's pretty ... I don't want to say dark, because that's a bit unfair. But it's not ... it's kind of like ... scary sometimes ... when you think about how much shit is going on on the earth, and how many wars and all that. And I think loving ...one other person is a, it's a good way of just, kind of, finding a meaning. You know, it feels like it's not all for nothing, and that there is a point.

From this and other parts of the interview, Neil's 'love-assemblage' can be populated with relations and affects. Along with Neil and his girlfriend were other relations: to the events in Neil's life that he might share; to world events; to a meaning for his life; and to his conception of a bubble secure and safe from circumstances; also to his male friends; to other girls he met but with whom he felt unable to have sexual relations; to former girlfriends, and to conceptions of male and female sexuality. But of course, we may also conjecture many other relations: the public and private places and spaces where lovers meet; the food, drink and other consumables that form a backcloth to their interaction, perhaps a ring or other relationship memorabilia. Then there are social norms and codes of love, relationships and 'going out' in Western culture, even of 'chivalry'; cultural models of masculinity and femininity; the commercialization and commodification of love; institutions and ideals of marriage and so forth. How these disparate relations affect each other critically determines if what emerges is a 'love-' assemblage, as opposed to a 'hate-', 'creativity-', 'health-' assemblage, or whatever.

Drawing on the principles for a materialist ontology already established in this book, we can identify three aspects of what part emotions play in assemblages and affective flows, and in territorializing capacities and desires.

First, an assemblage is produced and held together by affects. As in any other assemblage, we may uncover many different kinds of affects in a love-assemblage, producing all sorts of different capacities for action, desire or feeling. Some affects may be physical (for instance, a kiss or a hug from a lover can produce sensations in the recipient, which in turn may produce a further physical effect such as sexual arousal, perhaps alongside cognitive or emotional capacities). Affects can specify/territorialize desires, perhaps producing a decision to go out to an event or a 'romantic' meal, or create a subject-position (as boyfriend, partner, couple), or even to end the affair. Social and cultural affects such as norms of sexual behaviour or concepts such as 'romance' or monogamy will affect bodies in the assemblage. Some affects will produce a capacity in a body to *feel*, what is commonly called an emotional response such as love, sadness, jealousy or sexual desire (Deleuze, 1990: 246). All these capacities are themselves affects, representing the potential that a body has to act. As bodily capacities (to love, to care, and so forth), 'emotions' are thus produced in the same way as, and entangled with, other capacities.

Second, the affects in a love-assemblage *flow*. Because affects produce capacities in assembled relations, these capacities will result in single or multiple further affects, producing the affective flow in the assemblage. As emotions are themselves affects in the love-assemblage, they can alter, augment or reduce the lovers' capacities or desires, and consequently shape the potential for these bodies to affect other relations in the assemblage, contributing to the flow of affect. Emotions thus sit alongside physical actions, memories and ideas as part of the rhizomic flow of affects that may coerce, discipline, habituate, subjectify, provide meanings or otherwise territorialize bodies and the social world. Those such as love, anger or fear may be powerful motivators of action (Deleuze and Guattari, 1988: 240), while even a 'weaker' feeling associated with a kiss or a gift may lead to a decision to go to a movie, to have sex or get married. Because such flows are the means of production of bodies, the social world and human history (Thrift, 2004: 61), it is via this affective flow that emotions contribute to social production.

Third, a love-assemblage that incorporates bodies, things, social forms and abstract concepts cuts across natural and social worlds, and also across micro- and macro-levels, public and private, institutional and autonomous realms (Beckman, 2011: 10). So, for example, a love assemblage may link the bedroom to the boardrooms of Valentine's Day card companies; the clubs and pubs where attachments form, morph and evaporate; the legislatures and courts where the cultural limits on love are demarcated from stalking, sexual harassment and worse; the manufacturers and retailers of alcohol, beauty products and sex aids; even the pages of academic and medical journals and books that discuss sexuality or emotions. While this undermines any sense that emotions (as part of affective flows) are exclusively private, embodied phenomena, it also establishes the part they play within the flow of affect that produces cultures, social movements and the sweep of history, and also the very physiological way in which the social may engage with the physicality of bodies.

These elaborations establish a perspective on emotions that both constrains and massively enhances understanding of how they contribute to social life. In a love-assemblage, on one hand, a lover's feelings/emotions are merely one component in the wider affectivity that circulates through her/his body and life. Emotion is not a 'missing link' (as claimed by some theorists) between the biological and the social: actually such links must be ubiquitous and commonplace in assemblages in which bodies are affected or affect: physically, psychologically, socially or as reflexive subjects. Just because an emotion is 'felt' does not single it out from other ways bodies are affected by other bodies, things or ideas. On the other hand, emotions (alongside other affects) perform an important role within the flows that produce a lover, her/his unfolding life, and all the other relations that coalesce around her/his actions, feelings, desires and interactions. The significance of an emotion is not as a bodily response to an event, but as a *capacity to affect*.

Re-framing emotion as an element of affectivity draws a sociology of emotion back firmly to the wider processes of production of bodies and social life. Affects have the power to switch bodies 'from one mode to another in terms of attention, arousal, interest, receptivity, stimulation, attentiveness, action, reaction, and inaction' (Clough, 2004: 15). In this economy of affects, assemblages of bodies, subjectivities and experiences flow together with social movements and organizations, political doctrines and geo-economics, and emotions may be important elements of these affect economies. This can be illustrated by a second example not unrelated to love, from Fox and Ward's (2008) study of Viagra and erectile dysfunction (ED). This study reveals how bodies, technologies, markets and biomedicine assemble around a sexual capacity. One brief extract from an interview with a study respondent known as 'George' can provide a flavour of this economy.

> I was panicking because of not being able to maintain my erection ... sometimes it went down totally, (which) was really disappointing my partner. From that moment I guess I got performance anxiety. My best friend at the office introduced me to Viagra a week after he saw my attitude change at the office due to my noticeable depression. Thanks to Viagra, I feel I am gaining my manhood again, but now I'm lazy of doing sex without the blue pill. I am now becoming a big fan of Viagra, and afraid of having sex without (it).

The flow of affects in George's assemblage may readily be discerned: his erectile (in)capacity with his partner produced emotions – performance anxiety, and then feelings of depression that altered his behaviour. Seeing this led his colleague to suggest George used Viagra. The Viagra treatment had multiple affects, producing new physical capacities, a new subjectivity (as a Viagra-enhanced man), and further emotions: joy at his new-found erectile function and then a new performance anxiety: of attempting sex without pharmaceutical assistance.

The affective flow thus progressively transformed elements within the ED-assemblage. But within this affect economy were not only George, his partner, his penis, his colleague and the Viagra tablet, but also the pharmaceutical company that produced it; biomedical and scientific knowledge; the social relations of capitalist accumulation; government regulation and licensing of medicines; the flow of money between health services, manufacturers and consumers, and so forth (Fox and Ward, 2008: 862). Affects between George, Viagra and all these other elements in the assemblage linked bedroom and multinational corporation; sexual performance and financial performance; while emotions (performance anxiety, depression, self-esteem, admiration for the drug and more performance anxiety) played key parts in sustaining the flow that produced this unfolding sequence of events.

These two illustrations suggest how a materialist sociology of emotions connects into the wider affective sociological imagination that we have been developing in this book. It also establishes the means to analyse theoretically and empirically how emotions and desires may contribute to the on-going production of social life. Emotions are no longer oddities – throw-backs to a pre-rational social world – but fundamentally implicated in all aspects of social continuities and changes, from social divisions and inequalities, through work and citizenship to social movements and change (Clough, 2004: 19–20), and in the possibilities for lines of flight out of repression and oppression (Tamboukou, 2003: 222).

By looking at emotions in terms of affects and assemblages of human/ non-human relations, what this chapter has established so far is that emotions contribute to the production of social life, but crucially – as part of the general flow of affect that circulates between bodies, the physical and the social world. For the sociologist, the interest shifts from speculations about cognitive or neurochemical processes, or the biological or evolutionary purposes of emotionality (Dalgleish, 2004; Turner and Stets, 2005: 6) to consider how emotions and affects transform bodies and the world. Emotions are sociologically significant not because they are 'special', but because of their *potency* as products and producers of affect within the assemblages that create the social world. It is this latter characteristic that makes them sociologically interesting, particularly when it comes to social change.

Emotions, social continuity and social change

Having established a materialist sociology of affective flow in which emotions play a part, we want to return to where this chapter began, to examine afresh the many (perhaps all) areas of social life that possess an emotional component, but now informed by a holistic approach to generalized affect rather than one constrained by an anthropocentric focus predicated upon emotions as embodied responses to environmental stimuli. Though emotions have not been widely credited by sociologists as significant factors in social production, there are a range of studies that have revealed how emotions – amongst other factors – play a part in social change. Previous sociological research has revealed how emotions contribute to politics and protest (Jasper, 2011: 286), social movements (Ahmed, 2004: 42; Bensimon, 2012; Jasper, 1998) and social change (Summers-Effler, 2002), as well as in many aspects of daily life, from collective outpourings of grief over the death of a celebrity to the everyday laughter of children (Thrift, 2004: 57).

From the perspective of an affective sociology, we may attend to emotions as part and parcel of the affective flows that produce these sociological forms. Durkheim (1976: 218) might have described the integrative functions of 'collective effervescence' even in what appear quite dis-integrative phenomena, such as popular uprisings in the Middle East or civil unrest over austerity. By contrast, a materialist view would re-analyse the part that emotion plays in social protest in terms of assemblages within which reasoned argument, law, ideology, social organization, rights, physical coercion and emotions such as anger and joy flow together. Together these affect economies may produce lines of flight from aggregative authorities such as 'the State' or particular policies; within this flow of affect what bodies can *feel* is a key element of what they can 'do' (Jasper, 1998; Tamboukou, 2006). Reason and emotion are no longer opposed or contradictory as in many sociological analyses (Leys, 2011), but components together within the broad flow that drives a multiplicity of social processes, from political change to mob violence.

Areas ripe for sociological consideration include the interplay of emotion and reason in religion, faith and rituals (Riis and Woodhead, 2010: 94), or the role of national commemorations and celebrations such as Thanksgiving or May Day in producing and sustaining national identities or contributing to social integration. Sentiment has long been recognized as playing a key part in the movements of stock and commodity markets (Venn, 2010: 158), as dealers try to predict future trends to achieve a profit or avoid a loss – with impacts upon economies and governments. High-profile sporting set-pieces such as the American Football *Superbowl* or the 'Ashes' test matches between English and Australian cricket teams are emotionally charged events that can have consequences beyond the sports world, drawing people into collective reactions to victory or defeat of elation or despondency. Nick's study of the London 2012 Olympic Games (Fox, 2013) traced the part that emotions played from the moment in 2005 when the Olympics were awarded to London, through fears and anger concerning security arrangements and the highs and lows of sporting achievements, to the closing ceremony and the Games' 'legacy' of sporting facilities and the dramatic urban regeneration of a large tract of east London.

These studies, along with the Viagra example noted earlier, suggest the part emotions play in producing unfolding social life, their contribution to the affectivity of the world, and the need for sociology to attend to them seriously. However, while we wish to acknowledge emotions as elements in many social affect economies it would be wrong to attach too much weight to them, or to imply that social processes are driven by emotions alone. Rather, our analysis suggests that emotions need to be recognized as a contributory element in many event-assemblages, alongside memories, imagination, reflections, and of course the wider panoply of material relations and affects that we have been exploring throughout this book. To explore the affectivity of emotions in this broader context, and their impact on social change and continuity, we will draw the threads of our argument together by re-thinking one of sociology's early forays into emotion: the idea of the 'moral panic'.

Moral panics revisited

One of sociology's most evocative concepts (and one – which as earlier noted – has passed into popular discourse) is the 'moral panic', as set out in work by writers such as Stan Cohen (1973, 2002) and Jock Young (1971, 2009). The idea of a moral panic encompasses the outbreak of mass anxiety surrounding a perceived social problem, for instance in relation to migration, youth or sexualities (Cohen, 1973, 2002; Marsh and Melville, 2011; McRobbie and Thornton, 1995). They are of interest to us here because they appear to be founded upon 'irrational' or emotional reactions to an event (Cohen, 2002: 37–40; Young, 2009: 4), often with negative consequences that contributed to the creation, deployment and reproduction of social categorizations and mobilizations (Ahmed, 2004: 46–9).

We will focus here upon one of the earlier descriptions of a moral panic, Cohen's (1973, 2002) analysis of the anxieties experienced in 1960s Britain about rival youth gangs of 'mods' and 'rockers'. Crowds of young people – who identified themselves with these sub-cultures via dress, musical taste and outlook – gathered in seaside towns during holiday weekends, often fighting each other and the police, damaging property and disrupting the resorts. The mass media reported these incidents in text and pictures, fuelling both prurient fascination and anxieties in their (often older, middle-class or 'establishment') readers (Cohen, 2002: 37). This reaction contributed both to negative labelling of young people as anti-social or morally wayward, and to a pro-active and arguably heavy-handed response by police and magistrates when dealing with subsequent gatherings of young people (2002: 71–4).

Cohen's assessment of the societal reaction to these events – the 'moral panic' – was that this represented an exaggerated response (2002: 19), in part fuelled by media attention, but reflecting underlying and pre-existent anxieties, specifically concerning young, working-class men (2002: viii). These young men became a 'folk devil', a demonized category that provoked fear and uncertainty in others. For Cohen (2002: 1), from time to time, 'a condition, episode, person or group of persons emerges to become defined as a threat to societal values and interests'. Young, writing in 2009, has suggested that the fabrication of such folk devils (and the ensuing moral panics) are not random, but 'trigger points', reflecting underlying 'moral disturbances rooted in significant structural and value changes within society' (Young, 2009: 4). Other contemporary 'folk devils', Cohen argued in the 2002 edition of his book, include drug-users, paedophiles, welfare cheats, single mothers and asylum seekers (Cohen, 2002: xii–xviii), most of which are still demonized in some quarters of the media as we write in 2016.

In the context of the concerns of this chapter, moral panics such as those around the mods and rockers studied by Cohen, or more recently, around mass migration from Middle East war zones, pornography and paedophilia, are of interest because of how emotions are implicated. Emotions are involved both in demonizing a category of event or person, and in the subsequent reaction to the events that precipitate the moral panic. The emotions invoked in the former may include fear, anger, hostility, outrage resentment or jealousy (Cohen, 2002: 37, 160–5), while reactions to the latter may include any of these emotions, or a more generalized sense of outrage or moral indignation (2002: 167).

Returning to the contribution of emotions to processes of social production and social change, Cohen's case study suggests two ways in which this occurs during moral panics. First, moral panics may lead to demands for authorities to take punitive sanctions against the demonized group, and to responses by politicians, police and judges to address these demands through law-making and tougher sentencing – this is where moral panic translates into 'moral indignation', a response imbued with emotion (Young, 2009: 10). In more recent episodes of moral panic (most notably around paedophilia), there may also be vigilantism and violence directed against those demonized by members of the public. Second, in what Cohen (2002: 167) called 'deviancy amplification', a moral panic precipitated by specific events will confirm (demonized) stereotypes of the people or groups involved, sustaining society's continued emotional responses to that group. In both cases, we see emotions acting affectively, contributing to an affective flow that produces the social world and social identities.

However, the materialist analysis of emotions and affects that we have developed in this chapter suggests three divergences from Cohen's (and others') interpretations of these processes of demonization and moral panic, and the contribution emotions make to them. First, sociological analysis of moral panics treats the public's reactions to events such as the mod/rocker gatherings and violence as *outcomes* or 'warning signs' of a 'real, much deeper and more prevalent' social malaise (Cohen, 2002: viii; Young, 2009: 4). In the case of the mods and rockers, Cohen argued, the emotions of fear, resentment and so forth were markers of deep-seated antagonism between older people's experiences of wartime and post-war austerity and a new generation that appeared affluent, self-confident, sexually free and dismissive of traditional values (Cohen, 2002: 162). This analysis reflects the kind of sociological ontology that we criticized in Chapter 4, in which a particular element of social structure – operating at a 'deeper level' than everyday interaction – is promoted as the 'explanation' for a phenomenon. By contrast, the materialist 'sociology of association' we developed in that chapter considers that it is these explanations that actually need to be explained. In the case of the moral panic around mods and rockers, it is the gatherings, violence and damage, and the reactions they generate (including 'irrational' emotional reactions) in public and media that are themselves productive (alongside many other events at that time, such as rock music, popular culture and sexual liberation) of divergences between generations and challenges to the established social order, class systems and so forth.

Second, we would regard events such as the mod/rocker encounters and the reactions that followed as shot through with emotion, from beginning to end. The demonization of mod and rocker sub-cultures and the moral panic that followed their seaside encounters are not the start of a social process, but products of a much longer chain of emotions and affects, in which reactions by young people against post-war austerity, norms and establishment values, identification with certain musical and fashion genres, financial independence from their parents and so forth *produced* a range of different popular culture formations and social identities, including 'mods' and 'rockers'. These in turn led to events such as mass outings to seaside resorts, in which in-group camaraderie, antagonism to rival groups, music, drugs and sex provided a heady mix of emotions, as did the excitement and fear associated with violent encounters. We might also trace the affective chain forwards 'rhizomically' into the present, beyond the immediate media-fuelled panic and the reactions by police and politicians, into the future lives of those caught up in the events, in the laws that were passed to control mass gatherings and violence, and in the various youth cultures that succeeded mods and rockers.

Finally, however, our assessment does not elevate emotions above other affects, and the affect economies that produce the chains of events comprise a variety of affects, of which emotions are just one element. While a moral *panic* might imply an irrational or emotional reaction to events (cf. Cohen, 2002: xxviii), it is potentially patronizing and anti-democratic for sociologists to assert that people's reactions are exaggerated or disproportionate. These reactions may also be based upon firm evidence, or reasoned comparisons to past events, producing 'non-emotional' affects that contribute to a collective response labelled as a moral panic. Nor should the responses of law enforcers, judiciary or policy-makers be considered as purely 'emotional' (over-)reactions to moral panics. Rather, the assemblages that produce these chains of events and their consequences will comprise all manner of affects, including memories, reflections, scientific evidence and theories. Whether or not an emotion acts to trigger a moral panic, our analytical focus needs to be upon the wider flow of affect through events.

It is worth noting in conclusion that not all moral panics are 'negative' (or to be more precise, not all are reactions by conservative forces favouring social continuity over social change). While preparing this book during the summer of 2015, the UK government seemed slow to respond to the migrant crisis unfolding as thousands fled Middle East conflicts to try to gain asylum in Europe. It took a widely-viewed news picture of a drowned child on a Greek beach, and a powerful subsequent reaction from the public (fuelled by social media and online petitions) to kick-start the government into action, and grudgingly offer sanctuary to some refugees. As such, emotions can be agents for social change. Indeed, Cohen (2002: xxxiii) argued, in the introduction to the third edition of his book, that change might be achieved by 'encouraging moral panics about mass atrocities and political suffering' – though perhaps in such cases the label 'moral panic' for such social action may seem tenuous or even pejorative.

We have devoted significant space to considering moral panics, as they provide a useful (and sociologically well-documented) illustration of the part that emotions play in everyday life, and potentially how they influence social order and policy. Moral panics are, of course, the exception: most everyday events do not produce such extreme and widespread reactions, though they may be just as dramatic for individuals caught up in them. But by focusing on these extreme events we have sought to show emotions as one element (and often a significant one) within the affect economy of events. At the same time, however, we have also asserted that they are not qualitatively different from other affects in an event-assemblage. Emotions need to be taken seriously by materialist sociologists, particularly because on occasions they may be powerfully affective triggers for action and 'becoming', but always as part of a wider assemblage.

Summary

Our aim in this chapter has been to develop an intellectually-coherent materialist framework that steps away from considering emotion as an individualized embodied response to an environmental/social cue. Sociologically, emotions have to be appraised as more than simply an odd consequence of human evolution or the hard wiring of organs and nerve reflexes, or as a means to 'manage' individual or collective behaviour – for instance to produce docile air passengers or hospital patients.

Instead, we have explored the flows of affect within relational assemblages of animate and inanimate, material and abstract, within which emotions are one aspect of how bodies and things affect and are affected, alongside many others. Affects come in many forms, some governed by physical 'laws' of action and reaction, others by physiology or genetic codes that 'hardwire' responses to stimuli, others by cognition, learning and conditioned reflexes, and still others by the forces that social and cultural theorists have postulated from their studies of power, control and resistance in social formations, institutions and other collectivities. Within this panoply of affects, emotions should be firmly located as one sub-category of affectivity.

While this analysis displaces emotions from their supposed unique position between biology and society (as we saw in Chapter 2, a materialist analysis reveals myriad ways in which the body and the social world affect each other), it

(Continued)

(Continued)

reinvigorates sociological explorations of how emotions flow through social life, alongside instrumental and 'rational' engagements. It sets an agenda for an affective sociology that focuses not upon bodies, subjectivities and emotional responses, but upon capacities and social production. It requires sociology to take emotions seriously, as part of the processes that produce both social continuities and social change.

Further reading

Ahmed, S. (2004) *The Cultural Politics of Emotion.* Edinburgh: Edinburgh University Press.

Blackman, L. (2012) *Immaterial Bodies: Affect, Embodiment, Mediation.* London: Sage.

Fox, N.J. (2013) Flows of affect in the Olympic stadium, and beyond. *Sociological Research Online*, 18(2): 2. Accessed at: www.socresonline.org.uk/18/2/2.html

Wetherell, M. (2012) *Affect and Emotion: A New Social Science Understanding.* London: Sage.

8

Health

Beyond the Body-with-Organs

Introduction

In this chapter we consider another area that has been conventionally regarded as closely tied to individual human bodies – health and illness. As with the other topics in the middle section of this book (creativity, sexuality and emotions), our intention is to question the ways that sociology has linked health, bodies and the social world. We will use materialist analysis to break with an anthropocentric analysis, and to explore the issues in terms of the flow of affects that link bodies with a multitude of physical, psychological, sociocultural and abstract relations, and the associated affect economies. Once again, we will use the materialist toolkit of concepts and methods to re-think how sociology might engage with health and illness.

A thread that has run through this volume is the effort by materialist scholars to move beyond some of the dualisms that invest sociology: structure/agency, nature/culture, micro/macro. As a sociological topic that has struggled with this dualistic heritage, the study of health and illness is no exception; indeed, the shortcomings of this way of thinking about the world are particularly clear when it comes to health. Sociology has often sought to differentiate a social perspective on health that can establish clear water from biological or biomedical conceptions of the body. However, it has become clear in recent scholarship on the sociology of the body (Fox, 2012; Williams and Bendelow, 1998b) that the body is both cultural and natural, and that a subject such as health must be explored across this (artificial) divide. Furthermore, it has been widely acknowledged that health involves both human agency and other forces in the natural and social worlds, and that our analysis requires attention to both the experiential aspects of health and illness and the wider contexts that produce economic and social divisions and inequalities in health and healthcare.

So we shall apply the alternative, 'flat' ontology that we have developed earlier in the book to establish a materialist understanding that sees health and illness not as attributes possessed to greater or lesser extents by individual bodies, but as processes that link bodies to their social and natural environment and define their capacities to do and think and desire. We will use the framework of affects, assemblages and micropolitics to provide a perspective upon health and illness as assemblages of relationships and connectivities that may incorporate other bodies, inanimate objects, institutions and ideas. Within these assemblages, neither biology nor the social is privileged over the other (Deleuze and Guattari, 1988: 336).

This perspective, we would argue, holds substantial promise. 'Health' as assemblage is a process of *becoming*, concerned with maximizing capacities to do, think, desire and feel; illness a process that diminishes these capacities. Health and illness assemblages are disseminated effects, no longer properties of an organic body, but emergent features of relationships between bodies and other elements (Buchanan, 1997; Duff, 2010; Fox, 2002; Fox and Ward, 2006). Focusing on health as human becoming means exploring what bodies can do biologically, psychologically and socially, and the ways these capacities are shaped by forces that produce states we have learnt to call 'illness', 'ageing' and 'disability'. Later in the chapter we will explore the possibilities for a post-anthropocentric and posthuman health, and how the non-human (in the shape of cyborg technologies) may be developed to enhance a body's biological, social and political capacities.

Re-materializing health

Health and illness are phenomena that are material, experiential and culturally-contextual: diseases affect organs and cells, but also influence experience and identity, and manifest within contexts and across populations. Health and illness are shaped by social institutions and cultural beliefs (Cromby, 2004: 798; Turner, 1992: 36), as well as by biology, and the sociology of health and illness has provided myriad illustrations of the social character of health and illness (Armstrong, 1983; Conrad, 2007; Helman, 1978; Kleinman et al., 2006).

One strand of this sociological exploration, which might be called a 'sociology *in* health' perspective, offers sociological insights into patterns of health and illness. Perhaps best known is the contribution around the interactions between social class and health, which have assessed the positive association between various measures of poverty/social deprivation and ill-health and mortality (though see Chapter 4 for our materialist critique of social stratification theory). In an effort to explain why the burden of illness and early deaths falls unequally across populations, sociologists have investigated the factors linked to deprivation, including educational status, access to healthcare resources, work-related health hazards, as well as interactions with gender and race. As such, this work converges with the concerns of epidemiology, and has adopted many of the quantitative methodologies required to uncover significant associations.

This body of work has been complemented by a second thread of research and theory into the sociology *of* health, which has been more concerned with the structural, experiential and interactional aspects of health, illness and healthcare. This strand has focused upon the social and cultural processes such as labelling, stigma and compliance involved in episodes of illness, and upon the consequences of health and illness for people's experiences. It has also addressed the philosophy, shape, organization and politics of health and care services, including the ways in which medicine as a profession and a scientific discipline have impacted upon people in both health and illness through the 'medicalization' of their lives and troubles (Clarke et al., 2010; Conrad, 2007). This thread is more sociologically informed than the work on inequalities, and qualitative approaches have often been the methods of choice.

Social constructionism and post-structuralism grew in influence within these latter concerns, offering a critical assessment of biomedicine as a system of thought or 'discourse' that individualized health and healthcare, and extended a pathologizing 'gaze' into more and more aspects of life, from fertility (Franklin, 1990) to child behaviour (Tyler, 1997). Foucault and others described the emergence of this biomedical discourse as modern hospitals emerged as locations for observation (Foucault, 1976) and documentation (Foucault, 2002: 145) of the organic body. Biomedical models of the body have entered the popular domain, and medical advice or self-help books about the biomedical body are legion (Bunton, 1992: 232–4). This 'body-with-organs' (Fox, 1993: 145) or 'organism' (Deleuze and Guattari, 1988: 158) is also the focus for economic and political activity, for science, social science and the 'psy disciplines' (Rose, 1999) of psychotherapy, counselling, psychoanalysis and so on, and for the stratification of society by gender, ethnicity and age.

Despite their critical perspectives on health and medicine, and the elaborations of a social model of embodiment over the past 20 years, sociologists have not been immune to biomedical science's promulgation of such individualized, biologized body-with-organs as the location of 'health' and 'illness', and as the ontological unit of sociological analysis. Arguably, a biomedical ontology of the body has constrained sociological analysis of health and illness – health and ill-health have been too quickly accepted as attributes of an individual body, rather than as a wider, *ecological* phenomenon of body organization and deployment within social and natural fields. What is needed, we would argue, is a materialist, post-anthropocentric and post-human conception of health that breaks decisively with the body-with-organs, to understand health as an impersonal affective flow that links bodies into wider assemblages of relations.

Following the materialist model that we have set out in this book and used repeatedly, we start the task of re-materializing health by focusing not upon what bodies are, but what they can do; on bodies not as prior entities but always produced and materialized in their social and natural relations. We consider not structures or top-down forces that constrain or enable, but the micropolitical forces inherent in event-assemblages that produce capacities; and not fixed, stable states of health and illness but processes. Indeed, on this latter point, we might stop talking about health and illness and talk instead of 'healthing', or (as that is a fairly ungainly word) of health as *becoming*. Later we shall make a direct connection to a materialist perspective on 'health' as a quantitative measure of a body's capacity to form productive relations. To set the scene for that radically different view, we shall begin exploring the affectivity of health by looking at the 'ill-health assemblage'.

The ill-health assemblage

Within a relational ontology, an ill-health assemblage can be defined as comprising the myriad physical, psychological and social relations and affects that surround a body during an episode of ill-health. A simple ill-health assemblage, associated with an infection such as a cold, will comprise:

respiratory tract – virus – immune system – inflammation

In this simple assemblage, the virus affects the nose and other parts of a body's respiratory tract; the immune system will respond, attacking the virus and at the same time causing the inflammatory response that produces many of the symptoms of the infection. In this 'cold-assemblage', the capacity of the virus to attack body systems is relatively weak, and typically will be defeated eventually by the body's immune system, and the affect-economy will return the body to a pre-infection state after a few days.

Of course, sociology has taught us that health and illness cannot simply be reduced to physiology and immunology, and for an adult, many other psychosocial and cultural relations will contribute to the affect-economy, producing an assemblage that might look like this:

respiratory tract – virus – immune system – inflammation – pharmacist – pharmaceutical compound – theories of infection and inflammation – daily responsibilities – family members – social networks

This assemblage will impact variously on what a body can do physically, psychologically and socially, including infecting other bodies in contact with the sufferer – a feature that imparts a life of its own to this assemblage.

For a more serious illness, other relations will come into play, including health technologies, doctors, health facilities, as well as affective responses such as fear, anger or regret. Ill-health is not simply the product of disease, but is shaped by the affect economy between these multiple relations. It can have as much to do with the emotional meaning of illness and the cultural contexts of ill-health as with a disease agent such as a virus, tumour or genetic cause. Readers may recall that in Chapter 7, we looked briefly at an event involving 'erectile dysfunction' (ED) and 'George', a user of the drug Viagra. Within this assemblage were not only George, his partner, his penis, his work colleague (with whom he discussed using the drug) and the Viagra tablet, but also the pharmaceutical company that produced it; biomedical and scientific knowledge; government regulation and licensing of medicines; the flow of money between health services, manufacturers and consumers (Fox and Ward, 2008: 862). In this assemblage, a loss of penile erection rhizomically affected multiple relations, with all kinds of physical, psychological and pharmaceutical consequences across space and time (including the emotional flows we described in that chapter).

Ill-health assemblages are thus constituted from a mix of physical, psychological, social and cultural relations. Physical relations may include disease agents such as genes, pathogens, time, ageing and degenerative diseases, pollutants and environmental hazards, the body's biological responses such as the immune system and pain, and health technologies such as medicines, physical therapies, prostheses and devices. Psychological relations may include environmental stressors, health beliefs, psychological therapies, emotional reactions and attitudes to illness, as well as psychological and neurological pathologies. Sociocultural relations may include healthcare systems and professionals, culturally-specific explanatory models of illness and practices such as folk remedies, lay networks of family and friends, economics and politics of healthcare, and concepts deriving from science and biomedicine (Fox, 2011).

The relations in an ill-health assemblage can also vary across history, or from culture to culture, depending upon how diseases and illnesses are understood, and upon the institutions that cater for the sick. Reading Jane Austen's *Sense and Sensibility* can supply an insight into an 18th-century ill-health assemblage, in which forces of disease seem ready to strike at times of physical stress or emotional imbalance, thrusting a body into fever and danger of death. Foucault's (1967) *Madness and Civilisation* demonstrates the differing assemblages surrounding mental health in past times, while a history of sexualities reveals that the medical profession at one time pathologized all but adult heterosexual sexual contact (Alldred and Fox, 2015a). In addition, there will be many relations and affects within an illness event that are unique to the setting, circumstances, past experiences and other aspects of illness. The diversity of people's experiences and reactions to illness and healthcare are an outcome of these idiosyncrasies within their own particular ill-health assemblages.

Within this materialist perspective, the capacities that the ill-health assemblage produces are perhaps of greater sociological significance. Ill-health will tend to produce 'sickening-bodies', in which the capacities of the body will reflect differing patterns of biological and social engagements from that of a body in 'health'. What this sickening body can do is an outcome of the breadth of affects in an illness-assemblage, of which the physical/biological may not be the most significant, requiring that we move beyond a simplistic biomedical model of illness. For example, dependence on family or friends during illness can impact identity and self-confidence, undermining capacities to engage productively with the world (Fox, 2005). This is particularly important for understanding chronic illness, disability and ageing, in which the psychological and sociocultural relations may be powerfully affective in terms of what a person can do, think and feel.

This perspective on ill-health requires that we re-evaluate some of the fundamental building blocks of health sociology. Ontologically, bodies are not simply the locus upon which physical and social forces act, they are the *products* of the interactions of these forces. Ill-health does not act on a prior body; rather the body is an *outcome* of the ill-health assemblage, which now replaces the human body as the unit for sociological analysis. However, this post-anthropocentric and posthuman focus upon the illness-assemblage also requires that we look at the capacities that illness produces in the *non-human* elements of the ill-health assemblage.

These include social and cultural formations such as the social organization of healthcare services, the structure of employment (and hence the economy), family organization, policies and laws associated with health, illness and disability, all of which are shaped by the materiality of ill-health. But also affected are physical and biological relations, from the healthcare built environment, to the chemicals produced by pharmaceutical industry, and the consequent evolution of pathogens to counter these compounds. Human bodies may be the 'carriers' of health and illness, but the impacts of ill-health assemblages (and, as we will see in a moment, 'health-assemblages') have consequences across the social and natural worlds. A materialist analysis of health and illness demands a holistic understanding of how multiple relations (from a bacterium to a health belief) – all with material affectivity – assemble to produce and modify human capacities to do, think, feel and desire.

The 'health' assemblage

What, then, of the body in health? If there is an ill-health assemblage and a sickening-body, is there also a *health assemblage*, and a becoming-healthy body? And is this simply the obverse of the illness-assemblage? The answer to the former question is yes, but to the latter, no. We have listed the many physical, psychological and social relations that are in play during an episode of ill-health, and inevitably the relations during 'health' are mostly the same as those involved in the illness-assemblage. However, their intensities and affectivity may be much attenuated or in some case, wholly absent. On the other hand, there may be other relations that are much stronger during good health: these once again may be physical, psychological, social and cultural, economic, political or philosophical.

In order to explore the health-assemblage, we need to ask some foundational questions about health itself. Health has been argued over extensively. Biomedical science theorized health as merely an absence of disease (Wade and Halligan, 2004), and this view still dominates medical practice. The World Health Organisation (1985) offered a more holistic, if rather vague definition, considering health to be a state of 'complete physical, mental and social well-being'. From an anthropological perspective, Wright (1982) saw health as 'what it is to function as a human', with illness occurring when the body fails to function but continues to be seen as human. Canguilhem (1989) defined health and illness as positive and negative biological values. Illness is marked by increasing dependency, de Swaan (1990: 220) suggested, while health represented a 'maximization of potential and expression in everyday activities of life', according to Anderson (1991: 109).

Of these definitions, the latter has some congruence with a number of writers who have suggested a materialist understanding of health. If the sickening-body has restricted or re-directed capacities, health might be defined in terms of a body's widened capacities to make, resist and transform its relations. Ian Buchanan (1997: 82) draws on a Deleuzian reading of Nietzsche to define health as a body's 'actual measurable capacity to form new relations', relations that in turn lead to new assemblages and new possibilities for action. In an extensive contribution to an assemblage approach to health, Duff (2014: 67) finds in Sen's (1999) 'capabilities' model, a perspective on health as 'the sum effect of the adaptive advantages enacted in the acquisition of new capacities'. For Fox (2012: 99) what is important is that a body's relations enhance capacities ranging from its biological functions to its psychological well-being and the social and cultural resources it can draw upon. The 'health' of a body is affected by:

> ... refracted and resisted relations, biological capabilities or cultural mind-sets, alliances with friends or health workers, struggles for control over treatment or conditions of living. Health is neither an absolute ... to be aspired towards, nor an idealized outcome of 'mind-over-matter'. It is a process of becoming by (the body), of rallying relations, resisting physical or social territorialization, and experimenting with what is, and what it might become. (Fox, 2002: 360)

According to these perspectives, 'health' is not just an absence of particular 'ill-health' relations or affects (as might be assumed from a biomedical understanding), but the opposite – the proliferation of a body's capacities to affect and be affected. Health is neither a state nor a final outcome, but a process – a becoming-other that fluctuates according to the intensity of relations that impinge on the body. Rather than saying a body is healthy, we might talk about its 'becoming-healthy', to remind us of the active processes involved and the complex mix of relations in all assemblages. In this vein, Duff (2010: 624; 2014: 75) has suggested an explicit congruence between health and development, the latter being 'the expressed quality or manifestation of health', while health may be understood as 'a quantum of a body's power of acting'. This opens up the potential to explore health assemblages over the life-course, from cradle to grave (see, for instance Fox (2005) on the biological, psychological and cultural relations that influence what an ageing body can do).

The micropolitics of health

This analysis also draws us back to the earlier discussion of the ill-health assemblage, to consider further the impact of illness upon bodily capacities. Earlier in this chapter, we suggested that both scientific and social scientific perspectives on embodiment have struggled to move beyond locating health and illness in the *body-with-organs*. This understanding of the body, as an organic, individual entity, has been largely constituted by scientific, biological and mechanical models, and sustained by the professions and institutions of biomedical science (Fox, 2012: 22). It is manifested on a daily basis in the medicalizing processes that turn bodies into patients, healers and carers into health professionals, chemicals into medicines, and episodes of ill-health into case histories and archives of disease (Foucault, 2002: 145). The sick, the convalescent, the disabled and the aged are all part of this specification/territorialization, and the history of both disease and health have been written, and continue to be written within the territory of the body-with-organs.

In its most pared-down and emblematic formulation, the body-with-organs may be the product of an assemblage with just a handful of relations, for instance:

disease – patient – doctor – health technology – biomedical science

In the affect economy of this assemblage, biomedical science (materialized via medical training and health technologies) establishes the theoretical foundation for treatment and an expectation of cure. This allows a health professional to be defined as a healer; healthcare and health technologies (for instance, a medicine or a surgical procedure) as the means whereby the disease may be resolved; and the patient as a body-with-organs to be healed. Micropolitically, the affect-economy of these few relations is often so powerful that the affectivity of other relations in the ill-health-assemblage (for instance, family members or alternative theories of health) may be overwhelmed, minimizing any effect on a body's capacities.

The consequent body-with-organs is highly specified by these affects, with few possibilities to act. Thus becoming a 'patient' or receiving care within this biomedicalized assemblage can close down capacities. So, for example, the former cancer patient now free of disease is always 'in remission'; the noisy child is diagnosed as having attention deficit hyperactivity syndrome (ADHD) – to be treated by pharmaceuticals; the very old have become geriatric. This is the materialist analysis of the processes that have been called 'medicalization' by health sociologists (Clarke et al., 2010; Conrad, 2007).

Theorizing 'biomedicine'

In Chapter 4, we criticized the tendency of conventional sociology to offer 'structural' concepts such as 'neoliberalism' or 'patriarchy' as explanations of social processes, rather than posing these as the very things that need explaining. So it is important in our analysis here that we do not simply set up 'biomedicine' as some kind of all-powerful relation, solely responsible for specifying both the healthy and the sick as *bodies-with-organs*. 'Biomedicine' is sometimes used as a term merely to refer to the biomedical sciences (such as endocrinology, pharmacology or genomics), and we have used the term in this way already in this chapter. However, within the social sciences, 'biomedicine' is also used to describe a body of knowledge (what Foucault might call a 'discourse') or a scientific 'model' that explains how bodies and disease processes work in terms of biological structures and processes (Nettleton, 2006: 3). This biomedical model

(Continued)

(Continued)

is criticized by sociologists for its biological reductionism, excluding social and psychological processes and responses to illness and disease (Ogden, 1997), and as the ontological basis for health professional authority (Chamberlain, 2013: 21).

In this latter sense, 'biomedicine' offers a convenient target for sociologists to criticize medical dominance (Freidson, 1974) and medical 'power/knowledge' (Nettleton, 1992: 107), and it would be neat and easy to simply add 'biomedicine' or the 'medical model' as a relation when analysing health assemblages. However, the ontology we outlined in Chapter 4 requires that we explore power and resistance locally, in terms of relations within events. Let us consider, once again, the condition known to health professionals as 'erectile dysfunction' (ED). In her materialist analysis of men and their partners who used Viagra to overcome ED, Potts (2004: 22) described a 'Viagra machine', which we might term an 'erectile dysfunction/Viagra-assemblage'. This, at its simplest, might be represented as follows:

penis – pharmaceutical (Viagra) – partner – doctor

In this assemblage, Viagra (used according to medical advice) affects body tissues, producing an erection in a previously dysfunctional penis, in turn enabling penetrative sex with a partner.

It is tempting to add 'biomedicine' to this assemblage, to mark the theoretical source of a narrow, pathologizing territorialization of 'erectile dysfunction' (ED) – even this nomenclature reflects a biomedical model – as a condition to be resolved by medical intervention (a pharmaceutical compound). However, are there not other drivers also at work in this assemblage? Medical professions may feel powerless to address problems at the limit of what might be called disease, and welcome new treatments to meet their patients' complaints. The business model underpinning pharmaceutical companies means that success or failure will depend upon developing new technologies and generating new demand (Henry and Lexchin, 2002: 1591). Meanwhile, health consumerism fuels demand for effective treatments for problems and conditions such as ED, and creates a ready market for new products (Fox and Ward, 2008).

All these are contexts within which a user takes a blue Viagra tablet to gain an erection. So while the doctor diagnosing ED and prescribing a pharmaceutical compound has been trained within a biomedical model of sexuality and embodiment, the ill-health assemblage of a Viagra user is also shaped by relations as disparate as a drug company's business plan, a doctor's insecurity when faced with a patient with a hitherto untreatable condition, and demand from consumers and professionals for medications to treat ED.

Methodologically, materialist sociologists need to make sense of the affect economies that connect the relations within ill-health assemblages by exploring empirically what these relations do – what capacities they produce in other relations. Rather than speculating on which concepts and theories (such as 'biomedicine', or 'capitalism') may be influencing the relations in an assemblage, this requires detailed interrogation of research data, to disclose the specific affects and capacities in health and illness assemblages.

Though this materialist exploration of the micropolitics of health and illness suggests that the body-with-organs is a pervasive, highly specified or territorialized product of healthcare, our analysis does not inevitably lead to pessimism. Throughout this book we have emphasized that the materialist ontology we have presented recognizes that resistance and becoming-other are always options, and are only as far away as the next new relation in the assemblage. The body-with-organs can always be de-territorialized. Consequently, the sociological study of health and illness is also an exercise in discerning the micropolitics of specification and generalization, becoming and lines of light.

This has been revealed in a series of studies by Fox and colleagues, who identified the specifications and aggregations affecting older people in both familial and institutional care settings (Fox, 2005) and of obese and overweight people using health technologies such as weight-loss drugs (Fox et al., 2005c). These studies also disclose examples of dis-aggregation and lines of flight, including use of erectile dysfunction medicines to enable non-normative sexual activities (Fox and Ward, 2008). Perhaps the most dramatic examples were young women in the 'pro-anorexia' movement who rejected health professionals' efforts to 're-feed' them back to a 'normal' weight (Fox et al., 2005a), and instead found a line of flight in 'thinspirational' images and the managed use of diet medicines within a community that supported them to sustain very low body weights while not endangering their health. We explore this study in more detail in Chapter 10.

What these studies suggest is that understanding health and illness in terms of the assembling of disparate biological, psychological and social relations, and assessing illness and health not as states but as conditions of possibility and capacities for action, means shifting beyond both a (biomedicalized) body-with-organs and a focus on individual human bodies. Indeed, it makes sense to take illness- and health-assemblages as the units of analysis, looking at the consequences not just for human bodies, but for all the relations in the assemblage. Looking back to the examples we explored in Chapter 3 when we discussed the interactions between human health and the environment, we can see that the 'health' of an assemblage may have consequences not only for human bodies, but also for physical things like buildings or bikes, for social formations like families and schools, and for abstractions such as 'the economy' and 'sustainability'.

This re-focusing is an important antidote to a temptation to fall back into an anthropocentric view of either health (or development more generally) strictly in human terms. To emphasize this, we want to draw together the strands of our argument by exploring in some detail the interactions between bodies and technologies, to consider at an assemblage level how so-called 'personal health technologies' can be both territorializing and de-territorializing, and offer possibilities for health that can transform both individual bodies and the world about them.

Health and technology: cyborgs and citizen health

A materialist approach seems peculiarly suited to explore the interactions between bodies and physical objects such as medical technologies, and a number of actor-network theorists (ANT) have studied these interactions (see Chapter 2), including work by Prout (1996) on the development of the asthma metered-dose inhaler, and Hanseth et al.'s (2006) study of an electronic patient record system. In these studies, technologies were acknowledged as active and affective within relational networks of human and non-human elements, alongside human actors. From a different perspective, Deborah Lupton has drawn on Haraway's (1991) discussion of body/technology cyborgs to explore how mobile digital technologies produce hybrid bodies (Lupton, 2012: 229). Such 'cyborg bodies' are assemblages (2012: 237) that produce bodies with new capacities for self-monitoring. Nick's recent analysis of personal health technologies (N. Fox, 2015b) has been located firmly within a new materialist framework, and we will devote space to this, as it addresses explicitly the micropolitics of health technologies, but also sets out the possibilities for de-territorializing the body-with-organs, and promoting a posthuman approach to health via body/technology cyborgs.

Personal health technologies

Personal health technologies (PHTs) are near-body devices or applications designed for use by a single individual, principally outside healthcare facilities. They enable users to monitor physiological processes or body activity, are frequently communication-enabled, and sometimes also intervene therapeutically. They range from blood pressure or blood glucose monitors and implantable medical devices usually used under health professionals' supervision, to commercial devices such as the *Fitbit* and *Apple Watch*, purchased by individuals to monitor fitness and other body parameters.

PHTs have been of interest sociologically in part because they personalize and domesticate monitoring and therapy previously located in healthcare settings, sometimes with negative consequences. Older people may be coerced by care services to adopt telecare technologies such as alarms and falls monitors, or stigmatized for 'misusing' the technology in an attempt to increase their social contact with the outside world (Mort et al., 2013). Technologies can seem impersonal and unresponsive, can demand much of their users and create a sense of failure when the data they generate are not promising (Mol, 2009: 1757). Self-tracking technologies have been criticized for adding a further level of surveillance to contemporary society, producing data that render people's lives transparent as they are transmitted, collected and aggregated by biomedical or corporate interests (Lupton, 2014: 1353; Till, 2014).

We can analyse PHTs in terms of assemblages and affect-economies, and the micropolitics of specification and aggregation. So, for instance, a blood pressure monitor assembles at least the following relations:

vascular system – device – user – manufacturer – health professionals

The primary affectivity of the monitor is to provide feedback to a user concerning otherwise unobservable parameters. This produces a user capacity to assess blood pressure in relation to norms or to previous readings, and thereby to judge current risk level, or to manage body physiology or biochemistry (for instance, through diet or exercise, reducing sodium intake and so forth). Micropolitically, this assemblage makes a user responsible both for monitoring and acting in response to the readings; it extends a biomedical gaze over the user's body functions beyond clinical settings into domestic spaces; and furthermore, it both outsources and privatizes medical monitoring.

The *Fitbit* is one of a number of commercial products that can be worn or carried on the body, in order to monitor various body parameters including heart rate, motion and posture, hours slept and so forth. Data are sent wirelessly to a computer or mobile phone where they can be displayed graphically and calories burned and other functions calculated; data can also be shared. The *Fitbit*-user assemblage comprises at least the following relations

body movements – terrain – product – wearer – manufacturer – associates

The affect driving this assemblage is the *Fitbit*'s capacity to gather data on body parameters, turning these into quantifiable outputs that can be displayed, analysed and interpreted.

However, the affect economy also produces new user capacities to choose certain behaviours such as exercise or sleep, and new opportunities to share and compare behaviours with peers. In addition, as a commercial product, it provides its manufacturers with profit and a potential future market for related products. These affective flows generate a specific micropolitics that has the outcome of 'responsibilizing' (Muncie, 2006) the user. But, at the same time – by quantifying and making explicit certain aspects of daily life, and enabling comparisons with other users – such fitness PHTs encourage certain normative behaviours around fitness, sleep, weight etc., creating new body routines and regimens, and producing competitiveness with others and the user her/himself. In addition, by drawing users into an assemblage with commercial interests, private aspects of a user's life and health are privatized, commodified and commercialized.

Other PHTs may be subjected to similar analysis, but our materialist analysis suggests a further opportunity. If we can reverse engineer PHTs to reveal how they work and what capacities they produce, it should be possible also to forward-engineer technologies, to produce specific micropolitics and capacities. This may be done to meet specific objectives or from within different perspectives on health and illness. For instance, a technology may be designed to serve public health professionals: the aim here might be to design a PHT that enables surveillance of at risk individuals, reducing patient delay and encouraging individuals to take responsibility for their behaviour and activity. It might also allow health services to be managed more effectively to meet need, and potentially reduce costs (N. Fox, 2015b). An example of such a PHT might be a wireless-connected personal monitoring device issued to a target group of people. It would monitor a range of signs and parameters, notify wearers of health risks, invite people to attend primary care to address abnormal signs or to undergo appropriate screening or tests, remind people to take prescribed medications and so forth. Personal health technologies can also be designed to meet commercial objectives, or to care for individual patients at a distance.

However, Nick Fox (2015b) suggests a further possibility, which directly challenges the specifications and aggregations of bodies in biomedical and commercial paradigms, and opens up new opportunities for posthuman health, as conceived earlier in this chapter as a process of becoming. This 'resistance' paradigm would reject biomedicine's individualization of health; oppose surveillance, responsibilization and invasion of private or domestic spaces; and resist the commercialization and commodification of health and illness.

Engineering 'citizen health'

We can set out some objectives for a personal health technology designed to resist the body-with-organs. Such a PHT-assemblage would:

- Promote health and illness in terms of the capacities of people and collectivities to engage productively with their social, economic, political and cultural milieux.
- Enable people and communities to address health and illness threats and opportunities together, rather than as individuals.
- Provide data and analytical capacities and resources to inform health policy development or campaigns for health-related improvements to a locale or sector.
- Organize against health corporate interests such as environmental polluters, purveyors of fast and processed foods, and against corporate healthcare providers.
- Synchronize health and environmental sustainability – rejecting policy initiatives that seek human health or development gains at the expense of the environment and sustainability.

This kind of approach might be described as a 'citizen health' agenda (Rimal et al., 1997), in tune with ideas of health activism (Zoller, 2005) and critical public health (Green and Labonté, 2008). An example of a technology that could deliver on some or all of these objectives would be a network of wearable and free-standing PHTs (mountable on buildings and other structures), that could be used to gather and crunch relevant physiological, social, environmental health data. Instead of the many-to-one or 'hub-and-spoke' communication architecture that links bodies individually to health professionals or to corporate databanks, it would use a many-to-many communication protocol, to build networks of connected bodies and social formations. Specific functions might be to:

- assess health status and risks to health across a locality (or a specific sub-community such as LGBT citizens or teenage parents);
- notify participants of relevant policy or risks;
- access knowledge resources via local libraries and universities; and
- co-ordinate action and build coalitions with health professionals, politicians, researchers and others, and support policy development.

Such a 'citizen health' PHT is not fanciful, it can easily be developed using existing software such as Web 2.0 collaborative technologies, peer-to-peer file-sharing software and search tools (N. Fox, 2015b).

This exploration of personal health technologies has served to both reveal some of the ways in which bodies become specified as bodies-with-organs, but also to suggest the possibilities for generalizing (de-territorializing) a body-with-organs and the potential 'lines of flight' that are possible once a view of health as becoming is adopted. We will use these insights to draw together the various threads or argument we have discussed in this chapter.

Posthuman health

Our discussion of development of a 'resisting' personal health technology was not simply to promote the need for a specific device. Rather, it was to make a point that ideas such as 'citizen health' – that emerge from the materialist ontology we have set out in this chapter – offer an alternative to the way health has been conceptualized conventionally, both in the biomedical sciences and to an extent within sociology. This design for a 'citizen health PHT' addresses a number of the arguments we have made in support of a materialist, post-anthropocentric and posthuman perspective on health.

First, by subverting health paradigms deriving from biomedicine and commerce, it decentres health from being an attribute or possession of a body, locating it instead as the product of the affective flow between bodies, physical stuff, social formations, memories, ideas and abstract concepts. Second, it explicitly emphasizes the pursuit of health in terms of enhancing capacities and possibilities for action – for individuals, but also for collectivities and communities, and for the physical environment (see Chapter 3). Third, it is a practical manifestation of the cyborg character of bodies, demonstrating the 'health' that can be produced by drawing physical, social and cultural relations into assemblage. Finally this ecological understanding of health forms the basis for activism and social change, and firmly rejects the individualized body-with-organs promoted in biomedical theories of the body, health and disease, and the specifications and aggregations this produces.

These four points encapsulate the radical re-thinking of health and illness that derives from materialist sociology. In some ways it is a radical departure, in others it plays to sociology's strengths, by focusing not upon individual organic bodies but upon associations and assemblages that incorporate organic and inorganic, material and abstract. Health and ill-health are not attributes of individual bodies, but relational and ecological, concerned with the capacities produced by assemblages in both human bodies and other things. The endless permutations of living – of health, illness, sexual desire, ageing and death open up possibilities for exploring both continuities and change, power and resistance. The alternative perspective that we have suggested is not simply a philosophical and ontological exercise, but a means for the sociology of health and illness to embrace a posthuman perspective.

It is radical in a second way too, as this relational and ecological model of health sets out a powerful critique of biomedical thinking about bodies and health, and its negative consequences. It suggests that healthcare may – rather than creating opportunities – close down what a body can do by trammelling it within an individualized and medicalized framework. The body-with-organs has been a seductive model of embodiment: biological in essence, individualized, imbued with independent agency and located within a social, economic and political nexus that feeds on this model of embodiment (for instance, turning individuals into consumers), as do the medical professions (Deleuze and Guattari, 1988: 159). Sociology too is implicated in this specification, to the extent it has accepted the body-with-organs as its unit of analysis.

So for the most extensive critique of the body-with-organs, it is perhaps unsurprising that we must turn not to sociology, but to the materialist work of a philosopher and a psychoanalyst. In their two books on capitalism and schizophrenia, Gilles Deleuze and Félix Guattari set out a concerned attack on the body-with-organs or 'organism' (Deleuze and Guattari, 1984: 382–6; 1988: 158–9), which they saw as an impoverished and closed down entity, shorn of its breadth of connections and associations with the rest of the world.

Their objective in those books was to reconnect the body, to make it a 'body-*without*-organs', freed to re-connect in all kinds of ways, on all kinds of levels. In relation to mental health, they called their critique 'schizoanalysis' (Deleuze and Guattari, 1984: 273); more generally as a political strategy for living, they called it 'nomadology' (Deleuze and Guattari, 1988: 23).

This critique makes healthcare intrinsically political – on one hand closing down (post)human potential, while on the other engaging with and supporting the struggles of people to break free from specification by biology, culture or scientific theories. The 'health' of a body, in this view, is the outcome of associations and assemblages, alliances with friends or health workers, struggles for control over treatment or conditions of living; efforts to transform the social and natural environment to enable new associations and opportunities. It is a process of becoming, of rallying capacities, resisting physical or social specification, and experimenting with what is, and what might become. Health sociology can pull apart and re-make, intellectually and in practice, the ill-health assemblages that affect the material lives of people and the public health of nations.

Arguably, with this agenda for health as becoming, the true science of health is not medicine but sociology, though a sociology of association that is not obsessed with defending its boundaries, that acknowledges the biological and the psychological as key relations alongside the sociocultural in producing health, and that is willing to work alongside clinicians in the cause of health as becoming. This puts sociology on a collision-course with powerful groupings working within a biomedical perspective. Questioning the individualistic nature of ill-health and ill bodies may seem counter-factual to many, and intellectually-threatening to some. But to engage productively with such agendas actually collapses rather than reinforces disciplinary boundaries, and establishes a pressing need for collaboration between medical and caring professions, social and political scientists, social activists, indeed between every body – human, posthuman and non-human.

Summary

In this chapter we have used materialist ontology to re-think both illness and health. We have rejected the model of a body-with-organs used in the biomedical sciences to define these categories, and sought instead a relational and ecological approach in which health is to be seen as a process of becoming that opens up possibilities for action, both for human bodies and for their social and natural environments. We have argued for a posthuman focus that

(Continued)

(Continued)

recognizes health as not just about the condition of an individual body, but about the productiveness of the relations that humans have with others, and with all their physical, social and abstract relations. We suggest a new role for a sociology of associations in relation to health and healthcare, one that confronts individualistic approaches to health and promotes health as becoming, theoretically, and through research and activism.

Further reading

Buchanan, I. (1997) The problem of the body in Deleuze and Guattari, or, what can a body do? *Body & Society, 3*(3): 73–91.

Duff, C. (2010) Towards a developmental ethology: exploring Deleuze's contribution to the study of health and human development. *Health, 14*(6): 619–634.

Fox, N.J. (2012) *The Body.* Cambridge: Polity.

Part 3

Research, Policy and Activism

9

Research
Designs, Methods and the Research Assemblage

Introduction

Throughout this book we have used various examples to illustrate the different sociological topics we have explored, from social mobility to environmental change to health technology. Some have been based upon specific pieces of empirical research, and we have applied our toolkit of materialist concepts to offer new interpretations of the data, often drawing different conclusions from those of the original studies. However, until now we have resisted setting out explicitly a 'materialist' approach to social research. We now turn to this task, to address the methodological challenges facing those who wish to apply materialist ontology to social inquiry. Arguably, part of the added sociological value of the new materialism depends upon turning its novel perspectives on the social world into useable sociological methods for research.

Over the past ten years, a growing number of social scientific studies have applied research methodologies rooted in materialist perspectives. Social researchers have drawn on methodological concepts to be found in the work of materialist scholars, such as Karen Barad's ideas of 'intra-action' between researcher and researched (Barad, 1996: 179), and 'diffractive methodology' (2007: 90), and Deleuze and Guattari's 'schizoanalysis' (Deleuze and Guattari, 1984: 322) and 'cartography' (1988: 261). These concepts (see Glossary for definitions) have supplied novel and sometimes radical methods for collecting, analyzing and presenting data. A shift towards a materialist foundation for social inquiry also marks a move away from epistemological arguments (concerning how we may know the world) between realist and constructionist approaches to research (van der Tuin and Dolphijn, 2010), toward a concern with ontology (the kinds of things that exist in that world) (Barad, 1996: 162; Karakayali, 2015: 733).

Our point of entry into a materialist approach to social inquiry begins from an analysis of research as *assemblage*. From a materialist perspective, a research-assemblage (Coleman and Ringrose, 2013: 17; Fox and Alldred, 2013; Masny, 2013: 340) comprises the bodies, things and abstractions that get caught up in social inquiry, including the events that are studied, and the researchers. It will be this concept that will enable us to develop a materialist perspective on social inquiry, and form the basis of a methodology for materialist social inquiry. We shall not claim to offer the last word in materialist methodology, but what we shall provide is the means for students and researchers to translate ontological innovation into practical tools for social inquiry.

We begin by developing an analysis of research as an interaction between an event to be observed and the research assemblage. This will supply the foundation for understanding research micropolitics. But what is assembled can also be dis-assembled, and later in the chapter we will delve further inside the research-assemblage, opening up the research process to reveal both the workings of the various 'research-machines' that underpin data collection, analysis, writing and dissemination, and also the micro-political interactions between researcher and researched. We explore social research in terms of the interactions between events and the research-assemblage, and consider the micropolitics of these engagements and what they mean for the knowledge that is produced. This analysis will provide the basis for principles to conduct materialist research methodology.

Materialism and social inquiry

Social scientists have argued at great length over what kinds of knowledge can be generated by social inquiry. Generally, assessments of the capacity of social research to offer objective descriptions of events have polarized around a realist/constructionist dualism (Alvesson and Sköldberg, 2009; Barad, 1996), with the former perspective aspiring to a knowable reality independent of human concepts, while the latter position argues that what may be known is limited to conceptual/linguistic constructions of 'reality' produced within specific social and cultural contexts (Lau and Morgan, 2014: 574). However, these positions turn ultimately upon the ontology that links events, researchers and research tools (Danermark et al., 2002: 18; Stanley and Wise, 1993: 14). One of the attractions of the new materialisms has been its ontological focus on relationality rather than essence. As we shall show in this chapter, this has the effect of re-making the relationship between research data and the object of inquiry, cutting across the realist/constructionist dualism that has divided social research approaches (Coole and Frost, 2010: 26; van der Tuin and Dolphijn, 2010).

In Chapter 2, we established some foundational precepts for a materialist sociology that was relational, post-anthropocentric, and concerned with processes and becoming rather than essences and being. It is worth summarizing these principles as we set out to establish a materialist methodology. They are:

- an ontological orientation towards matter (as opposed to textuality or structures);

- a concern with what matter does, not what it is;

- a post-anthropocentric focus on the capacity of all matter (not just human bodies) to affect;

- acknowledgement that thoughts, memories, desires and emotions have material effects;

- power (and resistance to it) operates at the very local level of actions and events, rather than top-down; and

- sociology is itself part of the materiality of the social world.

These ontological shifts in emphasis inevitably influence how we understand the objects and methods of social inquiry, for instance by emphasizing non-human agency at the expense of human agency, cutting across micro/macro levels of analysis, and seeking explanation at the level of the event rather than in terms of structures or mechanisms. Conventionally, social inquiry (like other scientific inquiry) has been anthropocentric, regarding the researcher as the prime mover in the research enterprise, whose reason, logic, theory and scientific method gradually imposes order upon 'data' to supply an understanding, however imperfect, of the world. By contrast, this materialist perspective treats researcher and researched event (along with many other relations, including the tools, technologies and theories of scientific research) as an assemblage that produces a variety of material capabilities in its human and non-human relations.

After we introduced these abstract principles of materialist sociology in Chapter 2, we went on to set out the concepts that we would use to understand the workings of the social world. These included *assemblage*, *affect* and *territorialization/specification* deriving from Deleuze and Guattari (1988), Clough's (2004) notion of *affect economy*, and the idea of '*intra-action*' from Barad (1996). Now, to make sense of social inquiry, we will apply these same concepts once again, in order to explore the *micropolitics* of research, and to establish a materialist methodology. Readers may refer back to Chapter 2 if they wish to re-familiarize themselves with these concepts. However, before applying these principles for materialist social inquiry and a toolkit of concepts, there are a number of specific consequences of a materialist ontology that we need to consider when approaching empirical data.

First, these materialist principles shift the focus of social inquiry from human agents to the assemblage. Consequently, the concern is no longer with what bodies or things or social institutions *are*, but with the capacities for action, interaction, feeling and desire produced in bodies or groups of bodies by affective flows. The tools of interpretive research such as interviews or diary and narrative accounts, which conventionally attend to human actions, experiences and reflections, must be turned decisively to efforts to disclose the relations within assemblages, and the kinds of affective flows that occur between these relations (Fox and Alldred, 2013: 778–81; Juelskjaer, 2013: 759; Renold and Mellor, 2013: 26).

Second, materialist perspectives regard the social world as dynamic and relational, comprising affects, forces and desires, flows and intensities, aggregations and dis-aggregations, specifications (territorializations) and generalizations (de-territorializations), becoming rather than being (Deleuze and Guattari, 1988: 275). Social inquiry needs to have the tools to map these flows, intensities and intra-actions of relations and affects in assemblages ('cartography' or map-making is the preferred metaphor of Deleuze and Guattari (1988: 12) for exploring these affective movements).

Third, a 'flat' ontology of assemblages and affects undermines structural or systematic explanations of sociological data. Power resides in the affective flows between relations in assemblages, the aggregations and singularities these flows produce, and the capacities or constraints upon capacities produced in some – and not other – bodies, collectivities and non-human formations. Where analysis seeks to generalize from specific events (for instance, to set out the factors affecting migration or contemporary sexualities) this needs to be based in a micropolitical analysis of the affect economies within events.

Fourth, social inquiry needs to be open to the potential for assemblages to cut across micro, meso and macro levels of analysis (Taylor and Ivinson, 2013: 668). Take as an example Fox and Ward's (2008) study of the pharmaceuticalization of erectile dysfunction that we discussed in Chapter 7: there is nothing to prevent a relation such as a man's sexual performance (conventionally thought of as 'micro') and a 'macro' relation such as the financial performance of global pharmaceutical companies being drawn into assemblage, to the extent that one may affect or be affected by the other.

Finally, the posthumanism of the materialist perspective raises questions about human capacities to produce research knowledge: the view that knowledge can be gleaned from observation of the world is founded in the anthropocentric privileging of human cognitive processes (Paden, 1987: 129). Conventionally, social inquiry (like other scientific inquiry) has been considered from the point of view of the researcher, who through efforts of reason, logic and scientific method, gradually imposes order upon 'data', and in so doing, 'makes sense' of the world. If, on the other hand, we see researcher and data (along with many other relations) as a 'research-assemblage' with its own affect economy, we begin to recognize research as a micropolitical specification that shapes the knowledge it produces according to the particular flows of affect that its methodology and methods produce.

The research assemblage

The idea of research as an assemblage derives from the DeleuzoGuattarian view of assemblages as 'machines' that link elements together affectively to do something, to produce something (Deleuze and Guattari, 1988: 4). With this in mind, the research-assemblage will comprise a multiplicity of constituent (affective) relations between the 'events' to be researched (these can be any instance of bodies, things, settings or social formations, or of assemblages of these); research tools such as questionnaires, interview schedules or other apparatus; recording and analysis technologies, computer software and hardware; theoretical frameworks and hypotheses; research literatures and findings from earlier studies; the 'data' generated by these methods and techniques; and of course, researchers. To this list may be added contextual relations such as the physical spaces and establishments where research takes place; the frameworks, philosophies, cultures and traditions that surround scientific research; ethical principles and ethics committees; research assessment exercises; and all the paraphernalia of academic research outputs: libraries, journals, editors and reviewers, and readers.

By applying the conception of an assemblage to research, all the various stages in the research process (such as data collection or analysis, or techniques used to sample data or increase validity) can each be treated as a 'machine' that has been constructed to work in a specific way in order to produce certain outputs. Thus, a 'data collection machine' takes aspects of an event as its raw materials, and by the means specific to its design, generates 'data'. An analysis machine processes data according to specific rules of logic, deduction or inference to produce 'findings' in the form of generalities or summaries (Jackson and Mazzei, 2013). A reporting machine takes these outputs of data analysis and creates knowledge products for dissemination: theory, policy and practice implications and so forth. Furthermore, these machines can be 'plugged into' each other, to create the overall design of a research project.

So a research methodology may be seen as a particular arrangement of machines, designed to shape how affect flows between its constituent relations, and what capacities these flows produce (in researchers, and in research outputs). Precisely how event, instruments and researchers interact depends upon the affects designed into a specific machine. For example, a sampling frame determines which events are included in a study, while a thematic analysis separates data into categories. Theory is a further machine that plays a key part in research: a theoretical perspective brought to bear upon the research findings will establish specific capacities for how data are interpreted.

Unlike 'spontaneous' assemblages in daily life (for instance, the 'sexuality-assemblage' that we looked at in Chapter 6), such research machines comprise few relations and affects, making them amenable to 'reverse engineering', to understand how they work. To offer a simple example: a sampling frame is a machine that works by means of a single affect targeted at the various events available to social inquiry. This affect sorts events to be included in a study (for instance, teenagers) from those to be excluded (those under 13 or over 19). In other research machines, the affects may be more complex: the maths underpinning a summary statistic such as chi-squared comprises a series of arithmetic operations (affects) that progressively transform 'data' into a single indicator of statistical significance. By unpicking research machines, it is possible to assess how a change of data collection or analysis method, or of design (for instance, from survey to ethnography) alters the affective flow in the research-assemblage, and hence what kind of 'knowledge' it produces (Jackson and Mazzei, 2013: 263). Later in the chapter, we shall reverse engineer a range of designs and research machines.

This analysis of affects also opens to scrutiny the *micropolitics* of different research-assemblages, of who gains and who loses in the processes of research (Gillies and Alldred, 2012: 56). For example, in a randomized trial, controlling the experimental conditions and use of statistical techniques together limit the affective capacities of 'confounding' relations found in 'real-world' settings, empowering a researcher to model the 'uncontaminated' affect of an 'independent' upon a 'dependent' variable. By contrast, in qualitative studies a 'naturalistic' approach limits the researcher affective capacities, while enhancing the affectivity of respondents' accounts. We now offer a formal analysis of research-as-assemblage.

A materialist analysis of the research encounter

To understand more clearly what happens when a sociological researcher sets out to gather data about some aspect or other of the social world, we have chosen a specific event as an illustration – a school trip to the countryside – as described in Youdell and Armstrong's (2011) ethnographic account. We'll call this event E. From an assemblage perspective, E is an assemblage comprising a number of relations (which we will call 'ABC') linked by an affect economy that makes the assemblage do whatever it does. In this case, the relations included teachers, school students, the places they visited and so forth. What happens when this event becomes the focus for a research study?

The answer to this question requires that we also recognize the research process as an *event in itself*, and thus as a 'research-assemblage', which we shall call R. The aim of this research-assemblage is to apply techniques and methods that can somehow identify the relations within the E assemblage, explore the affects between these relations that make it work, and assess from some contextual perspective the capacities that these affects produce. The research-assemblage R comprises its own relations ('XYZ'), which are all the paraphernalia of academic inquiry: researcher, methodologies, research instruments, theories and so on.

Unlike the relations in the E event, a research-assemblage's relations need to be designed or engineered to establish a very specific affect economy – one capable of investigating the event-assemblage E (or other similar events), to produce an output that can be considered as research 'knowledge' of E. Critically, if R is to document, analyse and eventually report E, this requires that it can itself be affected in some way by the relations ABC within the event-assemblage, and the affects between them. This capacity is traditionally described in various ways: for instance in terms of the sensitivity and specificity that an instrument such as a thermometer or a questionnaire requires in order for it to be a useful measure, or of a researcher's understanding that enables events in a qualitative study to somehow 'speak' to her/his sensibilities.

This means that when an event E and a research process R engage together, the product is a third *hybrid* assemblage, which we might designate R/E, with an affect economy that incorporates relations A, B, C, X, Y and Z from the E and R assemblages. This flow is distinct from those in either E or R, producing research outputs in the form of 'knowledge' of the E assemblage. It may also produce effects on E itself, such as changes in behaviour due to a 'Hawthorne' effect from being observed, increased individual or collective reflexivity, or impacts on the event (for instance, a custom or tradition) due to attention from outsiders.

This way of understanding the intra-actions (Barad, 1996: 179) between event and research-assemblage enables a sophisticated understanding of the micropolitics of social research, and of two opposing hazards in social inquiry. Social researchers have devoted countless energy attempting to overcome the first of these – the risk of distorting the very events that research tries to describe and explain. This hazard arises when the XYZ relations from the research-assemblage dominate the affect-economy within R/E, asserting a powerful effect over the relations ABC of the event-assemblage E. This can happen in various ways: for example by a sampling strategy that excludes key aspects of E; by controlling out naturalistic contexts in an experiment; by imposing a theoretical framework on data; or by biased reporting or mis-representation of E. These affects radically re-specify the affective flow between ABC relations, to the extent that the 'knowledge' produced by R/E in research outputs no longer reflects the flow within E. The most extreme form of this hazard has been highlighted in social constructionist analyses that claim modernist research has *produced* rather than simply described its objects (for example, Foucault's (1981) and Kitzinger's (1987) analyses of the scientific construction of sexuality).

However, there is a contrary hazard, which occurs when the XYZ relations in the research-assemblage have so little affective capacity that the ABC relations dominate the flow within the R/E assemblage. Now the research process becomes a machine whose outputs are trivial or anodyne rather than analytical; descriptive or journalistic rather than critical. This may occur when affects in the research-assemblage are weak – for instance if the research design lacks a powerful (affective) analytical machine or is theoretically uninformed, the research instruments do not possess the capacity to differentiate the relations or affects in the event, or the reporting is literal rather than critical. Occasionally this affective weakness is intentionally exploited in a research design – for instance in case studies that set out to simply describe specific events; or in 'Delphi' methodologies that aim to gain consensus among experts and thereby offer a definitive statement on current knowledge (for example, scientific consensus on the effects of global climate change).

The aim of most research studies is to avoid these two extremes, and most social science R/E assemblages will achieve some kind of balance between the affects deriving from ABC and XYZ relations. However, the logic of this analysis asserts that, in each and every situation, there is a dynamic tension between the affective flow of E and that of R, a tension that has consequences for the knowledge and representations of the social world that research produces, and potentially for the social world itself.

If this were the final conclusion of this chapter, it would add little to our understanding of social research methodology and how it should be undertaken. However, a materialist analysis allows us to open up what has sometimes seemed like the 'black box' of social inquiry, to reveal a sophisticated *micropolitics* of the research process. This supplies insight into exactly how research designs and methods work, and what effects they may have upon the events they study. This is our next objective.

Dis-assembling social research

Considering research tools and techniques as machines whose capacities derive from their relations and affects means that research designs and methods can be unpacked, to reveal the affect economies and micropolitics of social inquiry. We can use the toolkit of materialist concepts we have developed in this book to delve into the specifications and generalizations, aggregations, singularities and lines of flight that occur when sociologists use different methods and research designs. We can thereby lay bare the social relations of contemporary research methodologies, examining these micropolitical effects for different data collection, analysis and writing machines, and the consequences for 'knowledge', for events, and for researchers.

Contemporary social research uses a wide range of methodologies and methods to explore the social world. The utility and validity of many of these are contested within contemporary social inquiry, for example, between enthusiasts for qualitative or quantitative designs, or between realists and constructionists. Rather than debating these traditional critiques, a materialist understanding of research-as-assemblage and the affect economies and micropolitics of the *R/E* assemblage allows us to explore how these designs and methods actually work. First we ask what a machine is designed to do, and what outputs it produces. From this, we apply a more critical assessment, using the materialist ontology of assemblages and affects to reverse engineer the machine and disclose the *affect economy* that enhances certain affective flows and mitigates or closes down others. From this, we can also identify the *micropolitics* of a research machine's effects.

To clarify this analysis, we will apply this approach to three methods or techniques (sampling, the questionnaire, and thematic qualitative analysis) and then two research methodologies often used in social inquiry: the survey and the qualitative interview. A comprehensive analysis of many of the other techniques, methods and methodologies used in social research are presented in Tables 9.1 and 9.2.

Techniques and methods

Sampling

A sampling machine performs a relatively simple task within a research-assemblage, selecting events (respondents, institutions, occurrences) for inclusion in or exclusion from a study, based upon two sequential affects. The first affect sets the choice of sampling approach (for example, representative sample, stratified sample, convenience sample, theoretical sample) for the researcher to implement. The second affect includes or excludes specific events, applying the appropriate means of selection (random inclusion for a representative sample; purposive inclusion across a range of events for a theoretical sample, and so forth), as set by the first affect. The affect economy in this machine acts upon study events, systematically including some in the sample and excluding others. Micropolitically, this economy empowers a researcher to achieve what is usually practically impossible – to assess an entire population – by restricting the affects from the event population entering the research assemblage according to specific, though arbitrary principles.

The questionnaire

The questionnaire is actually two separate machines: one for questionnaire construction, the other for its administration. The affect in the first transforms a variable to be measured (for example, political belief) into a question that will serve as an indicator (for example: how did you vote at the last election?), sometimes with pre-selected permissible responses. The affects in the second machine act on researcher and respondents, requiring a question to be asked, an answer to be supplied, this answer to be recorded and possibly allocated to a pre-coded category, and the instrument to be applied consecutively and independently to each respondent in turn, generating completed questionnaires ready to be fed into an analysis machine. The questionnaire's affective economy extracts information systematically from respondents to produce a dataset. Micropolitically, it acts as a filter on the affect economies of events being studied, extracting only certain data, and categorizing them according to the affect economy of the instrument rather than that of the event itself.

Thematic qualitative analysis

Thematic analysis of qualitative data is a machine that (manually, or with software assistance) organizes and reduces non-numerical data, making it more manageable and amenable to systematic reporting. It entails two affects: a code-generation affect that ascribes a code to a range of similar textual occurrences (for instance, to pieces of text that in some ways reference 'family finances'); and an affect that takes each piece of data in turn and codes it according to this scheme. The affect economy here acts on raw data from a study to aggregate it within coded categories, reducing variability for ease of reporting. The micropolitics of this machine serves to reduce the complexity of an event by aggregating data in ways defined by the analyst (for instance, in terms of a conceptual or theoretical framework).

Table 9.1 Materialist assessment of social research methods and techniques

A. Techniques

	Summary of what the machine produces:	Affective flow in the machine:	Micropolitics of the R/E assemblage:
Setting/Refining a Research Question	A delimited and therefore answerable research question.	Defines what is to be studied.	Asserts researcher's choice of which event affects are studied.
Internal Study Validity	Data that is relevant to the research question.	Selects the data to be gathered and analysed.	Justifies the machines selected for the research-assemblage.
External Study Validity	Data that is representative of a population.	Establishes rules for choice of events from a population.	Justifies inferences researchers make from findings to population.
Instrument Reliability	Data that is consistent and avoids random errors.	Quality assures tools used to measure an event.	Controls quality of tools and researcher conduct.
Instrument Validity	Data that is accurate and avoids systematic errors.	Assesses instrument accuracy against a defined standard.	Asserts the 'truth' of data from research tools and interpretations.
Ethics Approval	A study that meets cultural expectations for research conduct.	Assesses research against cultural principles and rules.	Justifies affects of researcher upon researched events.
Representative Sample	Equivalence between sample and population.	Determines which events are selected for study.	Justifies how events are included in the R/E assemblage.
Convenience Sample	Provides sufficient events to be studied.	Sets arbitrary cut-off point for recruiting events.	Justifies how many events are included in the R/E assemblage.
Theoretical Sample	Sample that reflects the breadth of affects in a population.	Applies a conceptual framework for including events.	Justifies which events are included in the R/E assemblage.

B. Data Collection Methods

	Summary of what the machine produces:	Affective flow in the machine:	Micropolitics of the R/E assemblage:
Individual Interview	Accounts of events supplied by human subjects.	Elicits accounts relevant to the research question.	Privileges human interpretations of event affects.

(Continued)

Table 9.1 (Continued)

	Summary of what the machine produces:	Affective flow in the machine:	Micropolitics of the R/E assemblage:
Group Interview	Interactive accounts of events supplied by human subjects.	Elicits interactive accounts relevant to the research question.	Privileges human interpretations of event affects.
Observation	Descriptions of events by a researcher.	Establishes researcher as data collection instrument.	Privileges researcher's perspective and analysis of events.
Questionnaire	Study sample scores on multiple measures.	Gathers and collates data on pre-selected indicators.	Imposes researcher categories and measures on event affects.
Experiment	Effect of a defined affect or affects within an event.	Tests affect(s) in an controlled setting.	Imposes arbitrary limits on which affects enter the R/E assemblage.

C. Analytical Methods

	Summary of what the machine produces:	Affective flow in the machine:	Micropolitics of the R/E assemblage:
Statistical Analysis	Numerical indicator of a study sample's characteristics.	Summarizes data by mathematical formulae.	Imposes statistical models of populations on data.
Thematic Analysis	Summary of data in terms of pre-selected themes.	Categorizes data in terms of similarities in attributes specified by a conceptual or theoretical framework.	Imposes researcher's categories on data.
Grounded Theory	Inductively-generated theory to explain an event.	Analyses event assemblage to disclose internal structure or processes.	Privileges coherence and structure in data over divergence and randomness.
Discourse Analysis	Social or cultural constructions and power relations in events.	Reveals relations and affects in linguistic representations of events.	Establishes a constructionist model and privileges the researcher's political analysis.

D. Study Presentation

	Summary of what the machine produces:	**Affective flow in the machine:**	**Micropolitics of the *R/E* assemblage:**
Writing up	A report of the events studied.	Summarizes and explicates the data collected and analysed.	Describes the event in terms of the affects in the *R/E* assemblage.
Peer Review	An assessment of research output quality.	Peers assess the research output against explicit or implicit criteria.	Incorporates the values of the community of researchers into the *R/E* assemblage.
Dissemination	An audience for the research report.	Presents the research report to selected audiences.	Uses the affective flow of the *R/E* assemblage to affect audiences.
Policy Application	An application to policy or practice.	Applies the conclusions of the research to affect policy or practice.	Uses the affective flow of the *R/E* assemblage to affect policy or practice.

Research methodologies

We now consider two common research designs, looking at each as a whole but also as constituted from a number of machines, including those described in the previous thumb-nail sketches and those listed in Table 9.1.

The survey

The survey is a social research design assemblage that typically produces a quantitative summary of specific aspects of a study population, as defined by a research question. This is done by a series of research-machines that:

1. draw a representative or stratified sample from a population;

2. use methods such as questionnaires to gather data on specified measures or indicators (often forcing responses into pre-specified categories);

3. submit these to descriptive or inferential statistical analysis; and

4. report a summary of the sample's features, often with a statistical assessment of generalizability to a population.

The affect economy that makes the survey design work derives from the economies of its constituent machines. Affects in the sampling machine supply a means to allocate events to the sample; those in the questionnaire machine select and categorize those features of events to be studied and record them in a form amenable to quantitative analysis; affects in the statistical analysis machine aggregate and manipulate the data mathematically, reducing it to summary values and statistical assessments of probability that efface the complexities and divergences in the events; the affects of the result-writing machine use these aggregated and de-contextualized findings and present them in an effort to answer the study's research questions.

Micropolitically, all these machines are highly aggregative, smoothing out variability and distinctiveness. As sampling and questionnaire machines systematize research selection and data collection, they restrict which affects from the event can become part of the *R/E* assemblage; the analysis machine aggregates the affective capacities of the event into numerical metrics, simplifying and thereby reducing the granularity of the event-affects represented in the research outputs; the writing machine imposes the constraints of a narrow research question on the affects in the event. In these ways, a survey powerfully privileges a researcher perspective over the events it studies.

The qualitative interview

Here we examine qualitative interviewing as a research methodology designed to provide 'rich descriptions' of a social event or events by interrogating accounts elicited from social actors. Within this research-assemblage are a number of machines that:

1. set and refine the research question;

2. select a sample – usually according to a purposive strategy to overcome the limitations of a relatively small sample size (Coyne, 1997: 629);

3. use individual or group interviews (based on an interview schedule designed to inform the research question) to gain in-depth data on interviewees' affective background, engagement with the issues being studied, and reflections on these issues;

4. undertake some kind of qualitative analysis, typically one that categorizes data into themes either 'grounded' in the data or deriving from a pre-defined theoretical or conceptual framework, or imposes some other structure upon the data; and

5. report these data in a textual format that often includes extracts from the interviews conducted.

The affect economy of this methodology is again provided by its constituent machines. The purposive sampling machine selects subjects to interview based on expectations of their affective economies, and often aims to maximize diversity rather than to ensure data is representative of a wider population. An interview schedule is a simple affect that determines which elements of the subjects' affective engagements with the topic can be reported, while the question/answer format underpinning the interview method also governs the material gathered. The qualitative analysis machine (as described earlier) organizes, aggregates and reduces the textual material, enabling themes to be developed or explanatory constructs to be developed. Report writing produces a second-order account of the events being studied, as interpreted first by interviewees and then by the researcher, and illustrates the account with representative or allusive quotations from the interviewees.

The micropolitics of qualitative interviewing reflect the interactions between researcher, interviewees and the events they describe. The researcher's questioning role and the answering role of subjects produce inequality in the research relationship, while the choice of research question, sampling and interview schedule machines all impose a framework on the affects admitted

Table 9.2 Materialist assessment of social research methodologies

	Summary of what the assemblage produces:	Affective flow in the assemblage:	Micropolitics of the R/E assemblage:
Randomized Controlled Trial	Truth or falsity of a hypothesis about a variable's effects.	Discounts effects of event affects other than test affect.	Justifies research claims to describe what individual event affects do.
Survey	Descriptive statistics on a population.	Describes and summarizes specific attributes of events.	Justifies inferences from sample data to a population.
Qualitative Interview	Summary of accounts concerning an event.	Organizes respondent accounts of events.	Privileges human accounts of events.
Ethnography	Detailed description of events in a specified setting.	Presents researcher/ academic assessment of a setting.	Privileges researcher account and analysis of an event.
Documentary/ Material Culture Analysis	Evaluation of an event from documentary sources or artefacts.	Organizes and interprets material culture or documents.	Imposes cultural meanings on selected artefacts or documents.
Case Study	Description of a single event.	Describes in detail specific aspects of one event.	Claims to provide full description of an event.
Delphi Study	Consensus among experts on a category of events.	Gathers and synthesizes opinions to negotiate agreement by selected experts.	Establishes an 'expert' assessment of a category of events.

into the *R/E* assemblage. However, the interview format does enable respondents to control the accounts they offer, and researchers may actively try to hand some power back to interviewees, to 'give them a voice'. As noted earlier, the systematizing and aggregating affects in the thematic analysis machine privilege the analyst's account over those of respondents; this is reflected in how the data are reported – typically within an imposed structure that establishes the researcher's unitary account of the event, with interviewees' accounts used selectively to justify the researcher's answer to the research question.

These detailed descriptions of methods and designs demonstrate how we have moved from what a machine does to how its affects make it work, and finally what this means for the micropolitics of the hybrid *R/E* assemblage. Tables 9.1 and 9.2 summarize other methods, techniques and designs that may be reverse engineered in the same way. The first table is divided into research techniques, data collection and data analysis methods, and aspects of data presentation. Table 9.2 analyses the principal research designs from across the spectrum of social inquiry. Of course, social research is continually innovating new designs and methods, often highly antagonistic to positivistic science, and these too are amenable to analysis, to reveal their unique affect economies and micropolitics.

The micropolitics of social inquiry

This analysis of research machines suggests how a materialist perspective may be applied to evaluate the wide range of research methods, techniques and designs in current use in sociology. It also offers new insights into the micropolitics of social inquiry that bear upon how social research is done. Most research-assemblages possess just the few relations and affects needed sequentially to perform the tasks of their interconnected machines. By breaking research-assemblages down in this way, a materialist analysis can exploit this sparseness, to reverse engineer research machines, revealing what is happening in the research process when different methods and techniques are applied. Generally speaking, most of the research assemblages and machines reviewed have in common that they produce simplicity where there was complexity, definition in place of indeterminacy, and evenness where there was variability, with consequences for the knowledge social inquiry produces.

However, there is one stand-out feature of many social research methods and techniques. Scrutinizing the two tables, it is striking how many research methods, techniques and designs have affective flows that *aggregate* events in one way or another. For example, aggregations occur when selecting a study sample based on particular attributes or properties of events; during coding survey or interview data into categories (whether pre-defined or inductively generated); in analytic methods that summarize data statistically or apply categories and themes in qualitative analysis; and in data reporting that generalize or summarize findings. From this perspective, quantitative survey and qualitative interview methodologies reveal less divergence than might be predicted from the rival claims of their advocates.

Aggregations are problematic because they produce a loss of detail or difference, and may exclude outliers and aberrations that may be extremely significant in social life – the world thus presented seems blander and less exceptional than it does to those immersed within it (see our discussion of social stratification in Chapter 4). But importantly, these aggregating affect economies within research machines and assemblages shift the micropolitics of the hybrid *R/E* assemblage firmly toward the researcher's agenda. This is unsurprising; after all research machines have been intentionally designed to enable researchers to do research; however, this assessment forces us to abandon claims that research is in some way a 'neutral' event.

This materialist analysis of the interactions between event, research process and researcher supplies a nuanced view of research micropolitics. By analysing the affects in the hybrid *R/E* assemblage, it is possible to assess in what ways, and to what extent, event affects have been specified and aggregated by the affect economy of the research process, and which machines and designs have done this. One outcome of such a micropolitical analysis of research is a refinement of a strict constructionist perspective on research, which has tended to regard research 'knowledge' as powerfully affected by the historical and cultural circumstances of its making by researchers (Thibodeaux, 2014: 830), or even constitutive of the objects it describes. So, for instance, Rose (1998: 55) has argued that historically 'evidence, results, arguments, laboratories, status and much else' contributed to the construction of differing 'truths' about LGBT sexualities – as pathology, then deviance, then diversity. Up to a point, a materialist analysis would assent to this assessment of the effects of research on its subject-matter: as has been seen, an aggregating and specifying (territorializing) research-assemblage can dominate the affective flow in a hybrid *R/E* assemblage, reshaping the event in the research's image. However, our materialist analysis diverges from a constructionist conclusion for two reasons.

The first concerns the suggestion that research re-constructs events in its own image. As noted earlier in this chapter, it is only in extreme cases that the affects in a research-assemblage will entirely overwhelm those in an event-assemblage. This may happen in intentionally fraudulent, ideologically-motivated or fictitious research reports, or where the machines in a research-assemblage are wildly inappropriate and entirely fail to engage with an event. However, in most studies the affects between ABC relations within an event-assemblage cannot be entirely erased from the *R/E* assemblage, and research outputs will inevitably contain something (even if not much) of the affect-economy of the studied event.

Second, it is widely recognized that research outputs (for example, a particular scientific understanding of non-normative sexuality) may sometimes impact on the events they describe – for instance, by producing guilt in people involved in what research has revealed to be a socially 'taboo' sexual practice. Research ethics codes seek ways to minimize such effects of social research. However, the micropolitical analysis we have used here supplies a means to assess such impacts more precisely; and while the aggregated and specified output of a research-assemblage may indeed affect the events they researched, this represents just one among the many affects that contribute to an event-assemblage. A research-assemblage's affective capacity would have to be exceptionally powerful to erase all these other affects.

These more sophisticated judgements of how research intra-acts with events derive from our micropolitical analysis of research-assemblages. We can pull apart a research process to interrogate its machines and their affect-economies, and specify and evaluate precisely what aggregations and specifications a research-assemblage has wrought upon its subject-matter. From this we can gauge the extent to which research outputs provide appropriate knowledge of events. Furthermore, analysis of the affect economies within a research-assemblage can enable precise assessment of the extent to which research has re-constituted an event in its own image. Though powerful cultural forces (including scientific orthodoxies) always have the potential to influence the affect economy of a research-assemblage, social inquiry is not doomed inevitably and uncritically to recapitulate these social and cultural forces.

Re-engineering methodology

We want to conclude this chapter by looking beyond the aggregations and specifications of contemporary social inquiry, to think about the kinds of research a materialist sociology might undertake. We have seen how a materialist ontology affords the opportunity to peer inside the machines and assemblages of social inquiry, and assess the research process micropolitically. Perhaps of greater significance though is the potential to manipulate these micropolitics. We can, if we so wish, design and re-engineer research-assemblages and machines (the data collection machine, the validity machine, the analysis machine and so on) to include or exclude specified aggregative and territorializing effects, and thereby innovate creative research-assemblages that produce specific capacities in researchers, data and the events studied.

From what has been said earlier about the aggregative tendencies of research methods, this could be treated simply as a charter to remove as many aggregating affects as possible from social inquiry (for instance, applying a sampling frame that takes uniqueness as its criterion; adopting a strictly descriptive approach to data analysis). However, we would suggest there is potential for a more nuanced engagement with the research process. The capacity to critically assess the affects that make research machines work means that researchers have the means to review reflexively, acknowledge and account for the aggregations and specifications they produce in *R/E* hybrid assemblages and hence in their findings (Gillies and Alldred, 2012: 57).

To help us in this task, we will return to the principles of materialist social inquiry we set out at the start of the chapter, and use these to reflect on how we might re-engineer different aspects of data collection, data analysis and reporting. We also reviewed a substantial number of recent social science studies applying materialist ontology, to inform our suggestions of the practical methods and techniques that can be adopted. We look first at research designs, and then at the machines that collect, analyse and report data, though this division is somewhat artificial, as some of the papers we review apply methods that intertwine the stages of data gathering and analysis, or analysis and reporting.

Research design

The principles of a materialist ontology suggest that in terms of design, a research assemblage should:

- attend not to individual bodies, subjects, experiences or sensations, but to assemblages of human and non-human, animate and inanimate, material and abstract, and to the affective flows within these assemblages;

- explore how affects draw the material and the cultural, and the 'micro', 'meso' and 'macro' into assembly together;

- explore the movements of specification and generalization, aggregation and disaggregation within the assemblages studied, and the consequent affect economies and micropolitics these movements reveal.

The objectives for designing materialist social inquiry are hence to reveal relations, affects and affect economies in assemblages, the capacities (and limits to capacities) produced in bodies, collectivities and social formations, and the micropolitics of these capacities and limits. Its orientation must be toward what things do, rather than what they 'are'; toward processes and flows rather than structures and stable forms; to matters of power and resistance; and to interactions that draw small and large relations into assemblage. A range of designs can fulfil some or all of those criteria, from ethnographic studies that explore the context in which events occur, through to surveys, which have the capacity to generate data at a population level on the incidence and prevalence of relations, affects and the capacities these produce, to methodologies such as Garfinkel's (1984) 'experiments with trust', in which participants tested the affects that shape daily life, and how small changes in interactions can destabilize affect economies and family assemblages.

However, the overwhelming preference among 40 recent materialist studies that we reviewed was for qualitative designs, with ethnography the favoured methodology (see for example, Blaise, 2013; Holford et al., 2013; Ringrose, 2011; Youdell and Armstrong, 2011). Others used in-depth qualitative interviewing (Cole, 2013; Masny and Waterhouse, 2011), and some a mix of qualitative approaches (Ivinson and Renold, 2013; Renold and Ringrose, 2011). The attraction of qualitative methodologies may lie in their capacity to contextualize events, thereby revealing the range of relations that comprise assemblages and affective economies. So, for example, Youdell and Armstrong (2011) detailed the geographical and physical environment that contribute to event assemblages, as well as the interactions that mark out the affective flows, revealing what bodies can and cannot do, and the specifications and generalizations that occur during the events they describe.

Some of these studies explicitly described their designs as 'schizoanalytic' or 'rhizomic' – terms deriving from Deleuze and Guattari (1988: 251) – to explore the affective movements and 'lines of flight' in the research settings (Cole, 2013: 235–6; Masny, 2013: 346; Renold and Ringrose, 2008: 320). For Masny (2013: 246), rhizoanalytic research was also about creating lines of flight in the research assemblage itself, emphasizing social inquiry's transformative capacities for all the bodies and other relations in the research-assemblage, and for thinking about events differently. A series of studies (Ringrose, 2011; Ringrose and Renold, 2012) of interactions between school-children, bullying, social networks, and activism around sexual violence applied an experimental schizoanalytic (and feminist) practice that created and mapped different formations and assemblages within events. Methodologically these studies linked together research, activism, art and writing to produce what Ringrose (2015: 406) calls 'new transversal flashes and disruptions' that both challenged hierarchies within schools (2015: 604) and reconfigured 'what research is ... and what it can do' (2015: 406).

Data collection

Materialist data collecting machines must be able to:

- identify assemblages of human and non-human, animate and inanimate, material and abstract, cutting across what are traditionally considered 'micro' and 'macro' levels;

- explore how elements in assemblage affect and are affected, and assess what bodies and other things do: the capacities these affective flows produce; and

- identify specifications and generalizations, aggregating and singular flows within assemblages.

These imperatives radically change the focus of data collection away from 'humanistic' objectives of researching experience, beliefs and reflections found in anthropocentric research, while also eliding boundaries between the material and the cultural (matter and meaning) and the micro/macro scales of social production. Cutting across matter/meaning and micro/macro dualisms suggests collecting data from a variety of sources, and using a variety of methods.

Recent materialist studies reflect this eclecticism. Taguchi and Palmer (2013: 673) used their own affective responses and memories as data on events, alongside photographs, media reports, research papers, interviews and other resources to research school life; Fox and Ward (2008) used interviews, online ethnography, media commentaries, official statistics and documentary sources as data to inform an analysis of pharmaceutical consumption. Renold and Ivinson (2014) melded contemporary ethnography and interviews with historical data to generate a rhizomic on Welsh Valleys mining culture in their study of horse/girl assemblages; while these researchers also used a creative mix including photography, film-making and walking tours alongside their interview data (Ivinson and Renold, 2013: 708). Other data sources include emotional, dream, and sensual data (St. Pierre, 1997); drawings made by the respondents (Masny and Waterhouse, 2011) and sound and music (Henriques, 2010).

Our earlier proposition that a variety of qualitative and quantitative designs might be used in materialist research suggests a broader range of data collection methods than represented in current materialist research, incorporating quantitative methods (possibly within a mixed-methods approach), and engineered to meet the objectives of identifying assemblages, affects (aggregating and singular) and capacities, while also encouraging reflexivity about how research is assembled.

Data analysis

Materialist data analysis needs to:

- take the assemblage as the primary focus for analysis, incorporating both non-human elements and human relations;

- explore affect economies and the specifying and generalizing capacities produced in bodies, collectivities and other relations in assemblages;

- examine how flows of affect within assemblages link matter and meaning, and 'micro' and 'macro' levels; and

- acknowledge the affective relations within the research-assemblage itself.

Materialist ontology shifts the focus of analysis from the ideas, actions and feelings of individualized subjects to the impersonal flows of affect through assemblages and the territorialized capacities these produce (Fox and Alldred, 2013: 778; Youdell and Armstrong, 2011: 145). Human accounts can no longer be accorded validity on the basis of their 'authenticity', and methods such as interviews should be treated not as means to collect subjective representations of the world but as evidence of how respondents are situated within assemblages (Fox and Alldred, 2013: 780; Juelskjaer, 2013: 759).

This shift in focus is reflected in the materialist studies we reviewed. Ringrose (2011) sought to 'map how desire flows and power operates in the relationships between school and online assemblages and bodies' in her interview and online data, while Renold and Ivinson (2014) used their 'transversal' insights to reveal affective flows between historical and contemporary horse/girl assemblages. The diffractive (Haraway, 1997: 16) analysis used by Juelskjaer (2013) and Taguchi and Palmer (2013) was an engaged and creative process that elided a strict distinction between data collection and analysis, incorporating the researchers' own experiences and insights into the analytic process, 'to collaboratively produce knowing in this rhizomatic zigzagging flow' (Taguchi and Palmer, 2013: 675).

The systematic methodology that we have used in a range of studies (Alldred and Fox, 2015b; N. Fox, 2015b; Fox and Bale, forthcoming) has taken a more formalized approach to analysing assemblages, affects and capacities. In this approach, empirical data sources (interviews, observations, documents, survey data and so forth) are 'dredged' to identify the relations and affects that comprise assemblages of bodies, things and social formations within a specific event, and also to assess the capacities that emerge from this assemblage. Analytically, the work required to piece together assemblages and affective flows is iterative and synthetic. It is based upon close reading of data sources to identify possible relations (which may be human, non-human or abstract) within assemblages, and how these affect or are affected by each other. Reading across and between field data progressively builds understanding of the assemblage, its affective flows, and the capacities these produce. This enables a micropolitical reading of data, to understand what bodies and things in assemblages can do, and what limits and opportunities for action are available within an event. We have illustrated this analytical methodology at various points throughout this book, as we have applied materialist analysis to sociological examples.

Reporting research

Presenting materialist social inquiry needs to:

- recognize that a research report is the product of a hybrid assemblage with an affect economy deriving from both the event and the machines of social research;

- problematize the highly ritualized conventions of academic research writing and publishing that transform multi-register event-assemblages into the uni-dimensional medium of written text;

- acknowledge and account for the effects that aggregations and specifications of events produced by the research process have upon accounts of events.

The earlier discussion of research-assemblage micropolitics has exposed the micropolitics of research machines and the consequences for how research represents events in its outputs. As noted, many of the research machines in use in contemporary social inquiry are highly aggregating, posing questions over the validity of research accounts. One solution to this has been to try to overcome these aggregations by connecting research audiences directly to events, for instance by using photographs (Ringrose and Renold, 2012) or drawings (Masny and Waterhouse, 2011). Whitaker (2010: 127) melded academic outputs with art installations, ecology and therapeutic activities, while the group of materialist scholars associated with Cardiff University have been collaborating with painters, sculptors and choreographers to explore multi-sensory research presentations (Renold and Ivinson, 2014).

We would suggest complementing such strategies with a more radical approach, shifting the purpose of a research report from a supposedly 'neutral' presentation of outputs of a research study to an audience, to a critical and reflexive assessment of research study micropolitics. This would both acknowledge and seek to account for the specifying and aggregating affects in the research-assemblage. While recognizing that research specifies and aggregates events in all sorts of ways, our analysis of research-assemblage micropolitics has argued that the various machines that comprise a particular research design can be mapped in detail, revealing precisely these specifications and aggregations, and the effects upon the data that is generated. Research reports are a means to document these research micropolitics, and partially redress these by contextualizing findings, re-privileging the affective flows of the event-assemblage, fostering affective flows between event and research audiences, and finding ways to enable lines of flight that 'produce genuinely new ways of being in the world' (Renold and Ivinson, 2014). Research-reporting in this conception is reflexive, recursive and rhizomic, offering lines of flight to event assemblages, and drawing research audiences into the research-assemblage, to contribute their own affects and capacities to its affective economy and micropolitics.

We have set out in this final section a programme for materialist social inquiry, founded firmly in the analysis of the research-assemblage that we have developed. Each stage of the research process is challenged by the micropolitical assessment of the various research machines that make up different research designs. This programme for materialist social inquiry suggests an eclectic and pragmatic approach to research design and methods, but one that is always aware of the micropolitics of the research assemblage as it engages with events, and is informed by the principles of materialism, post-anthropocentrism and posthumanism that we have been documenting throughout the book.

In this spirit, we encourage an approach to social inquiry that embraces flexibility and openness in research designs, and is guided by a posthuman sensibility to the event-assemblages that sociology takes as its focus. This may supply a new justification for applying a mix of methods within studies, some highly aggregative but analytically powerful, others less analytical but intentionally non- or even dis-aggregative. For instance, a study might combine a (minimally-aggregative) descriptive case study that produces a rich picture of the concerns and values of research participants in a setting with an intervention (highly aggregative) that attempts to alter aspects of the setting to address these concerns and values. A subsequent evaluation might combine aggregative quantitative measures with opportunities for participants to offer their own unmediated assessments of any improvements, and use the research outputs to challenge policy or improve their living environment. Mixing methods and methodologies in this way does not mean that the aggregations of particular methods are somehow 'cancelled out'. But because researchers can estimate precisely what aggregations their methods entail, the consequences for knowledge-production can be accurately predicted and acknowledged when reporting findings and drawing conclusions.

Summary

In this chapter we have taken the precepts of materialism and run with them, to explore what they mean for social inquiry. It would be a neat coda to the chapter to argue that our materialist analysis has resolved the contradictory perspectives on knowledge production between realism and constructionism (Coole and Frost, 2010: 26–7)! But this is not an appropriate conclusion; instead, what a materialist perspective on social inquiry has done is to change the terms of reference for the discussion. Rather than trying to answer an anthropocentric question of belief or scepticism about the possibility of gaining knowledge of the world independent of human culture, what our analysis has done is to look at what research actually does. We have used a 'turn to matter' and an ontology of assemblages and affects to disclose the micropolitical workings of the research-assemblage as it hybridizes with an event-assemblage.

Materialist analysis of research-assemblage micropolitics, we would simply conclude, opens up possibilities for how research is designed and undertaken, what capacities the research assemblage produces in researchers, research tools, audiences and events, and how a range of methodologies and methods may be critically applied and combined in the pursuit of useful understanding of the social world.

Further reading

Cole, D.R. (2013) Lost in data space: using nomadic analysis to perform social science. In: Coleman, R. and Ringrose, J. (eds.) *Deleuze and Research Methodologies.* Edinburgh: Edinburgh University Press, pp. 219–237.

Ringrose, J. (2015) Schizo-feminist educational research cartographies. *Deleuze Studies,* 9(3): 393–409.

Tamboukou, M. (2014) Archival research: unravelling space/time/matter entanglements and fragments. *Qualitative Research, 14*(5): 617–633.

10

Change
Action, Policy, Social Transformation

Introduction

The previous chapter focused upon social research – a core aspect of how a successful materialist sociology needs to engage with the social world – and set out an analytical approach to the development of a materialist research methodology. While a capacity for social inquiry may be necessary for a useable materialist sociology, particularly for those working in academic and research settings, social research is not the only potential engagement that sociology and its concepts, models and theories may have with the world (Dale and Kalob, 2006: 121). Some of the other potential involvements include:

- Practice (daily social interactions at work, home and personal relationships)
- Education and training
- Policy formulation and application
- Therapy and healing
- Assessment and evaluation
- Activism and social transformation

Some of these engagements have not traditionally been regarded as central to sociology, though all of us are caught up in daily social practices at work and in our private lives, and many sociologists are involved in one or more of the others, formally or informally. There are sociologists in all walks of employment – in local government, policy jobs, management, environmental protection, education, social services, human relations, the creative industries – all applying their knowledge and skills to an extent. In the US there are increasing numbers of both employed and independent consultants working as 'applied' and 'clinical' sociologists, using sociological concepts, models and research methods to provide solutions to social problems; though elsewhere the overwhelming majority of people with the title 'sociologist' in their job descriptions or on their business cards work in academic or research settings.

These various kinds of involvement between sociology and the world mark out different ways in which sociological concepts, theories and approaches may engage productively with events, from the practice of daily life through to more formal contributions. They define differing kinds of interactions – for instance, the development of workplace, local or national policies that can enhance the quality of people's lives or the local environment; educational initiatives to improve health or people's work opportunities; and interventions or campaigns to bring issues to society's attention in order to produce social change. In this chapter we shall concern ourselves with the possibilities provided by a materialist sociology in two of these arenas, policy and activism. Both of us, in different ways, have been involved in social transformation in these spheres, and for us, materialist ontology must be judged in part by its capacities to deliver a sociology that is capable of engaging in these ways.

In Chapter 2, we set out six propositions for a materialist sociology, addressing the foundational principles of a shift towards a relational, monistic and post-anthropocentric sociology. The breaks from a conventional sociological ontology that these mark out require that we re-think practical sociological interventions such as policy and activism. What, for instance, is the relationship between an event (such as a change in global climate patterns or social deprivation) and the policy developed to address it? How does activism occur when no longer bolstered by essentialism or identity politics?

At the heart of the exploration of social inquiry in the previous chapter was the analysis of the micropolitics underpinning engagements between events and the research process, or as we called it, the research-assemblage. We delved inside the processes of social research to disclose micropolitical movements of specification and generalization, aggregation and lines of flight that produce the outputs of research, including sociological knowledge. We concluded that chapter by suggesting how we might account for the affectivity of the research assemblage and its constituent machines by understanding the micropolitics that each machine brought into the research/event assemblage.

In this chapter we shall again apply a micropolitical analysis as we consider policy and activism – to make sense of what these activities entail, and to develop a materialist understanding. For policy and for activism, we need to ask what these different social engagements do, how they work, and what micropolitical movements and intensifications are involved. Before that, however, there is a piece of unfinished business to address, which we first touched upon in Chapter 2 as one of our six materialist propositions. If we are to develop a view on how sociology can contribute to social transformation, we need to have a firm grasp on two associated concepts – power and resistance.

Social action, power and resistance

Throughout its history, sociology has addressed issues of social order and disorder, and the related questions of how social continuity is sustained and how change may be effected (Boudon, 1991; Dale and Kalob, 2006). For most sociologists, these challenges have focused around the connected topics of power and resistance. What is the nature of power and how does it work? Why and how do people resist power, and where is resistance located? For a materialist sociology, understanding power and resistance is critical to how we might pursue social change and transformation, and address injustices or inequalities, whether by practice, by influencing policy or through activism.

Most of the early sociological ruminations upon power considered it to be a coercive, 'top-down' phenomenon. For Weber (1968: 53), power was a dynamic struggle between an individual or group's aspirations to achieve specific goals and others' resistance to these aspirations. Marx identified power in the control exerted by the capitalist class and capitalist state over the means of economic production, at the expense of the working class (Nigam, 1996: 9). Later generations of sociologists have drawn on these rival notions, forging Marx-inspired conflict models that have regarded society as an ongoing struggle between the powerful and the dispossessed, while Weberian perspectives have informed sociological studies of social organization in a complex modern society (Clegg, 1990: 157–8). For some, power has been seen as an essential and positive feature of social life. Thus, for Parsons (1963: 236), power was a necessary medium circulating through society, enabling a complex society to work effectively and resistance to be managed (1963: 232).

Post-structuralists deemed such top-down structuralist and functionalist analyses of power and resistance inadequate to make sense of the disparate power relations they saw in modern societies, or to supply a critical and radical stance to underpin struggles for social justice and plurality (Bonnell and Hunt, 1999: 8; Dean, 2010; Parker, 2002). Notable within this critique was Foucault's (1980) association of power with knowledge, and of technologies of power such as surveillance and archiving records. Foucault's earlier work focused on institutions such as schools, hospitals, prisons and workplaces, which he argued incorporated disciplinary regimes of surveillance and body control as a means to regulate and modify behaviour, and to produce 'docile bodies' (Foucault, 1979: 11; Fox, 2012: 134–6; Lupton, 1997: 101). His later work revealed an even more disseminated power, in which citizens policed their own conduct, thoughts and desires against societal codes and ethics, in a range of daily practices such as sexuality, spirituality or diet (Foucault, 1988: 18; Rose, 1998, 1999).

The sustained concern with issues of power and resistance in sociology was the reason that the fifth materialist proposition that we set out in Chapter 2 addressed these topics. 'New' materialism, as we saw in that chapter, and later in Chapter 4, rejects any sense of 'another level' of structures, systems or mechanisms working behind the scenes to establish order or produce regularities in social life. Instead, it works with a flat or 'monistic' understanding of social ontology, in which it is the events all around us – and nothing else – that produces the social world from minute to minute, year by year. Power, in such a flat ontology, must be *integral* to what goes on in this daily round of events, rather than some kind of amorphous stuff that somehow permeates the social world and the interactions that it comprises. Consequently, rather than being a unitary, 'downward' force upon citizens, power is disseminated, revealed and deployed at the very local level of actions and events (Barad, 2001: 94). This 'new' materialist analysis of power marks a clean break both with top-down ideas of power found in historical materialism, and models in which power is so diffuse it cannot be identified, traced or challenged.

The workings of power (and of resistance to power) consequently have to be sought at this localized level, focusing on actions, interactions and events, and within the relational ontology of assemblages and affects that we developed in earlier chapters. Throughout this book we have explored the micropolitics of how relations assemble in different events (creative, sexual, analytical and so on). These micropolitics reflect the specifications and generalizations, aggregations, lines of flight and becomings-other within assemblages; and the capacities all these micropolitical movements produce in bodies and other things. So, for instance, in Chapter 4 we noted how aggregations (groupings or classifications) of bodies into social classes, races or genders defined their opportunities and the limits on what they could do; in Chapter 7 how emotional affects produced all kinds of specifications and aggregations in the interactions between youth cultures and the forces of law and order. From a materialist perspective, the phenomena that sociologists have described as 'power' is nothing more nor less than these micropolitical interactions between assembled relations, as they affect and are affected (Patton, 2000: 52).

So power, in new materialist ontology, is a transient, fluctuating phenomenon – a momentary exercise of affectivity by one relation over another. Any apparent regularities or continuities in power (for instance, patriarchal power of one gender over another, or the dominance of market models of social interaction in areas of contemporary society such as education) depend upon continued replication of particular affects between assembled relations (Barad, 2001: 95). For example, a repeated categorization (aggregation) of bodies as 'female' or 'black' establishes the basis for sexist or racist power. Yet any regularity is illusory: power has continuity only as long as it is replicated in the next event, and the one after that, and may quickly evaporate as and when an assemblage's affect economy changes.

What then of resistance? Whether for structuralists or post-structuralists, sociologists have always recognized the intimate association between power and resistance: where there is one, there is always the potential for the other, by definition (Lupton, 1997: 102). This opposition of power and resistance has underpinned one of sociology's favourite dualisms, between *structure* and *agency*. Indeed, resistance has sometimes been conceptualized as the response of a plucky human agent, unwilling to be ground down by the coercive powers of social structures or Weber's (1930: 181) 'iron cage' of bureaucracy, or by the daily grind of employed work (Marx and Engels, 1952: 52). But as we have seen earlier in the book, new materialist ontology dispenses with this kind of privileged notion of human agency, according affective capacity to all kinds of animate and inanimate relations, with humans considered unexceptional. And as we have just noted, power is no longer to be considered as structural or top-down, but as a nexus of disseminated affects that may be either enabling or constraining in terms of the capacities they produce. We have conceptually dissolved both sides of this power/resistance dualism.

In order to develop a materialist perspective on resistance that articulates with this perspective on power, we need to explore the micropolitics of events again. We will use as an example Nick's ethnographic study of 'pro-anorexia' communities (Fox et al., 2005a).

Micropolitics and resistance in the pro-anorexia movement

The pro-anorexia or 'pro-ana' movement is a radical and transgressive lay approach to the management of anorexia, which has sought to re-define it outside of medical or other professional discourses. It has consequently often been the target of a powerful media backlash that brands it as a dangerous fad. Pro-ana has been facilitated by the development of Web 2.0 internet technologies, and exists within a shadowy world of semi-underground chat rooms and websites.

Fox and colleagues studied the '*Anagrrl*' website and forum (not its real name), which – despite having been closed down and re-opened under different names several times – was a thriving, supportive and lively community at the time of the research. The site offered information relating to anorexia and the pro-ana movement, recipes to promote healthy anorectic eating, advice on nutritional supplements to sustain well-being, and *'thinspiration'*: 'triggering' photographs of slim celebrities and encouraging tales that aimed to inspire and sustain anorectic behaviour. The users – who posted on a daily basis to multiple 'threads' – were overwhelmingly female, mostly between 17 and 20, in full-time education or working part-time, and predominantly from the US, UK, New Zealand and Australia.

This study found that participants in the pro-ana movement saw anorexia as a legitimate way to assert some control over the problems and troubles of daily life, and one that could be sustained while at the same time remaining physically healthy. In a disturbed life, this 'anti-recovery' stance provided the pro-ana movement's members with a safe and positive place to share experience and gain further insight into their condition, away from the territorializing and aggregating scrutiny and judgements of parents, boyfriends, husbands and the medical profession.

In this pro-ana community, the aim was no longer to 'recover' from anorexia, but to maintain both low body weight and good health, through a balanced diet and the use of dietary supplements, and within a supportive environment of like-minded people who acknowledged anorexia as a legitimate response to the troubles of daily life. The website creator 'Lily' described pro-ana as a means to enable participants to take an active role in living with what society considered a debilitating, dangerous and shameful disease. The community was regarded by some participants as a 'sanctuary' where they were not continually pressured to eat and gain weight.

This study offers an insight into the interactions between power and resistance in events. Sociologically, pro-ana may be understood as a challenge to, and a rejection of medical, social and feminist models that regard anorexia as a condition to be 'cured'. To understand the movements of power and resistance in pro-ana, we might first conjecture an 'anorexia assemblage':

> body – food – diet – body image – mirrors – clothes – hunger – social environment – cultural forces – media – significant others

People with anorexia are territorialized by relations in this assemblage in ways that produce the experience and events of anorexic lives. Medical, psychological and feminist assemblages aim to help sufferers to recover from an illness by gaining weight and addressing the underlying causes of disordered eating. For example, if they come to the attention of parents and health professionals, biomedical ideas, re-feeding diets and regimes, treatment strategies, health facilities and even genetics may become part of the assemblage. If involved with psychotherapy or counselling, the assemblage will include psychological perspectives on self-esteem, body image, empowerment, personal development and so forth.

Though those participating in pro-ana may have been previously caught up in these medical, psychological or feminist assemblages, the study indicated that their involvement in the movement drew them into a distinctive pro-ana assemblage with very different flows and specifications:

> body – food – diet – pro-ana philosophy – other anorexic people – 'thinspiration' images – recipes – health

Whereas relations in biomedical or other traditional approaches to resolving anorexia sought to territorialize and thereby reverse these desires, the physical and conceptual relations in a pro-ana assemblage produced a micropolitics that supplied the means to keep members both alive and anorexic. Participants used the lines of flight provided by pro-ana resources (recipes, thinspiration, support) to resist the forces that would lead to weight gain, and establish an alternative way of being anorexic, and away from the troubles of daily life.

We can see two movements of resistance within pro-ana. Participants described anorexia as itself a resistance: a micropolitical way for young people to gain some degree of control over lives beset by outside forces they could do little about. Second, the practices and perspectives of those involved in the pro-ana movement were a second resistance, a response to the forces of mainstream society that attempted to re-territorialize people with anorexia into a normative body shape. In both cases, a materialist analysis focuses upon the micropolitics of the assemblages within which anorexic bodies are a part. Resistance is not a negative reaction, rather it comes about by introducing new affects into assemblages, in ways that reduce existing forces ('power'), and open up new possibilities for action and subjectivity, of becoming–other and lines of flight away from these constraints on capacities. Like power, resistance is processual and transitory, and fully part of material affectivity.

This analysis of resistance in terms of affects complements our earlier analysis of power as affect, and suggests that power and resistance should be understood as two aspects of the same phenomenon. Attention to the micropolitics of assemblages means that both 'power' and 'resistance' must be explained by considering how particular relations affect or are affected by others, rather than invoking 'another level' of social structures or mechanisms where power circulates and against which resistance acts. Furthermore, a shift away from regarding ontologically-prior entities (for instance, a body, food, a skinny celebrity, a social institution) as sources of power or resistance, recognizes instead that relations (human and non-human) gain their capacities to act consequent upon other relations and affects within a particular event or action. This undermines notions of a fixed or stable reality in which power is asserted and resistance mounted. The fluctuating character of assemblage micropolitics means that 'power' and 'resistance' wax and wane, shift and reverse continually.

The pro-ana example illustrates this flux. Events are shaped by transitory affects such as pressure to eat experienced by an anorexic person attending a family meal (which might be labelled as an exercise of 'power'), or the use of thinspirational images to help a person fast (labelled as 'resistance'). These labels offer the impression of much more concerted social processes, whereas often the flux of forces in assemblages can shift the capacities of bodies or collections of bodies from moment to moment. As a person moves from an 'anorexia-assemblage' event (such as a family mealtime where they try to avoid eating) to a 'pro-ana assemblage' event (for instance, an online discussion about how to manage hunger pangs), the fluctuating affect economy between bodies, food, diets, family members, thinspiration and so on shifts bodily and other capacities from moment to moment. *What sociology has called power and what it has called resistance are both aspects of the affective flux between relations in particular assemblages; all events are sites in which both 'power' and 'resistance' may be discerned.*

Analysing an event in terms of its affects, capacities and consequent micropolitics allows us to move beyond these shorthand concepts to focus upon affects, and to unpack precisely how relations intra-act in assemblages and what the consequences are for the capacities of both human and non-human relations. Defining a certain affect as an assertion of power or an effort at resistance is less important than assessing the capacities that these affects produce. Rather than presenting certain events as examples of coercive or disciplinary power, and others as instances of resistance, the task of a materialist sociology is to bring its micropolitical concepts and tools to bear upon the daily actions and encounters between people, things and social formations. We can ask of any affect: does it close down capacities or open them up? This question addresses those foundational sociological questions that we are considering in this chapter, concerning order and disorder, continuity and change.

This question also, we would suggest, sets up both a materialist basis for us to confront oppression, exploitation and violence, inequalities and injustices, and to consider the possibilities for affective movements that may produce radical becoming-other or 'lines of flight' (Patton, 2000: 66). As such, this micropolitical analysis of power and resistance (which we will call a 'micropolitics of politics') supplies the foundation for the following explorations of policy and activism.

The micropolitics of politics and policy

With the benefit of this discussion of power and resistance, we are in a position to focus upon the first of the two sociological engagements that we consider here: policy. What can a materialist ontology bring to bear upon a sociological understanding of policy formulation and implementation? What are the limitations of policy, as seen from a materialist model of social continuities and change?

Policy may be defined as the responses of a collectivity – an informal group, an organization, an interest group or a government – to some aspect of life that is deemed significant: an issue, a value or a problem. The aim of policy is in some way to improve or reform the social or natural world, and may address issues bearing upon economic and political stability, continuity, security and cultural integrity, individual and collective safety, and liberty and rights to self-actualization of citizens (Shore and Wright, 1997: 30–1). Policy covers a range of interventions, from development of guidelines for conduct, to legislation and statutory regulation of individual or institutional activities, to enforcement and sanctions for policy transgression.

Social policy is principally concerned with issues associated with the needs or welfare of human beings (Coffey, 2004: 2), while policy may also be directed toward other living entities, the natural environment or technology, or to abstractions such as economics or politics. In the former category are matters such as health, housing, social divisions, care of the vulnerable; in the latter issues include animal welfare, loss of animal or plant habitats by human action, climate change, scientific and technological innovations and the conduct of economic and political life.

Sociological data, findings and theories have variously informed the development of policy, though with mixed responses from policy-makers (Davies, 2004: 449). However, policy development and implementation have themselves been a focus for sociological research, principally either in terms of interest groups or of institutional structures (Lascoumes and Le Gales, 2007: 4). According to the former, groupings including industry and commerce, professions, scientists and religious groups who are active within a social setting influence the shape of policy (Burstein and Linton, 2002; Macmillan, 2003). In the latter, structural factors within societies and governments and/or institutional history determine the shape of policy outcomes, shaping how interests exert influence, and what impact interest groups have on policy (Banchoff, 2005: 207; Lascoumes and Le Gales, 2007: 4; Wiktorowicz, 2003: 618).

The value of an interests perspective is that it supplies a critical position from which to assess policy, suggesting that policy is often compromised by a failure to address the interests of the broad range of stakeholders, and the differential powers of individuals and institutions (Macmillan, 2003: 188). A structural view provides an understanding of institutional influences upon policy, by suggesting that the structures and historical legacies of governments and states determine who has the power to set policy agendas, and which stakeholders' voices are heard (Banchoff, 2005: 230).

Both these perspectives focus upon what may be described as the 'macro' level of governments, states and institutional structures. As we have shown throughout this book, a materialist and monist sociology steps away from structural explanations, and – as we have already seen in this chapter – understands power and resistance in terms of affective movements within events. For these reasons, when it comes to policy (and politics more generally), a materialist sociology needs to shift from a macro-sociology of governments and states firmly back to the micropolitics of events. This micropolitical focus is a theme running through materialist scholarship on issues of policy and politics: for Widder (2012: 125) 'politics begins with micropolitics', while DeLanda (2006: 87) treats governments as assemblages in which some relations legitimate its authority, while others enable its enforcement. Patton (2000: 68) has pointed to the 'politics of desire' at the heart of Deleuze and Guattari's project, which included exploration of the micropolitics (territorializations and aggregations) of the State and its apparatuses of control (Deleuze and Guattari, 1988: 223).

This orientation, we suggest, is the basis for a *micropolitics of politics*, which aims to explore how legislation, governance and policy-making *events* work, in terms of the movements of power and resistance that derive from these political activities. What, for instance, are the consequences of consumer protection legislation for local traders and customers, how is the law enacted on a daily basis in shops and markets, and in what ways is it transgressed? What is significant about this move is that it emphasizes the *processual* character of policy: policy is not just something that is 'made' once and for all. Rather, policy-making needs to be understood as an always unfinished project; continually under review and revision in the myriad events that follow its initiation (McCann and Ward, 2012: 46). This suggests that policy implementation is of far more interest sociologically than its formulation, whether at the level of national policy or a policy initiative by an organization such as a school. To illustrate this approach to policy, we will explore the impact that the emergence of internet commerce had upon policy concerning the advertising of pharmaceutical medicines (Fox et al., 2006).

The internet and pharmaceutical advertising

Pharmaceutical products, particularly those only available to consumers/patients possessing a prescription from a doctor or nurse, are among the most highly regulated products in the market place. This is not surprising – many medicines are potent chemicals that can endanger human health or life if used inappropriately. National and supra-national (e.g. European Union) legislation governs the manufacture, testing, marketing and consumption of these compounds, with variations between

(Continued)

(Continued)

countries in the precise laws and regulatory frameworks in place. The emergence of the internet as a medium for commerce posed a major challenge to policy-makers and regulators during the 2000s, both in terms of control over prescribing and the marketing of prescription-only medicines (POMs) direct to users (Fox et al., 2006).

In the UK, two laws: the Medicines (Advertising) Regulations 1994 Act and the European Directive 2001/83/EC have prevented direct-to-consumer (DTC) advertising of POMs to UK citizens, though marketing to health professionals is permitted. All European countries have similar legislation; however, US laws permit manufacturers and retailers to promote a wide range of POMs directly to consumers. This difference was of marginal importance prior to the internet. However, when global pharmaceutical companies such as Pfizer or Novartis developed websites to advertise their products to US consumers, there was nothing to prevent UK and other EU citizens accessing this online material (Muscardini, 2001: 56). Meanwhile, overseas web-based pharmacies began to market directly to UK consumers, often with no medical oversight, and subject only to the laws of their host country. These developments raised issues of patient safety, as UK citizens may legally purchase and import POMs (apart from controlled substances) for personal use.

In the UK, the policy on DTC marketing is policed by an advertising unit within the Medicine and HealthCare Products Regulatory Agency (MHRA), which scrutinizes print and other media promotions of, and claims about, prescription medicines. As internet commerce developed, the MHRA stated that pharmaceutical websites (not intended exclusively for healthcare professionals) could publish only technical data on their products concerning dosage, drug interactions and contra-indications (Medicines Control Agency, 1999: 16). In an interview in Fox et al.'s (2006) study, a respondent from the MHRA confirmed that this extension to the UK's DTC advertising policy had been negotiated with UK-based pharmaceutical companies on a voluntary self-regulatory basis.

This response by the UK regulator, Fox et al. (2006) argued, indicated a pragmatism as far as the 'policing' of pharmaceutical advertising governance goes – a pragmatic reaction also noted in the regulation of online pharmacies (Fox et al., 2005b). The MHRA respondent acknowledged that their agreement with pharmaceutical companies did not cover overseas websites, but argued that where consumers accessed these sites, this was acceptable, as it represented a 'pull' rather than a 'push' in relation to accessing drug information.

> I think people are quite aware of the information they see on the internet, that they're looking at foreign information. I don't think that I would accept that that constitutes direct to consumer advertising in the UK. I accept that consumers can, if they search for the advertising material, but it would be a long step from companies targeting UK consumers. That's UK consumers trying hard to find the information. (Fox et al., 2006: 323)

This 'fix' ensured the continued viability of advertising policy as reasonable and legitimate, in the face of the global reach of the internet that arguably made a mockery of the UK's efforts to prevent marketing of pharmaceuticals to its citizens.

We would argue that the apparently casual response by the regulator to what appeared major challenges to policy on prescription medicines demonstrates that government policy is not a once-made entity, but an on-going project that must respond to shifts in power and resistance between material actors (in our ontology, in the micropolitics of the 'policy-assemblage'). Sustaining policy in the case of POMs and the internet entailed a substantial degree of behind-closed-doors discussion with industry, professional associations and so forth, leading to new agreements and adaptations to voluntary codes. The regulator responded to 'consumer power' (capacities to access information and purchase POMs online), which underpinned the need to adapt to new market forces and demands. This analysis supports a processual perspective on policy-making, based on 'continuing dialogue and resource-sharing' (Jessop, 2003: 101) among social actors to achieve beneficial outcomes and manage contradictions. Indeed, policy and its governance needs to be understood not as top-down activities, but as disseminated across the events and assemblages of civil society (McCann and Ward, 2012).

This is a view of policy as a dynamic process that is never fully achieved, and depends upon a broad base of consent from those within the 'policy-assemblage' (Prince, 2010). Thus, for example, policy-makers have negotiated consent from forest-owners to support biodiversity through voluntary agreements, even though the owners' underlying values and interests stand in opposition to this policy (Hysing and Olsson, 2005). We are reminded too of the lack of popular consent that led to the failure by UK Prime Minister Margaret Thatcher to successfully introduce a 'poll tax' (an annual flat-rate charge levied on all adult citizens) in the 1980s. This tax was generally regarded as contrary to fundamental (British) notions of individual liberty and fairness, and was repealed after wide scale protest, despite Thatcher's large parliamentary majority, a loyal civil service and a weak opposition (Butler et al., 1994).

This materialist perspective on policy reflects the position that we developed earlier on power and resistance as affective movements within the flux of an unfolding social world. What is clear is that policy, and politics and government more generally, can no longer be treated as top-down exercises of power, or as one-off events that determine the shape of social interactions. Policies and laws (for instance, a school policy against homophobic bullying, or a national policy to reduce the prevalence of obesity) may often be relations within assemblages, and will have an effect on the capacities of assembled bodies and other relations. Good policy can be productive of new opportunities and becomings, while poor or repressive policies or laws close these down.

But at the same time, in every event assemblage in which a policy, a law or a regulatory framework is a relation, the micropolitical flow between relations will impact upon the affective capacities of that policy or law itself. In other words, the effectiveness of a policy or law is continually subject to the micropolitics of events. What this suggests is a sociological engagement with policy that may begin with research or analysis of its formulation, but can also inform its practical delivery and impact on events, or offer insights that can aid its refinement, revision or – on occasions – its dissolution. This leads us neatly on to consider sociological activism.

Materialism and activism

There is a long tradition of sociological activism, motivated by sociologists' desires for social reform and improvements to the quality of life. After all, Karl Marx – one of the early influences upon sociology – had stated that the task facing society was not merely to interpret the world, but to change it (Marx, 1969). Sociologists have been involved in campaigns that have included women's suffrage, racism, child labour, union rights, educational reform and opposition to wars (Dale and Kalob, 2006: 121).

Activism, however, is not a core feature of contemporary sociology. Perhaps the subject's entrenchment into the relative security of academic institutions, and the progressive shaping of sociology by narrow evaluations of research knowledge and scholarship (Burrows, 2012; Freshwater, 2014: 328), has tempered the activist urge within the sociological imagination. However, this academic 'bunker' mentality has been challenged in recent years by sociologists such as Michael Burawoy (a past president of both American and International Sociological Associations) who has called for a more engaged 'public sociology' (Burawoy, 2005) that brings sociological knowledge to bear upon real-world issues. In addition, groups of sociologists inside and outside academia have emerged that consider activism as a direct means to demonstrate the 'impact' of sociological theories, models and research findings (some links are provided at the end of the chapter).

However, we would suggest that there is a further reason for sociological ambivalence to activism, deriving from divergence between the models of humans and society held by academics and activists, leading to different perspectives on social engagement. Over the past 40 years, sociology has become embroiled in epistemological debates between realists and constructionists over how to know the social world. One area of sociological theory at issue in this debate has been around the ways in which social identities (for instance, as 'woman', 'LGBT', 'British' and so forth) have been understood in sociology. In general, sociologists have favoured a model of identity as socially constructed, rather than innate or 'essentialist' (Brubaker and Cooper, 2000: 6). This has contrasted with some activist perspectives, for instance by feminists and anti-racism campaigners, for whom an essentialist approach to social identity (which has informed the consequent 'identity-politics') has sometimes underpinned activist campaigns (Alldred and Dennison, 2000: 126–7; Burman, 1990; El-Bushra, 2007: 142; Higgins, 1996: 99).

To explore this divergence in greater detail, and as the basis for developing a materialist approach to activism, we want to take as an example dissent between activist and academic responses to the perceived inappropriate 'sexualization' of young people in contemporary society (Fox and Bale, forthcoming).

Activist and academic perspective on sexualization

Anxieties over access to internet pornography and other media sexual content by children and teenagers, and their consequent precocious 'sexualization', has been the basis for an improbable activist coalition (Duschinsky, 2013) between religious organizations, conservative parent groups (such as 'Mumsnet' and the Mothers' Union in the UK) and some feminists concerned at the shaping of girls and women within a male model of sexuality, the commodification of sexuality and the objectification of girls' and young women's bodies (Gill, 2003: 105; Horvath et al, 2013). These diverse constituencies share a view of sexualization as a social problem to be addressed by policy initiatives and/or activism.

This activist analysis of sexualization possesses a realist flavour, as may be seen in two reports commissioned by the UK government – the 2011 *Bailey Review of the Commercialisation and Sexualisation of Childhood* and a report by psychologist Linda Papadopoulos (2010): the *Sexualisation of Young People Review*. A review of literature for the Office of the Children's Commissioner (Horvath et al., 2013: 7) suggests that increased access to pornography is linked to unrealistic attitudes to sex and relationships, more sexually permissive attitudes, beliefs that women are sex objects, less progressive gender role attitudes, and to children and young people engaging in risky sexual behaviours. Concern over increasing access to pornography by teenagers (Hines, 2011; Paul, 2005) features alongside other social issues concerning young people, including historical child sexual abuse (Mendelson and Letourneau, 2015) and sexting and cybersex (Levine, 2013; Mitchell et al, 2014; Phippen, 2012). Recommendations from these assessments have included tightening controls on music video content and broadcast media, and enhancing parental control over children's internet access (Bailey, 2011: 14–15).

Academic analyses of sexualization have diverged from these realist approaches. Drawing on post-structuralist, feminist and queer theory, scholars have argued that the ways that societies think about sexualization are influenced by cultural discourses and narratives that shape social and moral concerns about young people, sexuality and sexual conduct. Underlying contemporary societal anxieties and moral panics around sexualization of children (particularly girls) are underpinned by foundational, essentialist models that establish a distinction between 'innocent child' and 'responsible adult' (Barker and Duschinsky, 2012: 305; Duschinsky, 2013: 150). Egan (2013: 17)

(Continued)

(Continued)

identified four 'long-standing Anglophone anxieties' deployed in contemporary discussions of sexualization: concern over unfettered female heterosexuality; racialized concerns over sexual innocence and its corruption; middle-class anxieties about working-class sexuality; and disgust, anger and repressed desire over the eroticism of the child. These anxieties produced moral panics around children's access to pornography, safety of children from sexual predators and sexualization of young children, as reflected in the various policy reviews, strategies and sanctions noted earlier.

These academic perspectives have provided the basis for a critique of activist discourses on sex and sexualization, which they argue over-simplify concerns around girls, bodies, sex and sexuality in ways that 'flatten out social and cultural difference' (Renold and Ringrose, 2011: 391), and add a further constraint 'that fetters girls' (a)sexuality to morality, appearance and age' (Jackson and Vares, 2015). Gill (2012: 742) notes the 'profoundly classed, racialized and heteronormative framing of the sexualization debate, while Egan (2013: 134) points to how realist discourses on the media's role in sexualization depend upon constructing girls as deviant, rather than addressing the sexism, racism, classism and homophobia in popular culture.

This comparison between activist and academic responses reveals the divergence between essentialist and constructionist perspectives on sexualization. But critically for our discussion here, they also demonstrate very different propositions for policy and social change. The activist perspective advocates initiatives to counter a very real danger to young people, often founded upon an unproblematized assessment that society should 'let children be children' (the title of Bailey's (2011) review). By contrast, academic analyses have denied the notion of the essential nature of the child or the adult, and have concluded that activist responses to sexualization are themselves part of the problem or at best a distraction – to the extent that they mask more deep-seated issues. The problems to be addressed, in this latter view, concern contemporary society's attitudes to sex and sexuality, the marketization and commodification of sex and sexual bodies, and societal sexism, racism and homophobia.

The consequence of this divergence is that while activism has advocated direct policy initiatives, some of which have been readily adopted by Western governments eager to assuage voter concerns, academic approaches struggle to engage directly with issues of sexualization. Indeed, even the term 'sexualization' has been problematic for some feminist scholars, who prefer to focus more upon the workings of power in relation to sex and sexualities (Duschinsky, 2013: 152; Gill, 2012: 742). The propositions for action or for policy that follow from constructionist analyses (for instance, to eradicate gender inequalities or the commodification of female bodies) consequently lack immediacy, and may require a utopian (Ringrose et al., 2013: 319) shift in culture or dominant ideologies. Indeed, the immediate target for action in these academic studies have been the anti-sexualization campaign itself, which has been criticized for establishing a further constraining discourse on female sexuality and eroticism (Renold and Ringrose, 2013: 248), while leaving more fundamental issues of patriarchy and neoliberalism largely unaddressed (Attwood, 2009: xv–xvi; Egan and Hawkes, 2008: 294).

We should assure readers at this point that the example of sexualization is not an isolated case. We have written elsewhere (Alldred and Fox, 2015a) about the difficulties that social scientists have faced in relation to LGBT activism, which has similarly been underpinned by essentialized notions of sexual identities (as gay, lesbian, asexual and so forth). For constructionists (for instance, those informed by Foucault's (1990) analysis of sexuality), these identities are not fixed or stable, but constructed and culturally-contingent. Sociologists and psychologists have as a consequence found it problematic to engage uncritically with people's struggles against discrimination (Kitzinger, 1999). One solution was 'strategic essentialism' (Eide, 2010; Spivak, 1996: 214), an approach whereby politically-engaged social scientists 'bracketed' (temporarily set to one side) ontological problems of gender or sexuality essentialism, in order to build strategic alliances around notions such as 'woman' or 'lesbian' that could be a rallying-point to stage challenges to patriarchy or heteronormativity.

Throughout the book, we have noted that the 'new' materialist perspectives we have been exploring provide a space in which to cut across the traditional dualism between essentialism and constructionism. We have developed and worked with a dynamic understanding of assemblages of relations (bodies, things, social formations, ideas, memories) linked by a shifting network of forces that produce an ever-evolving skein of material possibilities constrained neither by fixed capacities of pre-existing entities (as in essentialism), nor within a fixed (social) context of choices (as in social constructionism) (Barad, 2001: 103). Now once again, we are going to invoke materialist ontology as a means to transcend the divergences between activist and academic perspectives that we have identified. To do this, we return to the previous example of sexualization, to consider how a materialist analysis by Fox and Bale (forthcoming) provides a new approach to sexualization.

This study explored the sexual development and conduct of young people, using in-depth qualitative interviews with 22 college students aged 16–19 years. During these interviews, participants were encouraged to tell their own stories and experiences, describe their sexual behaviours and sexuality, and how they engaged with sexual media content and pornography. The analysis was informed by materialist concepts and sought to identify the relations in the 'sexualization-assemblages' of individual participants, and to understand the affects that made these assemblages work, and the consequences in terms of what these young people could do, feel or desire. The aim of this analytical methodology was to make the assemblage rather than the student the focus of attention, and to investigate the range of forces in the assemblage that produced capacities.

The wide range of relations identified in this way included family, friends and peers; material things such as alcohol, condoms, social events, money, cars and sex education materials; social formations such as moral standards, norms and street culture; and idiosyncratic elements such as celebrities or skateboards. Sexualization assemblages varied, of course. So, for instance, 'Steve' (a 17-year-old male sports science student, in a heterosexual relationship since the age of 15) was part of an assemblage that included:

> friends – school – college – peers – media – parents – girlfriend – memories – fantasies – gender and sexual norms, beliefs and customs – learning – personal standards – parties and social events – alcohol – pornography – sex education – factual information about sex matters – sexual experiences and tastes

The analysis then looked more generally at the affects that linked these and other relations for the 22 participants. It explored how the affect-economies produced micropolitical effects on the young people, both constraining their sexualities and opening up possibilities for action. This detailed assessment suggested that sexualized media and pornography were components within a much wider range of materialities that affected young people's bodies and conduct.

Realist approaches to sexualization (such as those reviewed earlier) have tended to view children and young people as passive future-beings (Jenks, 2005), absorbing the differing messages that a society mediates, from the well-meaning efforts of parents, teachers and sex educators through to the insidious influences of consumer culture and pornographers. The materialist approach adopted by Fox and Bale recognized the affectivity of all these elements, but considered the young people not as compliant recipients of social forces, nor as people-in-waiting (Alldred and David, 2007: 118), but as 'becomings' within a continuously assembling and dis-assembling flux of relations. Young people's capacities to do, think and feel emerged and receded according to the mix at any one moment in time and space. Furthermore, the data suggested that, rather than being singularly pervasive and corrosive influences, media and pornography were relations in a broad, fluctuating affect economy that produced a multiplicity of capacities, sexual and non-sexual in young people, rather than some kind of monstrous 'sexualized' teenager.

Neither, however, did this materialist analysis recapitulate the conclusions of the constructionist approaches we have reviewed. On one hand it recognized that media and pornography contributed affects that might open up new possibilities for young people's emergent sexualities (for instance, as a source of information about sexuality or as an opportunity to explore possible sources of sexual pleasure), acting as a de-territorialization or even a sexual 'line of flight' from existing sexual repertories and capacities. But the analysis also disclosed affects deriving from media and pornographic materials that produced powerful specifications of sexuality. The limited and unimaginative practices portrayed in pornography and sexualized media imposed narrow and circumscribed definitions of what sex and sexuality comprise. By specifying and aggregating bodies into prescriptive formulations of sexuality, these definitions could reproduce and reinforce misogyny, sexual objectification and sexual consumerism, and constrain rather than promote sexual diversity.

The radical conclusion of this materialist assessment of the production and consumption of pornography and other sexual media content is not that they are good for some (consenting adults) and bad for others (children), but that they contribute to a pernicious sexualization-assemblage of bodies, body parts, money and desires that limits what is culturally understood as 'sexual' and contributes to broad sexual *grooming*. Genitalized pornography is a threat not to moral decency or to childhood innocence, but to all our capacities to enjoy and explore the full range of possibilities of sexualities and becoming-other (see also the discussion in Chapter 6 of body intensifications). This analysis consequently supplies the basis for activism and policy development around pornography and sexual media content that radically questions not only their effects on children, but their wider social consequences for adult sexualities too. This conclusion is quite distinct from those of both parties in the sexualization debates that we reviewed earlier.

We hope that this example demonstrates a materialist approach to social issues that overcomes the divergences between an essentialist, identity politics-driven agenda on one hand, and a constructionist sociological assessment on the other. The non-anthropocentric and posthuman approach that we have applied to this and to other social issues throughout this book shifts attention from individual bodies or human subjects to exploration of affective flows within assemblages of human and non-human relations whose capacities for action, feeling and desire are fluid and undetermined. It focuses on the micropolitics of assemblages, supplying the basis not only for academic theory, but also for application in settings beyond the academic, to actually engage and perhaps change the social world and human lives for the better. It feeds into, and off the materialist understanding of power and resistance that we explored earlier in the chapter, enabling micropolitical engagements with events.

Conclusion: an engaged sociology of materiality

Much of this book has had a strict academic orientation, very much concerned with setting out an alternative perspective on sociological theory and its application to a range of academic sociology topics. But in this chapter we have stepped beyond the confines of the university department, to focus on what is arguably the principal reason for doing sociology and social science in the first place, to make a difference to the world and to people's lives.

To that end, we have suggested that materialist sociology has some important tools that may be employed to seek social change, whether this is achieved by disseminating findings from research, influencing policy development, or working with people to enhance the quality of their lives or the lives of others. We began by developing a materialist model of power and resistance that recognizes both as integral to the events that produce the world from moment to moment, rather than some kind of amorphous stuff that shapes or structures social life. We then suggested how materialist ontology can break through divergences between popular movements based around identity-politics or other manifestations of essentialism and academic sociological models. Finally, we looked at policy and the challenges it poses for developing initiatives that engage with the issues that it seeks to address.

In our view, sociology – as seen through the materialist lens – cannot help but be engaged with the world in multiple ways. As we conclude this chapter and this book, we hope we have been able to suggest some possibilities that a materialist perspective offers, to extend a sociological imagination well beyond the confines of the academic lecture hall, out into the world.

Further reading

DeLanda, M. (2006) *A New Philosophy of Society*. London: Continuum. Chapter 4.
McCann, E. and Ward, K. (2012) Assembling urbanism: following policies and 'studying through' the sites and situations of policy making. *Environment and Planning A, 44*: 42–51.
Patton, P. (2000) *Deleuze and the Political*. London: Routledge. Chapter 5.

Relevant websites

Activism in Sociology Forum – www.britsoc.co.uk/groups/activism-in-sociology-forum. aspx
Everyday Sociology – www.everydaysociologyblog.com/

Glossary

Note: q.v. (*quod vide*, or 'see this item') indicates a term also appears within the glossary.

activism Action by citizens to effect social change or to improve or ameliorate social conditions.

actor-network theory, ANT Approach to social theory and research that recognizes objects as agents operating alongside humans in networks or assemblages.

affect economy The interaction of affective movements circulating within an assemblage that together establishes its capacities.

affect, affectivity May be used to refer to emotions, but in this book affect is used to connote 'something that affects or is affected'.

agency Used in sociology to describe action, usually associated with humans, and sometimes contrasted with social structure (q.v.).

aggregation A micropolitical movement within an assemblage that establishes similarities between persons, bodies or objects.

anthropocene An unofficial term used by some scientists to describe a subdivision of geological time during which human activity has affected the Earth's geology and ecosystems.

anthropocentrism A perspective that takes humans as the central focus and the standard against which other animate or inanimate entities are judged.

anti-humanism A philosophical position that rejects and seeks to overturn humanist assertions of the inherent value of human thoughts, beliefs and/or actions.

assemblage Common translation of *agencement* (arrangement) in Deleuze and Guattari's work, connoting an unstable coalescence of relations (q.v.).

base In Marxist dualist theory describes the economic foundations of a social system such as capitalism upon which a superstructure of social relations may be built.

becoming, becoming-other A process of transformation usually associated with an increase in or diversification of capacities to act.

biophilosophy A branch of philosophy focusing on biology, the biological and issues concerning life.

body-with-organs The body of biomedical theory, understood in terms of biological function, and comprised of inter-dependent organs.

body-without-organs A term used by Deleuze and Guattari to refer to the limits of what a body (a biological body or any assemblage of relations) can do, in terms of its capacities.

capacity An ability to do, think or desire; in new materialist theory capacities are not considered as fixed attributes but as properties of bodies or things emergent within particular contexts.

capital In Marxist theory, capital refers solely to economic resources such as money, raw materials and the means of material production (factories, machinery); this economic capital was supplemented in Pierre Bourdieu's analysis to incorporate symbolic capital (respect, reputation), social capital (social connections, mutual obligations) and cultural capital (knowledge, skills).

capitalism An economic and social system that establishes and promotes private ownership of the means of economic production, requiring workers to sell their labour to the owners of capital, in return for a wage.

cartography Map-making, used in Deleuzian and feminist materialist theory to describe an approach that aims to map the flows of affects, power and lines of flight (q.v.) in an event or assemblage, recognizing that mapping is itself experimental and a 'becoming' (q.v.).

constructionism A social theory of knowledge that focuses upon humans' construction of a shared understanding of the world. Extreme versions regard these social constructs as the only knowable entities, in contrast with realism (q.v.). See also 'post-structuralism'.

critical psychology A strand within psychology that questions the individualism of the subject's mainstream, to offer a more social and political analysis of psychological phenomena.

critical realism A philosophy of (social) science that seeks to disclose the mechanisms that underpin social events, though acknowledging that these mechanisms may be affected by social processes.

cultural capital See 'capital'.

cyborg In science fiction, an amalgam of living tissues and machines; in materialist theory also used as a metaphor to acknowledge that culture and nature are both material.

desire Conventionally understood as an absence to be filled by the acquisition of a desired object; used by Deleuze and Guattari to describe a force or affect productive of actions, interactions or ideas.

de-territorialization A generalizing process within an assemblage that counters specification, definition or territorialization (q.v.).

diffractive methodology An approach developed by Donna Haraway and Karen Barad in an effort to avoid linear representations and explore interferences, for instance by reading multiple data sources together, or reading different theorists alongside one another.

dualism, dualistic The division of a phenomenon into two opposed or contrasting aspects, such as male/female.

ecology The study of interactions between organisms and their environment.

empiricism An approach to social inquiry (q.v.) that emphasizes the importance of observations of events. In materialist ontology, an empiricist focus is underpinned by the proposition of the 'exteriority of relations' (q.v.) which considers that an entity's capacities depend entirely upon its relations to other assembled entities.

epistemology An aspect of the philosophy of science that addresses how these things can be known by an observer.

essence, essentialism A perspective that holds that an entity such as a body or a stone has intrinsic attributes or properties that define it absolutely.

event An occurrence in time and space marked by some kind of physical, social, cultural, psychological or other interaction by assembled relations; events comprise the flow of history and to social production and as such are the focus for materialist social inquiry.

evolutionary psychology An approach that explores which aspects of human psychology are associated with evolutionary processes of natural and sexual selection.

exteriority of relations A principle in materialist theory that an entity's capacities depend entirely upon its relations to other assembled entities, rather than because of essential or interior attributes or characteristics.

Gaia A hypothesis formulated by chemist James Lovelock in the 1970s that argues that the Earth is a complex, self-regulating ecosystem.

generalization A micropolitical process within an assemblage that increases a relation's capacities; synonymous with 'de-territorialization' (q.v.).

governmentality A Foucauldian concept that addresses the social shaping of conduct through the disseminated operation of power and knowledge throughout a society.

hegemonic masculinity A concept used by some sexualities theorists to refer to the dominant form/s of masculinity in particular societies; contemporary Western forms are founded upon heterosexuality, homophobia and misogyny.

heteronormativity A societal understanding that asserts heterosexuality as a norm and other sexualities as deviant.

historical materialism A theory of history most closely associated with Karl Marx, in which a society's organisation and development are understood in terms of the material processes associated with economic production.

humanism A view that asserts the inherent value of human thoughts, beliefs and/or actions.

idealism In sociology, a perspective that emphasizes the role played by human ideas, beliefs and values in shaping both society and our capacity to gain research knowledge of the social world.

intensity, intensification Used in this book to assess the strength of affectivity within assemblages; the process of increasing affective intensity.

intra-action A neologism coined by Karen Barad (as an alternative to 'interaction'), to stress her view that entities are not prior and independent, but themselves emerge from their 'intra-active' relationality with other entities.

line of flight An extreme de-territorialization (q.v.) – an 'escape route' from territorialization – that opens up hitherto untapped capacities for a body or thing, and may lead to the formation of novel assemblages.

linguistic turn A term sometimes used to describe the shift within the humanities and social sciences to post-structuralist (q.v.) concerns with language, texts and knowledge as the basis for social organisation and power.

materiality The quality of being composed of matter; also used as a plural noun in new materialist theory to describe the range of things capable of having material effects.

micropolitics Used here to describe the internal movements of power and resistance within assemblages; contrasted with 'macro' level politics applied in social science to examine social movements or governments.

modernism An era from about 1800 to the present day characterized by application of rational and/or scientific efforts to elucidate the world (for example by observation, experiment and the development of theoretical models), and linked to ideas of social and scientific progress through the exercise of these techniques.

molar A term (deriving from physical chemistry) used by Deleuze and Guattari to describe aggregated relations, or aggregative affects within assemblages (see aggregation).

molecular A term (deriving from physical chemistry) used by Deleuze and Guattari to describe unique or singular relations and affects in assemblages.

monism A philosophical perspective that considers that phenomena inhabit a single realm or are comprised of a single substance (for example, matter), in contrast to dualistic (q.v.) ontologies.

neo-liberalism A set of market-oriented practices, and a philosophical and policy orientation towards individualized self-interest and the market as the foundation for most if not all human interaction.

nomadology Deleuze and Guattari's philosophical project to develop a science and strategy for living that celebrates and encourages becoming and diversity rather than norms and aggregation (q.v.).

non-representational theory An approach developed in human geography by Nigel Thrift and others that focuses on events, activities and practices rather than representations such as human accounts, texts and images.

onto-epistemology A term introduced by Karen Barad to make the point that events and observation are part of the same phenomenon – their 'intra-action' (q.v.) means that issues of epistemology are intimately linked to ontology.

ontology Concerns propositions about the fundamental nature of things and the kinds of things that exist.

post-colonial studies Critical approach to the history and the cultural and material legacies of colonialism and imperialism.

posthumanism, posthuman A philosophical position – most clearly articulated by Rosi Braidotti – that acknowledges the continuities between human and non-human, nature and culture. The post-human is the assemblage reflecting these continuities (see also 'cyborg').

post-modernism Perspective in the arts, humanities and social sciences that is suspicious of the commitments of modernism (q.v.) to rationality, science and grand theories of the social and the human subject.

post-structuralism A range of philosophical perspectives in the arts, humanities and social sciences that reject structural explanations, seeking to explore the links between knowledge and power, as exemplified in the work of Foucault, Derrida and Lyotard.

quantum mechanics A branch of physics that explores the behaviour of sub-atomic particles and waves, recognising the interactions between events and observers.

queer theory Critical and deconstructive approach within social theory that acknowledges the constructed and therefore contextual character of the social world, rejects essentialism, and decouples and reverses the conventional relations between sex, gender and sexuality.

realism Philosophical perspective that asserts the existence of entities independent from human constructs; in contrast to constructionist (q.v.) approaches.

reductionism Approach that seeks explanations of complex events (such as social organization) in terms of more 'basic' processes (such as biology, biochemistry or genetics).

relations In Deleuzian theory, the components comprising assemblages, defined by their relational (rather than essential) capacities.

responsibilize, responsibilization A technique of power that seeks to make an individual responsible for their own actions and conduct.

re-territorialization See territorialization.

rhizome, rhizomic Metaphor used by Deleuze and Guattari to describe a branching, reversing, coalescing and rupturing flow, in contrast to linearity.

schizoanalysis Deleuze and Guattari's alternative to psychoanalysis, an approach that encourages complexity, de-territorialization (q.v.) and becoming-other.

singular Used in this book to describe an affect (q.v.) that acts uniquely upon a single relation, in contrast to aggregative (q.v.) affects that operate on multiple relations.

social capital See 'capital'.

social inquiry Use of research and theory to make sense of the social world.

social construct Idea or concept that contributes to a shared understanding of the world. See also 'constructionism'.

social structure A term used widely in sociology to denote processes or systems of social relations that influence (often constraining or limiting) human actions and interactions.

social stratification The categorizations or aggregations (for instance into classes, races or genders) by a society, culture or by social scientists.

sociobiology An approach that claims that much human social behaviour may be explained by evolutionary needs; in particular, the need to pass on genetic material through reproduction.

sociological imagination A term coined by C. Wright Mills to connote the insights that sociology can bring to the understanding of social processes.

sociology of associations A term used by Bruno Latour to assert his monist (q.v.) view that sociology should attend solely to the material connections between entities (both 'social' and 'natural').

specification Used in this book as an equivalent to the Deleuzian term 'territorialization' (q.v), to describe how affects (q.v.) circumscribe capacities.

superstructure In Marxist dualist theory, describes the culture, structures and social relations between people; contrasted with the economic base (q.v.).

territorialization A term in Deleuze and Guattari's work (related to the French concept of *terroir*, which recognizes the influence of environmental factors on the qualities of produce such as wine and honey) that addresses how an entity's capacities are specified by its relationships in assemblages.

text, textuality In post-structuralism used to describe any symbolic or representational system.

transgression A breach or contravention of a code, law or ethics of behaviour.

transversal, transversality Cutting across; used in this book to describe new materialist ontology's relation to sociological dualisms.

turn to matter Shorthand term for the move towards materialism in the social sciences, arts and humanities; contrasted with the 'linguistic turn' of post-structuralism (q.v.).

Bibliography

Ahmed, S. (2004) *The Cultural Politics of Emotion*. Edinburgh: Edinburgh University Press.

Albiston, C.R. (2010) *Institutional Inequality and the Mobilization of the Family and Medical Leave Act: Rights on Leave*. Cambridge: Cambridge University Press.

Alcadipani, R. and Hassard, J. (2010) Actor-Network Theory, organizations and critique: towards a politics of organizing. *Organization, 17*(4): 419–435.

Alldred, P. and David, M. (2007) *Get Real about Sex. The Politics and Practice of Sex Education*. Maidenhead: Open University Press.

Alldred, P. and Dennison, S. (2000) Eco-activism and feminism: do eco-warriors and goddesses need it? *Feminist Review, 64*: 124–127.

Alldred, P. and Fox, N.J. (2015a) From 'lesbian and gay psychology' to a critical psychology of sexualities. In: Parker, I. (ed.) *Handbook of Critical Psychology*. London: Routledge, pp. 200–209.

Alldred, P. and Fox, N.J. (2015b) The sexuality assemblages of young men: a new materialist analysis. *Sexualities, 18*(8), 905–920.

Allen, L. and Carmody, M. (2012) 'Pleasure has no passport': re-visiting the potential of pleasure in sexuality education. *Sex Education, 12*(4): 455–468.

Alvesson, M. and Sköldberg, K. (2009) *Reflexive Methodology (2nd edition)*. London: Sage.

Anderson, B.M. (1991) Mapping the terrain of the discipline. In: Gray, G. and Pratt, R. (eds.) *Towards a Discipline of Nursing*. Melbourne: Churchill Livingstone, pp. 95–123.

Anderson, B. (2009) Affective atmospheres. *Emotion, Space and Society, 2*(2): 77–81.

Anderson, B. and Harrison, P. (2010) The promise of non-representational theories. In Anderson, B. and Harrison, P. (eds.) *Taking-Place: Non-Representational Theories and Geography*. London: Ashgate, pp. 1–36.

Ansell Pearson, K. (1999) *Germinal Life*. London: Routledge.

Anthias, F. (1998) Rethinking social divisions: some notes towards a theoretical framework. *The Sociological Review, 46*(3): 505–535.

Armstrong, D. (1983) *The Political Anatomy of the Body*. Cambridge: Cambridge University Press.

Attwood, F. (2009) The sexualisation of culture. In: Attwood, F. (ed.) *Mainstreaming Sex: The Sexualisation of Western Culture*. London: I.B. Tauris.

Austin, J.I. (2016) Dancing sexual pleasures: exploring teenage women's experiences of sexuality and pleasure beyond 'sex'. *Sex Education, 16*(3): 279–293.

Bailey, R. (2011) *Letting Children be Children: Report of an Independent Review of the Commercialisation and Sexualisation of Childhood*. London: The Stationery Office.

Bale, C. (2011) Raunch or romance? Framing and interpreting the relationship between sexualized culture and young people's sexual health. *Sex Education, 11*(3): 303–313.

Ballantyne, A. (2007) *Deleuze and Guattari for Architects*. London: Routledge.

Banchoff, T. (2005) Path dependence and value-driven issues: The comparative politics of stem cell research. *World Politics, 57*(2): 200–230.

Barad, K. (1996) Meeting the universe halfway: realism and social constructivism without contradiction. In: Nelson, L.H. and Nelson, J. (eds.) *Feminism, Science and the Philosophy of Science*. Dordrecht: Kluwer, pp. 161–194.

Barad, K. (2001) (Re)configuring space, time and matter. In: Dekoven, M. (ed.) *Feminist Locations*. New Brunswick, NJ: Rutgers University Press, pp. 75–109.

Barad, K. (2003) Posthumanist performativity: toward an understanding of how matter comes to matter. *Signs, 28*(3): 801–831.

Barad, K. (2007) *Meeting the Universe Halfway. Quantum Physics and the Entanglement of Matter and Meaning*. Durham, NC: Duke University Press.

Barbalet, J. (2002) Introduction: why emotions are crucial. In: Barbalet, J. (ed.) *Emotions and Sociology*. Oxford: Blackwell, pp. 1–9.

Barker, M. (2005) 'This is my partner, and this is my … partner's partner': constructing a polyamorous identity in a monogamous world. *Journal of Constructivist Psychology, 18*(1): 75–88.

Barker, M. and Duschinsky, R. (2012) Sexualisation's four faces: sexualisation and gender stereotyping in the Bailey Review. *Gender and Education, 24*(3): 303–310.

Barrett, M. and McIntosh, M. (1982) *The Anti-Social Family*. London: Verso.

Beasley, C. (2015) Caution! Hazards ahead: considering the potential gap between feminist thinking and men/masculinities theory and practice. *Journal of Sociology, 51*(3): 566–581.

Becker, H.S. (1974) Art as collective action. *American Sociological Review, 39*(6): 767–776.

Becker, H.S. (1982) *Art Worlds*. Berkeley, CA: University of California Press.

Beckman, F. (2011) Introduction: what is sex? An introduction to the sexual philosophy of Gilles Deleuze. In: Beckman, F. (ed.) *Deleuze and Sex*. Edinburgh: Edinburgh University Press, pp. 1–29.

Belli, S., Harré, R. and Iniguez, L. (2010) What is love? Discourse about emotions in social sciences. *Human Affairs 20*(3): 249–270.

Bendelow, G. (2009) *Health, Emotion and the Body*. Cambridge: Polity.

Bendelow, G. and Williams, S. (1998) *The Lived Body: Sociological Themes, Embodied Issues*. London: Routledge.

Bennett, J. (2010) *Vibrant Matter*. Durham, NC: Duke University Press.

Bensimon, M. (2012) The sociological role of collective singing during intense moments of protest: the disengagement from the Gaza strip. *Sociology, 46*(2): 241–257.

Benton, T. (1991) Biology and social science: why the return of the repressed should be given a (cautious) welcome. *Sociology, 25*(1): 1–29.

Berezin, M. (2002) Secure states: towards a political economy of emotion. In Barbalet, J. (ed.) *Emotions and Sociology*. Oxford: Blackwell, pp. 33–52.

Berger, J. and Kellner, H. (1964) Marriage and the construction of reality: an exercise in the microsociology of knowledge. *Diogenes, 12*(46): 1–24.

Berger, P. and Luckmann, T. (1971) *The Social Construction of Reality*. Harmondsworth: Penguin University Books.

Best, S. (1995) Sexualizing space. In: Grosz, E. and Probyn, E. (eds.) *Sexy Bodies*. London: Routledge, pp. 181–194.

Blackman, L. (2012) *Immaterial Bodies: Affect, Embodiment, Mediation*. London: Sage.

Blackman, L. and Venn, C. (2010) Affect. *Body & Society*, 16(1): 7–28.

Blaise, M. (2013) Activating micropolitical practices in the early years: (re)assembling bodies and participant observations. In: Coleman, R. and Ringrose, J. (eds.) *Deleuze and Research Methodologies*. Edinburgh: Edinburgh University Press, pp. 184–200.

Bogue, R. (1989) *Deleuze and Guattari*. London: Routledge.

Bogue, R. (2011) Alien sex: Octavia Butler and Deleuze and Guattari's polysexuality. In: Beckman, F. (ed.) *Deleuze and Sex*. Edinburgh: Edinburgh University Press, pp. 30–49.

Bonnell, V.E. and Hunt, L. (1999) Introduction. In: Bonnell, V.E. and Hunt, L. (eds.) *Beyond the Cultural Turn*. Berkeley, CA: University of California Press, pp. 1–32.

Born, G. (2005) On musical mediation, ontology, technology and creativity. *Twentieth Century Music*, 21(1): 7–36.

Born, G. (2010) The social and the aesthetic, for a post-Bourdieusian theory of cultural production. *Cultural Sociology*, 42(2): 1–38.

Bottero, W. and Crossley, N. (2011) Worlds, fields and networks: Becker, Bourdieu and the structures of social processes. *Cultural Sociology*, 5(1): 99–119.

Boudon, R. (1991) *Theories of Social Change* (Trans. Whitehouse, J.C.). Cambridge: Polity.

Bourdieu, P. (1983) The field of cultural production, or, the economic world reversed. *Poetics*, 12(4/5): 311–356.

Bourdieu, P. (1984) *Distinction: A Social Critique of the Judgement of Taste*. Harvard University Press.

Bourdieu, P. (1990) *In Other Words: Essays Towards a Reflexive Sociology*. Cambridge: Polity.

Bowden, R. (2004) A critique of Alfred Gell on art and agency. *Oceania*, 74(4): 309–324.

Braidotti, R. (2000) Teratologies. In: Buchanan, I. and Colebrook, C. (eds.) *Deleuze and Feminist Theory*. Edinburgh: Edinburgh University Press, pp. 156–172.

Braidotti, R. (2006a) Posthuman, all too human: towards a new process ontology. *Theory Culture & Society*, 23(7–8): 197–208.

Braidotti, R. (2006b) *Transpositions*. Cambridge: Polity.

Braidotti, R. (2011) *Nomadic Theory*. New York: Columbia University Press.

Braidotti, R. (2013) *The Posthuman*. Cambridge: Polity.

Braidotti, R., Charkiewicz, E., Hausler, S. and Wieringa, S. (1994) *Women, the Environment and Sustainable Development: Towards a Theoretical Synthesis*. London: Zed Books.

Brubaker, R. and Cooper, F. (2000) Beyond 'identity'. *Theory and Society*, 29(1): 1–47.

Buchanan, I. (1997) The problem of the body in Deleuze and Guattari, or, what can a body do? *Body & Society*, 3(3): 73–91.

Bunton, R. (1992) 'More than a woolly jumper': health promotion as social regulation. *Critical Public Health*, 3(20): 4–11.

Burawoy, M. (2005) For public sociology. *American Sociological Review*, 70(1): 4–28.

Burman, E. (1990) *Feminists and Psychological Practice*. London: Sage.

Burrows, R. (2012) Living with the h-index? Metric assemblages in the contemporary academy. *The Sociological Review*, 60(2): 355–372.

Burstein, P. and Linton, A. (2002) The impact of political parties, interest groups, and social movement organizations on public policy: Some recent evidence and theoretical concerns. *Social Forces, 81*(2): 380–408.

Butler, D., Adonis, A. and Travers, T. (1994) *Failure in British Government – The Politics of the Poll Tax*. Oxford: Oxford University Press.

Butler, J. (1990) *Gender Trouble*. London: Routledge.

Butler, J. (1999) Revisiting bodies and pleasures. *Theory, Culture & Society, 16*(2): 11–20.

Callon, M. (1986) Some elements of a sociology of translation: domestication of the scallops and the fishermen of St. Brieuc bay. In Law, J. (ed.) *Power, Action and Belief* (Sociological Review Monograph 32). London: Routledge and Kegan Paul, pp. 196–233.

Canguilhem, G. (1989) *The Normal and the Pathological*. New York: Zone Books.

Carroll, J. (1993) *Humanism: the Wreck of Modern Culture*. London: Fontana.

Catton, W.R. and Dunlap, R.E. (1978) Environmental sociology: a new paradigm. *American Sociologist, 13*: 41–49.

Chamberlain, J.M. (2013) *The Sociology of Medical Regulation*. Dordrecht: Springer.

Cheyne, A. and Binder, A. (2010) Cosmopolitan preferences, the constitutive role of place in American elite taste for hip-hop music 1991–2005. *Poetics, 38*(3): 336–364.

Clarke, A.E., Shim, J.K., Mamo, L. et al. (2010) *Biomedicalization: Technoscience, Health, and Illness in the US*. Durham, NC: Duke University Press.

Clegg, S.R. (1990) *Modern Organizations*. London: Sage.

Clough, P.T. (2004) Future matters: technoscience, global politics, and cultural criticism. *Social Text 22*(3): 1–23.

Clough, P.T. (2008) The affective turn: political economy, biomedia and bodies. *Theory, Culture and Society, 25*(1): 1–22.

Coburn, D. (2014) Neoliberalism and health. In: Cockerham, W., Dingwall, R. and Quah, S.R. (eds.) *The Wiley Blackwell Encyclopedia of Health, Illness, Behavior, and Society*. Chichester: Wiley, pp. 1678–1683.

Coffey, A. (2004) *Reconceptualizing Social Policy: Sociological Perspectives on Contemporary Social Policy*. Maidenhead: Open University Press.

Cohen, S. (1973) *Folk Devils and Moral Panics: The Creation of the Mods and Rockers*. St Albans: Paladin.

Cohen, S. (2002) *Folk Devils and Moral Panics: The Creation of the Mods and Rockers* (3rd Edition). London: Routledge.

Cole, D.R. (2013) Lost in data space: using nomadic analysis to perform social science. In: Coleman, R. and Ringrose, J. (eds.) *Deleuze and Research Methodologies*. Edinburgh: Edinburgh University Press, pp. 219–237.

Colebrook, C. (2013) Face race. In: Saldanha, A. and Admans, J.M. (eds.) *Deleuze and Race*. Edinburgh: Edinburgh University Press, pp. 35–50.

Coleman, R. and Ringrose, J. (2013) Introduction. In: Coleman, R. and Ringrose, J. (eds.) *Deleuze and Research Methodologies*. Edinburgh: Edinburgh University Press, pp. 1–22.

Connell, R.W. (1987) *Gender and Power: Society, the Person, and Sexual Politics*. London: Allen & Unwin.

Connell, R.W. and Messerschmidt, J.W. (2005) Hegemonic masculinity: rethinking the concept. *Gender & Society, 19*(6): 829–859.

Connolly, W.E. (2010) Materialities of experience. In: Coole, D.H. and Frost, S. (eds.) *New Materialisms: Ontology, Agency, and Politics.* Durham, NC: Duke University Press, pp. 178–200.

Connolly, W.E. (2011) The complexity of intention. *Critical Inquiry, 37*(4): 791–98.

Conrad, P. (2007) *The Medicalization of Society.* Baltimore, MD: Johns Hopkins University Press.

Coole, D.H. and Frost, S. (2010) Introducing the new materialisms. In: Coole, D.H. and Frost, S. (eds.) *New Materialisms. Ontology, Agency, and Politics.* London: Duke University Press, pp. 1–43.

Cooper, R. and Burrell, G. (1988) Modernism, postmodernism and organizational analysis: An introduction. *Organization Studies, 9*(1): 91–112.

Coyne, I.T. (1997) Sampling in qualitative research. Purposeful and theoretical sampling: merging or clear boundaries? *Journal of Advanced Nursing, 26*(3): 623–630.

Crenshaw, K. (1989) *Demarginalising the intersection of race and sex: A black feminism critique to antidiscrimination doctrine, feminist theory and antiracist politics.* University of Chicago Legal Forum, pp. 139–167.

Cromby, J. (2004) Between constructionism and neuroscience: the societal co-constitution of embodied subjectivity. *Theory and Psychology 14*(6): 797–821.

Cutler, A. and MacKenzie, I. (2011) Bodies of learning. In: Guillaume, L. and Hughes, J. (eds.) *Deleuze and the Body.* Edinburgh: Edinburgh University Press, pp. 63–72.

Dale, C. and Kalob, D. (2006) Embracing social activism: Sociology in the service of social justice and peace. *Humanity & Society, 30*(2): 121–152.

Dalgleish, T. (2004) The emotional brain. *Nature Reviews Neuroscience, 5*(7): 583–589.

Danermark, B., Ekstrom, M., Jaokobsen, L. and Karlsson, J. (2002) *Explaining Society. Critical Realism in the Social Sciences.* London: Routledge.

Davidson, M. and Wyly, E. (2012) Class-ifying London. *City, 16*(4): 395–421.

Davies, P. (2004) Sociology and policy science: just in time? *British Journal of Sociology, 55*(3): 447–450.

De Castro, E.B.V. (2004) Exchanging perspectives: the transformation of objects into subjects in Amerindian ontologies. *Common Knowledge, 10*(3), 463–484.

De Fillippi, R., Grabher, G. and Jones, C. (2007) Introduction to paradoxes of creativity, managerial and organizational challenges in the cultural economy. *Journal of Organizational Behavior, 28*(5): 511–521.

De La Fuente, E. (2007) The new sociology of art: putting art back into social science approaches to the arts. *Cultural Sociology, 1*(3): 409–425.

De La Fuente, E. (2010) The artwork made me do it, introduction to the new sociology of art. *Thesis Eleven, 103*(1): 3–9.

de Swaan, A. (1990) *The Management of Normality.* London: Routledge.

De Visser, R.O. and Smith, J.A. (2007) Alcohol consumption and masculine identity among young men. *Psychology and Health, 22*(5): 595–614.

Dean, M. (2010) *Governmentality: Power and Rule in Modern Society.* London: Sage.

Dean, M. (2014) Rethinking neoliberalism. *Journal of Sociology, 50*(2): 150–163.

DeLanda, M. (2006) *A New Philosophy of Society.* London: Continuum.

DeLanda, M. (2013) *Intensive Science and Virtual Philosophy.* London: Bloomsbury Academic.

Deleuze, G. (1988) *Spinoza: Practical Philosophy.* San Francisco: City Lights.

Deleuze, G. (1990) *Expressionism in Philosophy: Spinoza.* New York: Zone Books.

Deleuze, G. (2003) *Francis Bacon, The Logic of Sensation* (Translated by D.W. Smith.). London: Continuum.

Deleuze, G. and Guattari, F. (1984) *Anti-Oedipus: Capitalism and Schizophrenia.* London: Athlone.

Deleuze, G. and Guattari, F. (1986) *Kafka. Toward a Minor Literature.* Minneapolis: University of Minnesota Press.

Deleuze, G. and Guattari, F. (1988) *A Thousand Plateaus.* London: Athlone.

Deleuze, G. and Guattari, F. (1994) *What is Philosophy?* New York: Columbia University Press.

DeNora, T. (1999) Music as a technology of the self. *Poetics, 27*(1): 31–56.

Diamond, L.M. (2004) Emerging perspectives on distinctions between romantic love and sexual desire. *Current Directions in Psychological Science, 13*(3): 116–119.

Douglas, M. (1992) *Risk and Blame. Essays in Cultural Theory.* London: Routledge.

Duff, C. (2010) Towards a developmental ethology: exploring Deleuze's contribution to the study of health and human development. *Health, 14*(6): 619–34.

Duff, C. (2014) *Assemblages of Health. Deleuze's Empiricism and the Ethology of Life.* Dordrecht: Springer.

Duncombe, J. and Marsden, D. (1993) Love and intimacy: the gender division of emotion and 'emotion work': a neglected aspect of sociological discussion of heterosexual relationships. *Sociology, 27*(2): 221–41.

Dunlap, R.E. (1998) Lay perceptions of global risk public views of global warming in cross-national context. *International Sociology, 13*(4): 473–498.

Dunlap, R.E. and Catton, W.R. (1979) Environmental sociology. *Annual Review of Sociology 5*: 243–73.

Dunlap, R.E. and Catton, W.R. (1994) Struggling with human exemptionalism: the rise, decline and revitalization of environmental sociology. *The American Sociologist, 25*(1): 5–30.

Dunlap, R.E., Liere, K.V., Mertig, A. and Jones, R.E. (2000) Measuring endorsement of the new ecological paradigm: a revised NEP scale. *Journal of Social Issues, 56*(3): 425–442.

Durkheim, E. (1976 [1915]) *The Elementary Forms of the Religious Life.* London: Allen and Unwin [first published London: George Allen and Unwin, 1915].

Durkheim, E. (1984) *The Division of Labour in Society.* London: Macmillan.

Duschinsky, R. (2013) The emergence of sexualization as a social problem: 1981–2010. *Social Politics, 20*(1): 137–156.

Edwards, J. (2010) The materialism of historical materialism. In: Coole, D.H. and Frost, S. (eds.) *New Materialisms. Ontology, Agency, and Politics.* London: Duke University Press, pp. 281–298.

Egan, R.D. (2013) *Becoming Sexual. A Critical Appraisal of the Sexualisation of Girls.* Cambridge: Polity.

Egan, R.D. and Hawkes, G.L. (2008) Endangered girls and incendiary objects: Unpacking the discourse on sexualization. *Sexuality & Culture, 12*(4): 291–311.

Eide, E. (2010) Strategic essentialism and ethnification: hand in glove? *Nordicom Review, 31*(2): 63–78.

El-Bushra, J. (2007) Feminism, gender, and women's peace activism. *Development and Change, 38*(1): 131–147.

Eng, D.L., Halberstam, J. and Munoz, J.E. (2005) Introduction: what's queer about queer studies now? *Social Text, 23*(3): 84–85.

Fish, J.S. (2005) Talcott Parsons and the sociology of emotion. *Sociological Perspectives, 48*(1): 135–152.

Fitzgerald, J.I. (1998) An assemblage of desire, drugs and techno. *Angelaki: Journal of the Theoretical Humanities, 3*(2): 41–57.

Flax, J. (1990) *Thinking Fragments: Psychoanalysis, Feminism and Postmodernism in the Contemporary West.* Berkeley: University of California Press.

Ford, C.M. (1996) A theory of individual creative action in multiple social domains. *Academy of Management Review, 21*(4): 1112–1142.

Foucault, M. (1967) *Madness and Civilisation.* London: Tavistock.

Foucault, M. (1976) *Birth of the Clinic.* London: Tavistock.

Foucault, M. (1979) *Discipline and Punish.* Harmondsworth; Peregrine.

Foucault, M. (1980) The eye of power. In: Gordon, C. (ed.) *Power/Knowledge.* Brighton: Harvester.

Foucault, M. (1981) *The History of Sexuality Vol.1: The Will to Knowledge.* Harmondsworth: Pelican.

Foucault, M. (1982) The subject and power. *Critical Inquiry, 8*(4): 777–795.

Foucault, M. (1987) *The Use of Pleasure (Vol. 2 of the History of Sexuality).* Harmondsworth: Peregrine.

Foucault, M. (1988) Technologies of the self. In: Martin, L.H., Gutman, H. and Hutton, P.H. (eds.) *Technologies of the Self: A Seminar with Michel Foucault.* Amherst, MA: University of Massachusetts Press.

Foucault, M. (1990) *The Care of the Self (Vol. 3 of the History of Sexuality).* Harmondsworth: Penguin.

Foucault, M. (2002) *The Archaeology of Knowledge.* London: Routledge.

Fox, B. (2015) Feminism on family sociology: interpreting trends in family life. *Canadian Review of Sociology/Revue canadienne de sociologie, 52*(2): 204–211.

Fox, N.J. (1991) Green sociology. *Network, 50*: 23–4.

Fox, N.J. (1993) *Postmodernism, Sociology and Health.* Buckingham: Open University Press.

Fox, N.J. (2002) Refracting health: Deleuze, Guattari and body/self. *Health, 6*(1), 347–64.

Fox, N.J. (2005) Cultures of ageing in Thailand and Australia (what can an ageing body do?) *Sociology, 39*(3): 501–518.

Fox, N.J. (2011) The ill-health assemblage: beyond the body-with-organs. *Health Sociology Review, 20*(4): 359–371.

Fox, N.J. (2012) *The Body.* Cambridge: Polity.

Fox, N.J. (2013) Flows of affect in the Olympic stadium, and beyond. *Sociological Research Online, 18*(2): 2. Available at: www.socresonline.org.uk/18/2/2.html

Fox, N.J. (2015a) Creativity, anti-humanism and the 'new sociology of art'. *Journal of Sociology, 51*(3): 522–536.

Fox, N.J. (2015b) Personal health technologies, micropolitics and resistance: a new materialist analysis. *Health.* DOI: 10.1177/1363459315590248

Fox, N.J. (2016) Health sociology from post-structuralism to the new materialisms. *Health, 20*(1): 62–74.

Fox, N.J. and Alldred, P. (2013) The sexuality-assemblage: desire, affect, anti-humanism. *Sociological Review, 61*(6): 769–789.

Fox, N.J. and Alldred, P. (2014) New materialist social inquiry: designs, methods and the research-assemblage. *International Journal of Social Research Methodology, 18*(4): 399–414.

Fox, N.J. and Alldred, P. (2015) Inside the research-assemblage: new materialism and the micropolitics of social inquiry. *Sociological Research Online, 20*(2): 6. http://www.socresonline.org.uk/20/2/6.html

Fox, N.J. and Bale, C. (forthcoming) Bodies, pornography and the circumscription of sexuality: a new materialist study of young people's sexual practices.

Fox, N.J. and Ward, K.J. (2006) Health identities: from expert patient to resisting consumer. *Health, 10*(4): 461–479.

Fox, N.J. and Ward, K.J. (2008) Pharma in the bedroom … and the kitchen. The pharmaceuticalisation of daily life. *Sociology of Health and Illness, 30*(6): 856–868.

Fox, N.J., Ward, K. and O'Rourke, A. (2005a) Pro-anorexia, weight-loss drugs and the internet: an 'anti-recovery' explanatory model of anorexia. *Sociology of Health and Illness, 27*(7), 944–971.

Fox, N.J., Ward, K. and O'Rourke, A. (2005b) The birth of the e-clinic. Continuity or transformation in the UK governance of pharmaceutical consumption? *Social Science & Medicine, 61*(7): 1474–1484.

Fox, N.J., Ward, K.J. and O'Rourke, A.J. (2005c) The 'expert patient': empowerment or medical dominance? The case of weight loss, pharmaceutical drugs and the Internet. *Social Science and Medicine, 60*(6): 1299–1309.

Fox, N.J., Ward, K.J. and O'Rourke A.J. (2006) A sociology of technology governance for the information age: the case of pharmaceutical consumption. *Sociology, 40*(2): 315–334.

Francis, B. (2002) Relativism, realism, and feminism: an analysis of some theoretical tensions in research on gender identity. *Journal of Gender Studies, 11*(1): 39–54.

Francis, B. and Paechter, C. (2015) The problem of gender categorisation: addressing dilemmas past and present in gender and education research. *Gender and Education, 27*(7): 776–790.

Franklin, S. (1990) Deconstructing 'desperateness': The social construction of infertility in popular representations of new reproductive technologies. In: McNeil, M., Varcoe, I. and Yearley, S. (eds.) *The New Reproductive Technologies*. London: Palgrave, pp. 200–229.

Fraser, M. (1998) 'The face-off between will and fate': artistic identity and neurological style in de Kooning's late works. *Body & Society, 4*(4): 1–22.

Freshwater, D. (2014) What counts in mixed methods research: algorithmic thinking or inclusive leadership? *Journal of Mixed Methods Research, 8*(4): 327–329.

Freidson, E. (1974) *Professional Dominance: The Social Structure of Medical Care*. New Brunswick NJ: Transaction Publishers.

Freund, P.E.S. (1990) The expressive body: a common ground for the sociology of emotions and health and illness. *Sociology of Health and Illness, 12*(4): 452–477.

Friedland, R. and Mohr, J. (2004) *Matters of Culture: Cultural Sociology in Practice*. Cambridge: Cambridge University Press

Frosh, S., Phoenix, A. and Pattman, R. (2002) *Young Masculinities*. Basingstoke: Palgrave.

Game, A. (1991) *Undoing the Social*. Buckingham: Open University Press.

Garfinkel, H. (1984) *Studies in Ethnomethodology* (2nd edition). Cambridge: Polity.

Gatens, M. (1996a) *Imaginary Bodies*. London: Routledge.

Gatens, M. (1996b) Through a Spinozist lens: ethology, difference, power. In: Patton, P. (ed.) *Deleuze: a Critical Reader*. Oxford: Blackwell, pp. 162–187.

Gatens, M. (2000) Feminism as 'password': re-thinking the 'possible' with Spinoza and Deleuze. *Hypatia, 15*(2), 59–75.

Gauntlett, D. (2011) *Making is Connecting, The Social Meaning of Creativity, from DIY and Knitting to YouTube and Web 2.0*. Cambridge: Polity.

Gell, A. (1998) *Art and Agency*. Oxford: Oxford University Press.

Giddens, A. (1981) *A Contemporary Critique of Historical Materialism*. London: Macmillan.

Giddens, A. (1982) *Sociology: A Brief but Critical Introduction*. London: Macmillan.

Giddens, A. (1992) *The Transformation of Intimacy*. Cambridge: Polity.

Gill, R. (2003) From sexual objectification to sexual subjectification: the resexualisation of women's bodies in the media. *Feminist Media Studies, 3*(1): 100–106.

Gill, R. (2012) Media, empowerment and the 'sexualization of culture' debates. *Sex Roles, 66*(11–12): 736–745.

Gillies, V. and Alldred, P. (2012) The ethics of intention: research as a political tool. In: Miller, T., Birch, M., Mauthner, M. et al. (eds.) *Ethics in Qualitative Research*. London: Sage, pp. 43–60.

Goffman, E. (1968) *Stigma. Note on the Management of Spoiled Identity*. London: Pelican.

Goffman, E. (1969) *The Presentation of Self in Everyday Life*. London: Allen Lane.

Goldthorpe, J. H. and McKnight, A. (2006) The economic basis of social class. In: Morgan, S.L., Grusky, D.B. and Fields, G.S. (eds.) *Mobility and Inequality: Frontiers of Research in Sociology and Economics*. Stanford, CA: Stanford University Press, pp. 109–124.

Gordo-López, A.J. (1996) The rhetorics of gender identity clinics: transsexuals and other boundary objects. In: Burman, E., Aitken, G., Alldred, P. et al. (eds.) *Psychology, Discourse and Social Practice: from Regulation to Resistance*. London: Taylor and Francis, pp. 171–193.

Gordo-López, A.J. and Cleminson, R.M. (2004) *Techno-Sexual Landscapes: Changing Relations Between Technology and Sexuality*. London: Free Association Books.

Grace, W. (2009) Faux amis: Foucault and Deleuze on sexuality and desire. *Critical Inquiry, 36*(1): 52–75.

Green, J. and Labonté, R. (2008) Introduction: from critique to engagement. In: Green, J. and Labonté, R. (eds.) *Critical Perspectives in Public Health*. London: Routledge, pp. 1–11.

Grosz, E. (1994) *Volatile Bodies*. Bloomington: Indiana University Press.

Guattari, F. (2000) *The Three Ecologies*. London: Athlone.

Guillaume, L. and Hughes, J. (2011) *Deleuze and the Body*. Edinburgh: Edinburgh University Press.

Hall, S. (1996) New ethnicities. In: Morley, D. and Chen, K–H. (eds.) *Stuart Hall: Critical Dialogues in Cultural Studies*. London: Routledge.

Halpern, D. (2013) *Mental Health and the Built Environment: More Than Bricks and Mortar?* London: Routledge.

Hanseth, O., Jacucci, E., Grisot, M., et al. (2006) Reflexive standardization: side effects and complexity in standard making. *MIS Quarterly, 30*: 563–581.

Haraway, D. (1991) *Cyborgs, Simians And Women*. London: Free Association Books.

Haraway, D. (1992) Otherworldly conversations; terran topics; local terms. *Science as Culture*, 3(1): 64–98.

Haraway, D. (1997) *Modest_Witness@Second_Millennium. Femaleman_Meets_Oncomouse*. New York: Routledge.

Helman, C.G. (1978) 'Feed a cold, starve a fever': folk models of infection in an English suburban community, and their relation to medical treatment. *Culture, Medicine and Psychiatry*, 2(2): 107–137.

Henriques, J., Hollway, W., Urwin, C. et al. (1998) *Changing the Subject: Psychology, Social Regulation and Subjectivity*. London: Routledge.

Henriques, J.F. (2010) The vibrations of affect and their propagation on night out on Kingston's dancehall scene. *Body & Society*, 16(1): 57–89.

Henry, D. and Lexchin, J. (2002) The pharmaceutical industry as a medicines provider. *Lancet, 360*: 1590–95.

Herdt, G. (2012) *Third Sex, Third Gender. Beyond Sexual Dimorphism in Culture and History*. New York: Zone Books.

Hickey-Moody, A. (2013) *Youth, Arts and Education: Reassembling Subjectivity Through Affect*. London: Routledge.

Higgins, T. E. (1996) Anti-essentialism, relativism and human rights. *Harvard Women's Law Journal*, 19: 89–126.

Hines, G. (2011) *Pornland: How Porn Has Hijacked Our Sexuality*. Boston, MA: Beacon.

Hines, M. (2006) Prenatal testosterone and gender-related behaviour. *European Journal of Endocrinology*, 155(Supplement 1): S115–S121.

Hird, M.J. (2000) Gender's nature: intersexuality, transsexualism and the 'sex'/'gender' binary. *Feminist Theory, 1*(3): 347–364.

Hochschild, A.R. (1983) *The Managed Heart*. Berkeley: University of California Press.

Hochschild, A.R. (1989) *The Second Shift*. New York: Viking Penguin.

Hodder, I. (1994) The interpretation of documents and material culture. In: Denzin, N.K. and Lincoln, Y.S. (eds.) *Handbook of Qualitative Research*. London: Sage, pp. 393–402.

Hoehner, C.M., Brennan, L.K., Brownson, R.C., et al. (2003) Opportunities for integrating public health and urban planning approaches to promote active community environments. *American Journal of Health Promotion, 18*(1): 14–20.

Holford, N., Renold, E. and Huuki, T. (2013) What (else) can a kiss do? Theorizing the power plays in young children's sexual cultures. *Sexualities*, 16(5–6): 710–729.

Holland, J., Ramazanoglu, C., Sharpe, S. and Thompson, R. (1998) *The Male in the Head*. London: Tuffnell Press.

Horvath, M.A.H., Alys, L., Massey, K. et al. (2013) *Basically Porn is Everywhere*. London: Office of the Children's Commissioner.

Hysing, E. and Olsson, J. (2005) Sustainability through good advice? Assessing the governance of Swedish forest biodiversity. *Environmental Politics, 14*(4): 510–526.

Isaki, B. (2013) Colourblind colonialism in the '50th state of America'. In: Saldanha, A. and Adams, M. (eds.) *Deleuze and Race*. Edinburgh: Edinburgh University Press, pp. 113–128.

Ivinson, G. and Renold, E. (2013) Valleys' girls: re-theorising bodies and agency in a semi-rural post-industrial locale, *Gender and Education, 25*(6): 704–721.

Izard, C.E. (1991) *The Psychology of Emotions*. New York: Plenum.

Jackson, A.Y. and Mazzei, L.A. (2013) Plugging one text into another: thinking with theory in qualitative research. *Qualitative Inquiry, 19*(4): 261–271.

Jackson, S. (1993) Even sociologists fall in love: an exploration in the sociology of emotions. *Sociology, 27*(2): 201–220.

Jackson, S. and Vares, T. (2015) 'Too many bad role models for us girls': girls, female pop celebrities and 'sexualisation'. *Sexualities, 18*(4): 480–498.

Jaggar, A.M. (1992) Love and knowledge: emotion in feminist epistemology. In: Jaggar, A.M. and Bordo, S.R. (eds.) *Gender/Body/Knowledge*. New Brunswick, NJ: Rutgers University Press, pp. 145–171.

Jagose, A. (1996) *Queer Theory: An Introduction*, New York: New York University Press.

Jagose, A. (2010) Counterfeit pleasures: fake orgasm and queer agency. *Textual Practice, 24*(3): 517–539.

James, N. (1989) Emotional labour: skill and work in the social regulation of feelings. *Sociological Review, 37*: 15–42.

James, V. and Gabe, J. (1996) Introduction. In: James, V. and Gabe, J. (eds.) *Health and the Sociology of Emotions*. London: Routledge, pp. 1–24.

Jasper, J.M. (1998) The emotions of protest: affective and reactive emotions in and around social movements. *Sociological Forum, 13*(3): 397–424.

Jasper, J.M. (2011) Emotions and social movements: twenty years of theory and research. *Annual Review of Sociology, 37*: 285–303.

Jeanes, E.L. (2006) Resisting creativity, creating the new. A Deleuzian perspective on creativity. *Creativity and Innovation Management, 15*(2): 127–134.

Jenks, C. (2005) *Childhood (2nd edition)*. London: Routledge.

Jessop, B. (2002) Liberalism, neoliberalism, and urban governance: a state–theoretical perspective. *Antipode, 34*(3): 452–472.

Jessop, B. (2003) Governance and metagovernance: on reflexivity, requisite variety and requisite irony. In: Bang, H. (ed.) *Governance as Social and Political Communication*, Manchester: Manchester University Press, pp. 101–116.

Jessop, B. (2012) Marxist approaches to power. In: Amenta, E., Nash, K. and Scott, A. (eds.) *The Wiley-Blackwell Companion to Political Sociology*. Oxford: Blackwell, pp. 3–14.

Jordan, T. (1995) Collective bodies, raving and the politics of Gilles Deleuze and Felix Guattari. *Body & Society, 1*(1): 125–144.

Juelskjaer, M. (2013) Gendered subjectivities of spacetimematter. *Gender and Education, 25*(6), 754–768.

Karakayali, N. (2015) Two ontological orientations in sociology: building social ontologies and blurring the boundaries of the 'social'. *Sociology, 49*(4): 732–747.

Kaufman, J.C. and Beghetto, R.A. (2009) Beyond big and little: the four C model of creativity. *Review of General Psychology, 13*(1): 1–12.

Kimmel, M.S. (2008) *Guyland: The Perilous World Where Boys Become Men*. New York: Harper.

Kirchner, J.W. (2002) The Gaia hypothesis: fact, theory, and wishful thinking. *Climatic Change, 52*(4): 391–408.

Kirton, M.J. (1994) *Adaptors and Innovators: Styles of Creativity and Problem-Solving*. London: Routledge.

Kitzinger, C. (1987) *The Social Construction of Lesbianism*. London: Sage.

Kitzinger, C. (1999) Lesbian and gay psychology: is it critical? *Annual Review of Critical Psychology, 1*: 50–66.

Klausen, S.H. (2010) The notion of creativity revisited: a philosophical perspective on creativity research. *Creativity Research Journal,* 22(4): 347–360.

Kleinman, A., Eisenberg, L. and Good, B. (2006) Culture, illness, and care: clinical lessons from anthropologic and cross-cultural research. *Focus: the Journal of Lifelong Learning in Psychiatry,* 4(1): 140–149.

Lacey, C. (1966) Some sociological concomitants of academic streaming in a grammar school. *British Journal of Sociology*, 17(3): 245–262.

Lambert, G. (2011) The 'non-human sex' in sexuality: 'what are your special desiring-machines?' In: Beckman, F. (ed.) *Deleuze and Sex*. Edinburgh: Edinburgh University Press, pp. 135–152.

Lambevski, S.A. (2004) Movement and desire: on the need to fluidify academic discourse on sexuality. *GLQ: A Journal of Lesbian and Gay Studies,* 10(2): 304–308.

Lambevski, S.A. (2005) Bodies, schizo vibes and hallucinatory desires – sexualities in movement. *Sexualities, 8*(5): 570–586.

Landecker, H. and Panofsky, A. (2013) From social structure to gene regulation, and back: a critical introduction to environmental epigenetics for sociology. *Annual Review of Sociology, 39*: 333–357.

Lange, I.G., Daxenberger, A., Schiffer, B. et al. (2002) Sex hormones originating from different livestock production systems: fate and potential disrupting activity in the environment. *Analytica Chimica Acta*, 473(1): 27–37.

Lascoumes, P. and Le Gales, P. (2007) Introduction: understanding public policy through its instruments – from the nature of instruments to the sociology of public policy instrumentation. *Governance*, 20(1): 1–21.

Latour, B. (1999) On recalling ANT. *The Sociological Review*, 47(S1): 15–25.

Latour, B. (2005) *Reassembling the Social. An Introduction to Actor Network Theory*. Oxford: Oxford University Press.

Lau, R. and Morgan, J. (2014) Integrating discourse, construction and objectivity: a contemporary realist approach. *Sociology*, 48(3): 573–589.

Law, J. (1992) Notes on the theory of the actor-network: ordering, strategy and heterogeneity. *Systems Practice*, 5(4): 379–93.

Law, J. (1999) After ANT: complexity, naming and topology. *The Sociological Review*, 47(S1): 1–14.

Law, J. (2009) Actor network theory and material semiotics. In: Turner, B. (ed.) *The New Blackwell Companion to Social Theory*. Oxford: Blackwell, pp. 141–158.

Lawrence, G., Richards, C. and Lyons, K. (2013) Food security in Australia in an era of neoliberalism, productivism and climate change. *Journal of Rural Studies*, 29(1): 30–39.

Lee-Treweek, G. (1996) Emotion work in care assistant work. In: James, V. and Gabe, J. (eds.) *Health and the Sociology of Emotions*. London: Routledge, pp. 115–132.

Lees, S. (1993) *Sugar and Spice. Sexuality and Adolescent Girls*. Harmondsworth: Penguin.

Lemke, T. (2015) New materialisms: Foucault and the 'government of things'. *Theory, Culture & Society, 32*(4): 3–25.

Levine, D. (2013) Sexting: a terrifying health risk ... or the new normal for young adults? *Journal of Adolescent Health, 52*(3): 257–258.

Leys, R. (2011) The turn to affect; a critique. *Critical Inquiry,* 37(3): 434–472.

Linstead, S. and Pullen, A. (2006) Gender as multiplicity: desire, displacement, difference and dispersion. *Human Relations,* 59(9): 1287–1310.

Lipman, P. (2011) *The New Political Economy of Urban Education: Neoliberalism, Race, and the Right to the City.* Abingdon; Routledge.

Lockie, S. (2016) Sustainability and the future of environmental sociology. *Environmental Sociology,* 2(1): 1–4. DOI: 10.1080/23251042.2016.1142692

Lorenz, C. (2012) If you're so smart, why are you under surveillance? Universities, neoliberalism, and new public management? *Critical Inquiry,* 38(1): 599–629.

Lorraine, T. (2008) Feminist lines of flight from the majoritarian subject. *Deleuze Studies,* 2(Suppl): 60–82.

Lovelock, J. (2007) *The Revenge of Gaia: Earth's Climate Crisis and the Fate of Humanity.* London: Penguin.

Luhmann, N. (1982) *The Differentiation of Society.* New York: Columbia University Press.

Lupton, D. (1997) Foucault and the medicalisation critique. In: Petersen, A. and Bunton, R. (eds.) *Foucault, Health and Medicine.* London: Routledge, pp. 94–110.

Lupton, D. (2012) M-health and health promotion: The digital cyborg and surveillance society. *Social Theory & Health,* 10(3): 229–244.

Lupton, D. (2014) Critical perspectives on digital health technologies. *Sociology Compass,* 8(12): 1344–1359.

Lyon, M. (1996) C. Wright Mills meets Prozac: the relevance of social emotions to the sociology of health and illness. In: James, V. and Gabe, J. (eds.) *Health and the Sociology of Emotions.* London: Routledge, pp. 55–78.

Mac an Ghaill, M. (1994) *The Making of Men.* Buckingham: Open University Press.

MacKinnon, C.A. (1982) Feminism, Marxism, method, and the state: an agenda for theory. *Signs,* 7(3): 515–544.

Macmillan, T. (2003) Tales of power in biotechnology regulation: the EU Ban on BST. *Geoforum,* 34(2): 187–201.

Marks, S.R. (1974) Durkheim's theory of anomie. *American Journal of Sociology,* 80(2): 329–363.

Marsh, B.I. and Melville, G. (2011) Moral panics and the British media – a look at some contemporary 'folk devils'. *Internet Journal of Criminology,* 267–272. Accessed at www.internetjournalofcriminology.com/index.html

Martin, J.L. (2014) *Social Structures.* Princeton, NJ: Princeton University Press.

Martin, P.Y. (2004) Gender as social institution. *Social Forces,* 82(4): 1249–1273.

Marx, K. (1959) *Economic & Philosophic Manuscripts of 1844.* Moscow: Progress.

Marx, K. (1969) *Theses on Feuerbach.* Moscow: Progress.

Marx, K. (1971) *A Contribution to the Critique of Political Economy.* London: Lawrence & Wishart.

Marx, K. (1975) *Early Writings.* Harmondsworth: Penguin.

Marx, K. and Engels, F. (1952) *The Communist Manifesto.* Moscow: Progress.

Masny, D. (2013) Rhizoanalytic pathways in qualitative research. *Qualitative Inquiry,* 19(5): 339–348.

Masny, D. and Waterhouse, M. (2011) Mapping territories and creating nomadic pathways with multiple literacies theory. *Journal of Curriculum Theorizing,* 27(3): 287–307.

Massey, D.S. (2002) A brief history of human society: the origin and role of emotion in social life. *American Sociological Review, 67*(1): 1–29.

Massumi, B. (1988) Translator's foreword. In: Deleuze, G. and Guattari, F. *A Thousand Plateaus*. London: Athlone, pp. ix–xix.

Massumi, B. (1992) *A Users Guide to Capitalism and Schizophrenia*. Cambridge, MA: MIT Press.

Massumi, B. (1996) The autonomy of affect. In: Patton, P. (ed.) *Deleuze: a Critical Reader*. Oxford: Blackwell, pp. 217–239.

Massumi, B. (2002) Navigating movements. In: Zournazi, M. (ed.) *Hope: New Philosophies for Change*. Annandale: Pluto Press, pp. 210–244.

Matten, D. (2004) The impact of the risk society thesis on environmental politics and management in a globalizing economy – principles, proficiency, perspectives. *Journal of Risk Research, 7*(4): 377–398.

McCann, E. and Ward, K. (2012) Policy assemblages, mobilities and mutations: toward a multidisciplinary conversation. *Political Studies Review, 10*(3): 325–332.

McLean, C. and Hassard, J. (2004) Symmetrical absence/symmetrical absurdity: critical notes on the production of actor-network accounts. *Journal of Management Studies, 41*(3): 493–519.

McMichael, A.J. (2013) Globalization, climate change, and human health. *New England Journal of Medicine, 368*(14): 1335–1343.

McRobbie, A. and Thornton, S.L. (1995) Rethinking 'moral panic' for multimediated social worlds. *British Journal of Sociology, 46*(4): 559–574.

Medicines Control Agency (1999) *Advertising and Promotion of Medicines in the UK*. London: Stationery Office.

Meloni, M. (2014) How biology became social, and what it means for social theory. *The Sociological Review, 62*(3): 593–614.

Mendelson, T. and Letourneau, E.J. (2015) Parent-focused prevention of child sexual abuse. *Prevention Science, 16*(6): 844–852.

Mills, C.W. (2000 [1959]) *The Sociological Imagination*. New York: Oxford University Press.

Mills, M.B. (2003) Gender and inequality in the global labor force. *Annual Review of Anthropology, 32*: 41–62.

Mitchell, K.J., Jones, L., Finkelhor, D. and Wolak, J. (2014) *Trends in Unwanted Online Experiences and Sexting: Final Report*. Durham, NH: Crimes against Children Research Center.

Mitchell, R. and Popham, F. (2008) Effect of exposure to natural environment on health inequalities: an observational population study. *Lancet, 372*(9650): 1655–1660.

Mol, A. (2009) Living with diabetes: care beyond choice and control. *Lancet, 373*(9677): 1756–1757.

Mol, A.P. and Spaargaren, G. (1993) Environment, modernity and the risk-society: the apocalyptic horizon of environmental reform. *International Sociology, 8*(4): 431–459.

Mort, M., Roberts, C., and Callén, B. (2013) Ageing with telecare: care or coercion in austerity? *Sociology of Health & Illness, 35*(6): 799–812.

Moscheta, M.S., McNamee, S. and Santos, M.A. (2013) Sex trade among men: Negotiating sex, bodies and identity categories. *Psicologia & Sociedade, 25*(1): 44–53.

Mulcahy, D. (2012) Affective assemblages: body matters in the pedagogic practices of contemporary school classrooms. *Pedagogy, Culture & Society, 20*(1): 9–27.

Mulkay, M. (1985) *The Word and the World.* London: Allen & Unwin.

Mumby, D.K. and Stohl, C. (1991) Power and discourse in organization studies: absence and the dialectic of control. *Discourse and Society, 2*(3): 313–332.

Muncie, J. (2006) Governing young people: Coherence and contradiction in contemporary youth justice. *Critical Social Policy, 26*(4): 770–793.

Murphy, R. (1995) Sociology as if nature did not matter: an ecological critique. *British Journal of Sociology, 46*(4): 688–707.

Muscardini, C. (2001) Written question: electronic sales of drugs. *European Union Commission Official Journal, C151E (22/05/2001):* 56–57.

Nash, K. (2001) The 'cultural turn' in social theory: towards a theory of cultural politics. *Sociology, 35*(1): 77–92.

Navaro-Yashin, Y. (2009) Affective spaces, melancholic objects: ruination and the production of anthropological knowledge. *Journal of the Royal Anthropological Institute, 15*(1): 1–18.

Nayak, A. (2006) Displaced masculinities: Chavs, youth and class in the post-industrial city. *Sociology, 40*(5): 813–831.

Nayak, A. and Kehily, M.J. (2006) Gender undone: subversion, regulation and embodiment in the work of Judith Butler. *British Journal of Sociology of Education, 27*(4): 459–472.

Nettleton, S. (1992) *Power, Pain and Dentistry.* Buckingham: Open University Press.

Nettleton, S. (2006) *The Sociology of Health and Illness.* Cambridge: Polity.

Newton, T. (2003) Crossing the great divide: time, nature and the social. *Sociology, 37*(3): 433–457.

Niewöhner, J. (2011) Epigenetics: Embedded bodies and the molecularisation of biography and milieu. *BioSocieties, 6*(3): 279–298.

Nigam, A. (1996) Marxism and power. *Social Scientist, 24*(4/6): 3–22.

Niven, K., Totterdell, P. and Holman, D. (2009) Affect regulation and well-being in the workplace: an interpersonal perspective. In: Antoniou, A., Cooper, C., Chrousos, G. et al. (eds.) *Handbook of Managerial Behavior and Occupational Health.* Cheltenham: Edward Elgar, pp. 218–228.

Office for National Statistics (2012) *Population Ageing in the United Kingdom, its Constituent Countries and the European Union.* London: ONS.

Ogden, J. (1997) The rhetoric and reality of psychosocial theories of health a challenge to biomedicine? *Journal of Health Psychology, 2*(1): 21–29.

Osborne, T. (2003) Against 'creativity', a philistine rant. *Economy and Society, 32*(4): 507–525.

Paden, R. (1987) Foucault's anti-humanism. *Human Studies, 10*(1): 123–141.

Paechter, C. (2006) Reconceptualizing the gendered body: learning and constructing masculinities and femininities in school. *Gender and Education, 18*(2): 121–135.

Pakulski, J. (1993) The dying of class or of Marxist class theory? *International Sociology, 8*(3): 279–292.

Papadopolous, L. (2010) *Sexualisation of Young People Review.* London: Home Office.

Papoulias, C. and Callard, F. (2010) Biology's gift: interrogating the turn to affect. *Body & Society, 16*(1): 29–56.

Parker, C. (2002) *The Open Corporation.* Cambridge: Cambridge University Press.

Parker, I. (1992) *Discourse Dynamics: Critical Analysis for Social and Individual Psychology*. London: Routledge.

Parr, A. (2009) *Hijacking Sustainability*. Cambridge, MA: MIT Press.

Parsons, T. (1951) *The Social System*. New York: Free Press.

Parsons, T. (1963) On the concept of political power. *Proceedings of the American Philosophical Society, 107*(3): 232–262.

Pascoe, C.J. (2005) 'Dude, you're a fag': adolescent masculinity and the fag discourse. *Sexualities, 8*(3): 329–346.

Patton, P. (2000) *Deleuze and the Political*. London: Routledge.

Patton, P. (2006) Order, exteriority and flat multiplicities in the social. In: Fuglsang, M. and Sørensen, B.M. (eds.) *Deleuze and the Social*. Edinburgh: Edinburgh University Press, pp. 21–38.

Paul, P. (2005) *Pornified: How Pornography is Damaging our Lives, our Relationships, and our Families*. New York: Owl Books.

Phippen, A. (2012) *Sexting: An Exploration of Practices, Attitudes and Influences*. London: NSPCC.

Piller, I. and Cho, J. (2013) Neoliberalism as language policy. *Language in Society, 42*(1): 23–44.

Poland, B. and Dooris, M. (2010) A green and healthy future: the settings approach to building health, equity and sustainability. *Critical Public Health, 20*(3): 281–298.

Potts, A. (2004) Deleuze on Viagra (Or, what can a Viagra-body do?) *Body & Society, 10*(1): 17–36.

Pretty, J. and Ward, H. (2001). Social capital and the environment. *World Development, 29*(2): 209–227.

Prince, R. (2010) Policy transfer as policy assemblage: making policy for the creative industries in New Zealand. *Environment and Planning A, 42*(1): 169–186.

Prior, N. (2011) Critique and renewal in the sociology of music, Bourdieu and beyond. *Cultural Sociology, 5*(1): 121–138.

Prout, A. (1996) Actor-network theory, technology and medical sociology: an illustrative analysis of the metered dose inhaler. *Sociology of Health & Illness, 18*(2): 198–219.

Puar, J. (2007) *Terrorist Assemblages: Homonationalism in Queer Times*. Durham, NC: Duke University Press.

Rasmussen, M.L. (2012) Pleasure/desire, sexularism and sexuality education. *Sex Education, 12*(4): 469–481.

Ratner, B.D. (2004) 'Sustainability' as a dialogue of values: challenges to the sociology of development. *Sociological Inquiry, 74*(1): 50–69.

Renold, E. (2002) Presumed innocence: (hetero)sexual, heterosexist and homophobic harassment among primary school girls and boys. *Childhood, 9*(4): 415–434.

Renold, E. and Ivinson, G. (2014) Horse-girl assemblages: towards a post-human cartography of girls' desire in an ex-mining valleys community. *Discourse: Studies in the Cultural Politics of Education, 35*(3): 361–376.

Renold, E. and Mellor, D. (2013) Deleuze and Guattari in the nursery: towards an ethnographic multi-sensory mapping of gendered bodies and becomings. In: Coleman, R. and Ringrose, J. (eds.) *Deleuze and Research Methodologies*. Edinburgh: Edinburgh University Press, pp. 23–41.

Renold, E. and Ringrose, J. (2008) Regulation and rupture: Mapping tween and teenage girls' resistance to the heterosexual matrix. *Feminist Theory, 9*(3): 313–338.

Renold, E. and Ringrose, J. (2011) Schizoid subjectivities? Re-theorizing teen girls' sexual cultures in an era of 'sexualization'. *Journal of Sociology, 47*(4): 389–409.

Rich, A. (1980) Compulsory heterosexuality and lesbian existence. *Signs, 5*(4): 631–660.

Riis, O. and Woodhead, L. (2010) *A Sociology of Religious Emotion.* New York: Oxford University Press.

Rimal, R.N., Ratzan, S.C., Arnston, P. et al. (1997) Reconceptualizing the 'patient': health care promotion as increasing citizens' decision-making competencies. *Health Communication, 9*(1): 61–74.

Ringrose, J. (2011) Beyond discourse? Using Deleuze and Guattari's schizoanalysis to explore affective assemblages, heterosexually striated space, and lines of flight online and at school. *Educational Philosophy and Theory, 43*(6): 598–618.

Ringrose, J. (2015) Schizo-feminist educational research cartographies. *Deleuze Studies, 9*(3): 393–409.

Ringrose, J., Harvey, L., Gill, R. et al. (2013) Teen girls, sexual double standards and 'sexting': Gendered value in digital image exchange. *Feminist Theory, 14*(3): 305–323.

Ringrose, J. and Renold, E. (2012) Slut-shaming, girl power and 'sexualisation': thinking through the politics of the international SlutWalks with teen girls. *Gender and Education, 24*(3): 333–343.

Rojek, C. and Turner, B. (2000) Decorative sociology: towards a critique of the cultural turn. *The Sociological Review, 48*(4): 629–648.

Rolnik, R. (2013) Late neoliberalism: the financialization of homeownership and housing rights. *International Journal of Urban and Regional Research, 37*(3): 1058–1066.

Rose, N. (1998) *Inventing Our Selves: Psychology, Power, and Personhood.* Cambridge: Cambridge University Press.

Rose, N. (1999) *Governing the Soul* (2nd edition). London: Free Association Books.

Ryan, C. and Rivers, I. (2003) Lesbian, gay, bisexual and transgender youth: victimization and its correlates in the USA and UK. *Culture, Health & Sexuality, 5*(2): 103–119.

Saldanha, A. and Adams, J.M. (2013) (eds.) *Deleuze and Race.* Edinburgh: Edinburgh University Press.

Sarmah, A.K., Meyer, M.T. and Boxall, A.B. (2006) A global perspective on the use, sales, exposure pathways, occurrence, fate and effects of veterinary antibiotics (VAs) in the environment. *Chemosphere, 65*(5): 725–759.

Savage, M., Devine, F., Cunningham, N., et al. (2013) A new model of social class? Findings from the BBC's *Great British Class Survey* experiment. *Sociology, 47*(2): 219–250.

Sayers, S. (2003) Creative activity and alienation in Hegel and Marx. *Historical Materialism, 11*(1): 107–128.

Schalet, A.T. (2011) *Not Under my Roof. Parents, Teens and the Culture of Sex.* Chicago, IL: University of Chicago Press.

Scheff, T.J. (1994) *Microsociology: Discourse, Emotion, and Social Structure.* Chicago, IL: University of Chicago Press.

Scheff, T.J. (2005) Looking-glass self: Goffman as symbolic interactionist. *Symbolic Interaction, 28*(2): 147–166.

Schulz, A. and Northridge, M.E. (2004) Social determinants of health: implications for environmental health promotion. *Health Education & Behavior, 31*(4): 455–471.

Schweizer, T.S. (2006) The psychology of novelty-seeking, creativity and innovation: neurocognitive aspects within a work-psychological perspective. *Creativity and Innovation Management*, *15*(2): 164–172.

Sedgwick, E.K. (1990) *Epistemology of the Closet*. Berkeley, CA: University of California Press.

Seidman, S. (1992) Postmodern social theory as narrative with a moral intent. In: Seidman, S. and Wagner, D.G. (eds.) *Postmodernism and Social Theory*. Oxford: Blackwell, pp. 47–81.

Sen, A. (1999) *Development as Freedom*. Oxford: Oxford University Press.

Shalin, D.N. (1990) The impact of transcendental idealism on early German and American sociology. *Current Perspectives in Social Theory*, *10*(1): 1–29.

Shilling, C. (1997) The undersocialised conception of the embodied agent in modern sociology. *Sociology*, *31*(4): 737–754.

Shilling, C. (2002) The two traditions in the sociology of emotions. In: Barbalet, J. (ed.) *Emotions and Sociology*. Oxford: Blackwell, pp. 10–32.

Shilling, C. (2012) *The Body and Social Theory*. London: Sage.

Shore, C. and Wright, S. (1997) Policy: a new field of anthropology. In: Shore, C. and Wright, S. (eds.) *Anthropology of Policy*. London: Routledge, pp. 3–36.

Shrivastava, P. (1995) Ecocentric management for a risk society. *Academy of Management Review*, *20*(1): 118–137.

Silk, M.L. and Andrews, D.L. (2012) Sport and the neoliberal conjuncture: complicating the consensus. In: Andrews, D.L. and Silk, M.L. (eds.) *Sport and Neoliberalism: Politics, Consumption, and Culture*. Philadelphia, PA: Temple University Press, pp. 1–20.

Simonton, D.K. (1997) Creative productivity: a predictive and explanatory model of career trajectories and landmarks. *Psychological Review, 104*(1): 66–89.

Smedley, A. and Smedley, B.D. (2005) Race as biology is fiction, racism as a social problem is real: Anthropological and historical perspectives on the social construction of race. *American Psychologist*, *60*(1): 16–26.

Spinks, L. (2001) Thinking the post-human: literature, affect and the politics of style. *Textual Practice*, *15*(1): 23–46.

Spivak, G.C. (1988) Can the subaltern speak? In: Nelson, C. and Grossberg, L. (eds.) *Marxism and the Interpretation of Culture*. Chicago: University of Illinois Press, pp. 271–313.

Spivak, G.C. (1996) Subaltern studies: deconstructing historiography. In: Landry, D. and MacLean, G. (eds.) *The Spivak Reader*. London: Routledge, pp. 203–235.

St. Pierre, E.A. (1997) Methodology in the fold and the irruption of transgressive data. *International Journal of Qualitative Studies in Education, 10*(2): 175–189.

Standing, G. (2014) *The Precariat: The New Dangerous Class*. London: Bloomsbury.

Stanley, L. and Wise, S. (1993) *Breaking Out Again (2nd edition)*. London: Routledge.

Steffen, W., Crutzen, P.J. and McNeill, J.R. (2007) The Anthropocene: are humans now overwhelming the great forces of nature? *AMBIO: A Journal of the Human Environment*, *36*(8): 614–621.

Stevens, P. (2012) Towards an ecosociology. *Sociology*, *46*(4): 579–595

Strandvad, S.M. (2011) Materializing ideas: a socio-material perspective on the organizing of cultural production. *European Journal of Cultural Studies*, *14*(3): 283–297.

Strangleman, T. (2001). Networks, place and identities in post-industrial mining communities. *International Journal of Urban and Regional Research*, *25*(2): 253–267.

Strangleman, T., Rhodes, J. and Linkon, S. (2013) Introduction to crumbling cultures: deindustrialization, class, and memory. *International Labor and Working-Class History*, *84*(Fall): 7–22.

Stringer, R. (2007) A nightmare of the neo-colonial kind: politics of suffering in Howard's Northern Territory intervention. *Borderlands*, *6*(2). Accessed online at www.ntne.ws/#/article/500f70fac5b261906c000480.

Summers-Effler, E. (2002) The micro-potential for social change: emotion, consciousness, and social movement formation. *Sociological Theory*, *20*(1): 41–60.

Swinburn, B., Egger, G. and Raza, F. (1999) Dissecting obesogenic environments: the development and application of a framework for identifying and prioritizing environmental interventions for obesity. *Preventive Medicine*, *29*(6): 563–570.

Taguchi, H.L. and Palmer, A. (2013) A more 'livable' school? A diffractive analysis of the performative enactments of girls' ill-/well-being with(in) school environments. *Gender and Education*, *25*(6): 671–687.

Tamboukou, M. (2003) Interrogating the emotional turn: Making connections with Foucault and Deleuze. *European Journal of Psychotherapy Counselling and Health*, *6*(3): 209–223.

Tamboukou, M. (2006) Power, desire and emotions in education: revisiting the epistolary narratives of three women in apartheid South Africa. *Gender and Education*, *18*(3): 233–252.

Tamboukou, M. (2014) Archival research: unravelling space/time/matter entanglements and fragments. *Qualitative Research*, *14*(5): 617–633.

Taylor, C.A. and Ivinson, G. (2013) Material feminisms: new directions for education. *Gender and Education*, *25*(6): 665–670.

Thacker, E. (2005) Biophilosophy for the 21st century. In: Kroker, A. and Kroker, M. (eds.) *Critical Digital Studies, a Reader*. Toronto: University of Toronto Press, pp. 132–142.

Thibodeaux, J. (2014) Three versions of constructionism and their reliance on social conditions in social problems research. *Sociology*, *48*(4): 829–837.

Thomas, J.M. (2014) Affect and the sociology of race: A program for critical inquiry. *Ethnicities*, *14*(1): 72–90.

Thompson, P., Jones, M. and Warhurst, C. (2007) From conception to consumption, creativity and the missing managerial link. *Journal of Organizational Behavior*, *28*(5): 625–640.

Thrift, N. (2004) Intensities of feeling: towards a spatial politics of affect. *Geografiska Annaler Series B Human Geography*, *86*(1): 57–78.

Till, C. (2014) Exercise as labour: quantified self and the transformation of exercise into labour. *Societies*, *4*(3): 446–462.

Tooby, J. and Cosmides, L. (1989) Evolutionary psychology and the generation of culture, Part I: theoretical considerations. *Ethology and Sociobiology*, *10*(1): 29–49.

Turner, B. (1984) *The Body and Society*. London: Sage.

Turner, B. (1992) *Regulating Bodies*. London: Routledge.

Turner, J.H. (2001) Towards a general sociological theory of emotions. *Journal of the Theory of Social Behaviour*, *29*(2): 133–162.

Turner, J.H. and Stets, J.E. (2005) *The Sociology of Emotions*. Cambridge: Cambridge University Press.

Tyler, D. (1997) At risk of maladjustment: the problem of child mental health. In: Petersen, A. and Bunton, R. (eds.) *Foucault, Health and Medicine*. London: Routledge, pp. 74–93.

United Nations (2013) *World Population Ageing 2013* (ST/ESA/SER.A/348). New York: UN Department of Economic and Social Affairs Population Division.

Urry, J. (2009) Sociology and climate change. *The Sociological Review*, 57(s2): 84–100.

van der Tuin, I. and Dolphijn, R. (2010) The transversality of new materialism. *Women: A Cultural Review*, 21(2): 153–171.

van Krieken, R. (1991) The poverty of social control: explaining power in the historical sociology of the welfare state. *The Sociological Review*, 39(1): 1–25.

Venn, C. (2010) Individuation, relationality, affect: rethinking the human in relation to the living. *Body & Society*, 16(1): 129–161.

Wade, D.T. and Halligan, P.W. (2004) Do biomedical models of illness make for good healthcare systems? *British Medical Journal*, 329(7479): 1398–1401.

Walker, G. (2005) Sociological theory and the natural environment. *History of the Human Sciences*, 18(1): 77–106.

Walley, C.J. (2013) *Exit Zero. Family and Class in Postindustrial Chicago*. Chicago: University of Chicago Press.

Wandersman, A.H. and Hallman, W.K. (1993) Are people acting irrationally? Understanding public concerns about environmental threats. *American Psychologist*, 48(6): 681–686.

Watkins, F. and Jacoby, A. (2007) Is the rural idyll bad for your health? Stigma and exclusion in the English countryside. *Health & Place*, 13(4): 851–864.

Weber, M. (1930) *The Protestant Ethic and the Spirit of Capitalism*. London: George Allen & Unwin.

Weber, M. (1968) *Economy and Society* (Trans. Roth, G. and Wittich, C.). New York: Bedminster Press.

Westhoek, H., Lesschen, J.P., Rood, T., et al. (2014) Food choices, health and environment: effects of cutting Europe's meat and dairy intake. *Global Environmental Change*, 26(May): 196–205.

Wetherell, M. (2012) *Affect and Emotion: A New Social Science Understanding*. London: Sage.

Whitaker, P. (2010) Groundswell: the nature and landscape of art therapy. In: Moon, C.H. (ed.) *Materials and Media in Art Therapy*. London: Routledge, pp. 119–136.

Whitaker, P. (2012) The art therapy assemblage. In: Burt, H. (ed.) *Art Therapy and Postmodernism*. London: Jessica Kingsley, pp. 344–366.

Widder, N. (2012) *Political Theory after Deleuze*. London: Continuum.

Wiktorowicz, M. (2003) Emergent patterns in the regulation of pharmaceuticals: institutions and interests in the United States, Canada, Britain, and France. *Journal of Health Politics, Policy and Law*, 28(4): 616–58.

Williams, S. and Bendelow, G. (1996) Emotions, health and illness: the 'missing link' in medical sociology? In: James, V. and Gabe, J. (eds.) *Health and the Sociology of Emotions*. London: Routledge, pp. 25–53.

Williams, S. and Bendelow, G. (1998a) In search of the missing body: pain, suffering and the postmodern condition. In: Scambler, G. and Higgs, P. (eds.) *Modernity. Medicine and Health*. London: Routledge, pp. 125–146.

Williams, S. and Bendelow, G. (1998b) *The Lived Body: Sociological Themes, Embodied Issues*. London: Routledge.

Willis, P. (1977) *Learning to Labour*. Farnborough: Saxon House.

Willis, P. (2004) Twenty-five years on: old books, new times. In: Dolby, N. and Dimitriadis, G. (eds.) *Learning to Labor in New Times*. Abingdon: Routledge, pp. 167–196.

Winant, H. (2000) Race and race theory. *Annual Review of Sociology*, 26: 169–185.

Wolff, J. (2006) Groundless beauty: feminism and the aesthetics of uncertainty. *Feminist Theory*, 7(2): 143–158.

World Health Organisation (1985) *Targets for Health for All*. Geneva: World Health Organisation.

Wright, W. (1982) *The Social Logic of Health*. New Brunswick: Rutgers University Press.

Wrong, D. (1961) The pitfalls of social reductionism; the over-socialised conception of man. *American Sociological Review*, 26: 183–193.

Youdell, D. and Armstrong, F. (2011) A politics beyond subjects: the affective choreographies and smooth spaces of schooling. *Emotion, Space and Society*, 4(3): 144–150.

Youdell, D. and McGimpsey, I. (2015) Assembling, disassembling and reassembling 'youth services' in Austerity Britain. *Critical Studies in Education*, 56(1): 116–130.

Young, J. (1971) The role of the police as amplifiers of deviance. In: Cohen, S. (ed.) *Images of Deviance*. Harmondsworth: Penguin, pp. 27–61.

Young, J. (2009) Moral panic: its origins in resistance, ressentiment and the translation of fantasy into reality. *British Journal of Criminology*, 49(1): 4–16.

Zoller, H.M. (2005) Health activism: communication theory and action for social change. *Communication Theory*, 15(4): 341–364.

Index